GREAT
BRITISH
WALKIES

National Trust

Jen and Sim Benson

GREAT BRITISH WALKIES

100 brilliant dog walks through
beautiful countryside

Published by National Trust Books
An imprint of HarperCollins Publishers
1 London Bridge Street
London SE1 9GF
www.harpercollins.co.uk

HarperCollins Publishers
Macken House
39/40 Mayor Street Upper
Dublin 1
D01 C9W8
Ireland

First published in 2024

ISBN 978-0-00-864133-7

10 9 8 7 6 5 4 3 2 1

A catalogue record for this book is available from the British Library.

Printed and bound in Bosnia and Herzegovina by GPS.

Typeset by Simon Letchford.

If you would like to comment on any aspect of this book, please contact us at the above address or national.trust@harpercollins.co.uk

National Trust publications are available at National Trust shops or online at Nationaltrustbooks.co.uk

Contents

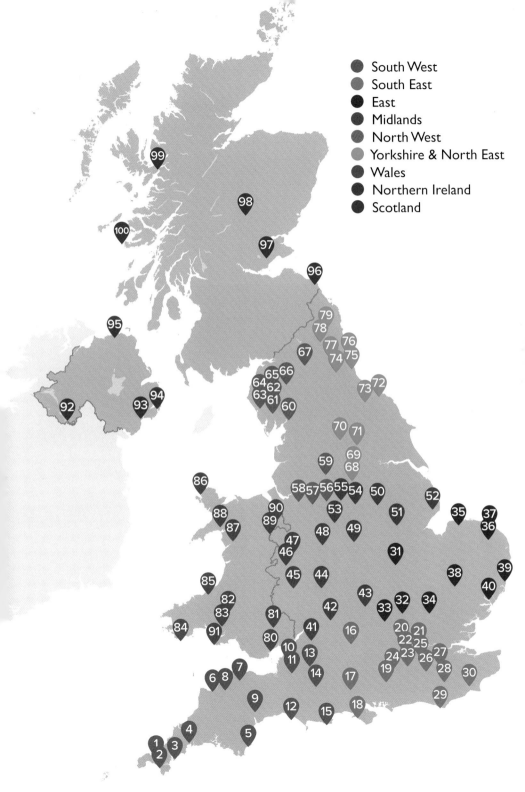

South West
South East
East
Midlands
North West
Yorkshire & North East
Wales
Northern Ireland
Scotland

Foreword
by Matt Baker

I simply cannot remember a time without dogs. They've been by my side all of my life. Growing up on a working sheep farm, they were my adventure companions and workmates. From St Bernards to giant schnauzers, from Border collies and Labradors to cairn and Biewer terriers, the walks we took, and which I continue to take, are time that I value greatly. It's a chance for contemplation, to collect my thoughts, to be inspired and to recover. I love the joys of sharing the landscape with my dogs, as it gives a completely different appreciation of where you are. Rain or shine, winter or spring, walking our dogs is a different way to explore our countryside and a reason to get out there.

I hope the pages of this book inspire you to take your four-legged friends to explore the places that are protected by the National Trust, and that the dog walkers of the future will continue to share the joys of our landscape that have made me who I am.

Introduction

Here in Britain, we're a nation of dog lovers. Recent figures from the PDSA reveal that 29% of UK adults have a dog – that's around 11 million pet dogs in total. For many people, having a dog provides invaluable company and companionship, and at no time in recent history has this been more evident than during the Covid-19 pandemic.

Since taking on an energetic black-and-white springer spaniel nearly seven years ago, our daily dog walks have become an important and cherished part of our lives. Walking the dog gives us time to be together, and time to be by ourselves. And however bad the weather is, it gets us out of the house.

Borrowdale, Lake District.

We think walks are always better for being shared with the dog, whether we're wandering through the fields and woods close to home, exploring hidden coves and sandy bays on the coast path, or seeking steep trails and far-reaching views in the mountains. And we're clearly not the only ones.

Looking after a dog takes time, money and energy, but the rewards are great. A 2022 study by researchers at the University of Liverpool, published in *Frontiers in Psychology*, found that owning a dog improves our wellbeing and happiness; provides us with purpose, companionship, self-acceptance, pleasure and distraction; and can even lessen emotional pain and suffering.

There's a social benefit, too. Daily walks bring us into contact with other people – often other dog owners – in our local communities. We've made many new friends while out walking or running with our dog, when he's trotted up to their dog to say hello, and sparked a conversation. Regular walks also bring us closer to nature, another well-evidenced mental health and wellbeing booster.

Glendurgan Garden, Cornwall.

Dogs and the National Trust

The National Trust has a long and illustrious doggy past, and the stories of beloved and important dogs are woven through the history of many of their places. From Gelert, the faithful dog of Welsh folk legend, whose statue stands outside the village of Beddgelert in north Wales, to Churchill's miniature poodles – both called Rufus – who took pride of place at his Chartwell home. Today, dogs still live and work at many National Trust properties, from family pets to farm dogs, and they're treasured as much as ever.

While walking is part of life for dog owners, sometimes a walk can be a little extra special. Working with Forthglade to develop a pawprint rating system – how dog-friendly a place is – the National Trust has unearthed some of the very best places for dogs, right across Britain. In the name of research, we've walked our spaniel in every corner of the country, met dog-loving bloggers and scone-loving doggies, and tried and tested the best dog-friendly cafés, pubs and places to stay along the way. We're delighted to share the results with you in the pages that follow.

About the walks

The walks in this book range from 2 to 10 miles, taking in a variety of different terrains, settings and levels of difficulty. Some are accessible – perfect for those visiting with buggies or wheelchairs – while others are particularly family-friendly, with play areas that work well for the kids as well as their canine friends. For each walk, we've included full details on how to find the start/finish, what to expect, including how challenging the walk is, and what facilities are available for you and your dog. You'll find comprehensive directions and a handy map to help you find your way. Some walks require a ticket or National Trust membership to access, while many are free for all.

The Christmas trail at Seaton Delaval Hall, Northumberland.

Key to symbols & maps

 Pawprint Rating

 Seasonal restrictions

 Refreshments

 Accessible

 Water provided

 Off-lead area

 Stiles

•••• Walk route

▬ Road

▭▬▭ Railway

 Parking

 Toilets

 Café/restaurant

 Country house

 Castle

 Lighthouse

Let the adventures begin

The National Trust and Forthglade have teamed up to offer dogs and their owners the best possible outdoor adventures. It's a partnership based on a shared love of dogs, and a knowledge that open spaces are important for exploring, training and bonding.

Together they are making Trust spaces even better for dogs, such as providing more waste bins and wash-down areas, improving access to gardens and cafés, and providing dog welcome packs in holiday cottages.

PAWPRINT RATINGS

The National Trust's new pawprint system makes it even easier to plan days out with your dog, with each place rated for its dog-friendliness. You can find the ratings alongside each walk in this book.

 One pawprint: dogs are welcome here, but facilities are limited. They can stretch their legs in open spaces, depending on the season.

 Two pawprints: these places are good for dogs. They have water bowls and dog bins, with dog access in some areas. You can have a cup of tea with them, probably outside.

 Three pawprints: these walks are considered the very best for dogs. Clumber Park, for example, is one your dog won't want to miss with the 'Central Bark' dog-friendly café, agility course, dog shower and more on offer.

THE CANINE CODE

Whether you're a new or experienced dog owner, take a look at the Canine Code – a guide to help you have a fun and stress-free day with your pup, as well as protect farm animals and precious wildlife habitats, making sure everyone can enjoy the countryside.

Keep them close
Using a short lead helps to keep your dog from disturbing ground-nesting birds and farm animals. It's essential to use a short lead around sheep. But if cattle approach you, it's best to let your dog off the lead, and call them back when it's safe to do so.

Pick up poo
Picking up your dog's waste keeps the area clean for everyone to enjoy. Pop it in the bin, or if there isn't one, take it home with you.

Watch the signs
Keep an eye on local signs and notices wherever you're walking. They'll tell you if you're in an area where dogs can run off-lead, for instance, or if a beach has a dog ban, or if a path has been diverted.

Stay on the ball
While lots of us love dogs, some of us don't. That's why it's important to make sure your dog doesn't run up to other people, especially children.

TIPS FOR HAPPY WALKS ON THE LEAD

Invest in a comfy collar or lead
A front-fastening harness or head collar can help dogs learn to walk on the lead, making for a more enjoyable walk.

Keep the lead loose
Instead of using a taut lead, start with your dog at your side (but be consistent with your choice of side) and make sure there's no tension in the lead when they're next to you.

Walk forward with purpose
Lead training is all about getting your dog used to walking calmly next to you. If they creep forward and start to pull, stop and encourage them back to your side with a tasty treat. Swiftly praise them and then walk purposefully forwards again.

When it's not going so well, try these simple steps:

1. If your dog has too much energy to focus on learning, find a safe, enclosed place to burn off some of their energy, then start training.

2. Pull up on the lead rather than backwards, as this enables you to better communicate with your dog.

3. Dogs pick up on our emotions – so if you're feeling tense, your dog probably is too. Take a few minutes to stop, stroke and fuss over your dog to relieve the tension.

Walking your dog on the lead gives you both time to enjoy the outdoors and deepen your bond. Why not spend time practising tricks or simply sit together and take in the view?

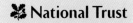

In partnership with

South West

01. Godolphin Hill Walk

**Godolphin Cross
Helston
Cornwall
TR13 9RE
01736 763194**

godolphin@nationaltrust.org.uk

ABOUT THIS WALK

Distance 2.4 miles (3.8km)
Difficulty Moderate
Terrain A moderate climb; some uneven paths, muddy in winter
Stiles Yes
Interest Wildlife, history

Godolphin Hill.

Godolphin is a place rich in history and wildlife, developed over the centuries from the Bronze Age right through to modern times. Proceeds from its tin mines funded the building of the house standing today, and the estate is included in the mining landscape that is now UNESCO's Cornwall and West Devon World Heritage Site. The 16th-century garden is one of the most important historic gardens in Europe. The wider estate boasts Leeds engine house and stack – the remains of the Godolphin family mine – and acres of woodland, shaped by historic mining activity.

This gentle walk climbs to the top of Godolphin Hill to take in gloriously impressive views over West Cornwall. On a clear day you can see to St Michael's Mount on the south coast and St Ives bay on the north coast from this spot.

THINGS TO SEE

On and around Godolphin Hill you'll discover evidence of prehistoric enclosures, early mine workings and rabbit warrens. The mineshafts around Godolphin are about 400 years old and include an old adit (entrance tunnel) which carries the water supply to Godolphin from the workings. These are now home to lesser horseshoe bats and The Slips provide an excellent night-time feeding area for them.

The old deer park was created when the family was at its most wealthy, around the 16th century. It was very much a status symbol as the park extended down to the garden, making it prominent for any important visitors.

Much of Godolphin estate is still a working farm and the National Trust tenant farmer has cattle and sheep grazing. This includes Red Devon cows grazing on the hill helping to improve this habitat for nature, by trampling and nibbling on the more dominant species, opening up space for more wildflowers such as bluebells and wood anemones. The top of the hill, visible from many miles around, was once used for lighting a beacon. It's also home to a prehistoric enclosure from the neolithic period, 4,000–3,000BC, similar to those at Carn Galver, Carn Brea, Trencrom and St Michael's Mount.

HOW TO GET HERE

Public transport Nearest train stations are Hayle 5 miles, Camborne 9 miles or Penzance 9.6 miles. Bus No. 39 from Helston to Camborne; alight at Goldolphin Cross. Or Bus No. 39A from Penzance to Townshend then change to Bus No 39.
Car From Helston take A394 to Sithney Common, turn right onto B3302 and follow the brown signs.
OS map Explorer 102
Start/finish Godolphin car park, TR13 9RE, grid ref: SW599320

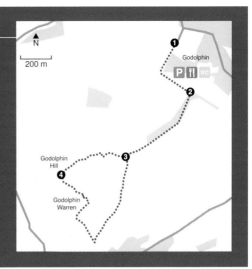

DIRECTIONS

Start/finish: Godolphin car park

1. Leave the car park and turn right, up the track past the path in the hedge on your left. Continue past the barns and where the track curves to the right, go over the cattle grid on the far left and follow the path across the field. At the far end, go over the stile to enter the wide tree-shaded lane known as The Slips.

2. Turn right and follow the path up The Slips to reach an arrangement of gates and walls, developed over centuries to give livestock access to the estate's main water supply, which follows the line of the avenue. Continue through the gate and uphill, passing fenced-off pits on your left and mineshafts protected by 'collars' of moss-covered stone walls. Follow the path through a gateway and continue uphill until you reach the junction with the path encircling the base of Godolphin Hill.

3. Turn left and take the path around the hill. Follow the path until, close to Leeds Shaft, a path forks left down to Park Gate, an opening in the old deer park pale. Ignore this path and take the one on the right up towards the summit of Godolphin Hill.

4. When you reach the top of the hill, the full panorama is revealed. On a clear day you can see both coasts: to the south views of Mounts Bay and the iconic St Michael's Mount and to the north, views of St Ives Bay. Leaving the summit take the path north, on the right, which will lead you down towards The Slips, from where you can retrace your steps to the car park.

Paws for thought
Godolphin estate is a working farm run by farm tenants, so you may find cattle and sheep on the hill and in the fields. Please keep dogs on a lead throughout – unless cattle approach closely, in which case let your dog go. Please pick up after your dog, and close gates behind you. Keep to the footpaths.

Other walkies nearby
The South West Coast Path offers a wealth of walking opportunities, stretching around the entirety of Cornwall's coast. Trengwainton Garden – a two-pawprint property – is a 30-minute drive away.

DOG-FRIENDLY AMENITIES

Dogs on short leads are welcome everywhere within Godolphin's garden and outbuildings, including the tea-room. Dogs are not allowed in the house. There's a dog water bowl outside the Piggery Café and dog poo bags available at Godolphin Welcome Hut, as well as a dog poo bin opposite the Welcome Hut.

Spring bluebells at Godolphin.

02. Loe Pool Circular, Penrose

Penrose
Helston
Cornwall
TR13 0RD
01326 222170
penrose@nationaltrust.org.uk

ABOUT THIS WALK

Distance 7 miles (11.3km)
Difficulty Moderate
Terrain Gravel and surfaced lakeside and woodland trails, section of pebble and sand beach
Stiles No
Interest Wildlife, coastline

Penrose covers over 1,500 acres (607ha) of farmland, parkland, woodland, creeks and trails on the south coast of Cornwall. At its centre is Loe Pool, the largest natural freshwater lake in Cornwall, cut off from the sea by a broad shingle bar heaped up by the relentless Atlantic Ocean.

The restored wetlands at Willow Carr, adjacent to the pool, are wonderful to walk around and a perfect place for spotting wildlife from bats and birds to dragonflies.

THINGS TO SEE

Loe Bar is a long mound of shingle, formed by the Atlantic and separating the freshwater Loe Pool from the salty sea. It's a site of many historical shipwrecks, and legend has it that this is where King Arthur was mortally wounded and died. It's also a fascinating place to walk, with the calm pool to one side and the pounding waves to the other.

Loe Bar, separating Loe Pool from the Atlantic.

Paws for thought

Penrose is a popular destination for walkers, runners and families, especially during holidays and weekends, so it can get busy. During these times, it's especially important to have your dog on a short lead. The beach at Porthleven Sands is a great place for your dog to run free, but the area around Loe Pool is home to fragile flora and fauna, so dogs should be kept under close control. The beach shelves steeply and there are strong currents at Porthleven Sands, so swimming isn't advised here and is strictly prohibited in Loe Pool.

Other walkies nearby

The Higher Penrose Bridleway connects nearby Porthleven with the Penrose estate. Following recent work to improve accessibility, the full stretch of the bridleway is now surfaced and suitable for buggies, bikes and horses, as well as for year-round, stile-free walking without the mud!

HOW TO GET HERE

Public transport Penzance train station is 10 miles (16km) away. From the train station, take First 2/2A or 7/8 bus Penzance–Falmouth via Porthleven.

Car Penrose Estate is 2 miles (3.2km) south-west of Helston on the B3304, just south of Porthleven. Satnav: TR13 0RD

OS map Explorer 103

Start/finish Penrose Hill car park, TR13 0RD, grid ref: SW638258

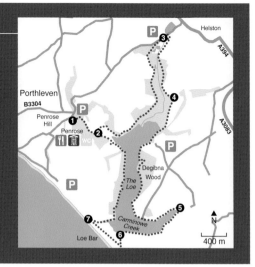

DIRECTIONS

Start/finish: Penrose Hill car park

1. From the car park follow the downhill path to the main drive. Turn right and follow the drive down and take the next left to the waymarked path.

2. Continue along the surfaced path, there's a natural bend to the right which takes you between the fenced parkland.

3. At the junction there are way-marked signs, you can turn right to go over the bridge and to the Stables and Walled Garden. Or continue along the path following the signs for Helston with Loe Pool on your right and a tree-lined path next to the River Cober.

4. At the path junction at Lower Nansloe, where you'll see farm buildings to your left, turn right, staying on the bridleway and following it alongside the woodland to reach the eastern shore of Loe Pool. Follow the obvious path along the shore, continuing along the arm of Carminowe Creek.

5. Turn right, crossing Carminowe Creek via a footbridge, turning right again after the bridge to follow the bridleway along the southern shore of Loe Pool, crossing another footbridge as you go.

6. At the pebbly stretch of Loe Bar, join the South West Coast Path, following this across the Bar towards Porthleven and up the hill to the clifftop.

7. Follow the path all the way to the Stables. The path takes a turn to the right across the bridge. At the junction take a left and follow the path back to the car park.

DOG-FRIENDLY AMENITIES

The Stables café is dog-friendly, with water bowls and biscuits on offer. The café serves hot and cold drinks, sweet treats and snacks, which can be enjoyed in the outdoor seating area. There's also dog-friendly accommodation here. Dogs are allowed in all parts of the Penrose estate, and bins are provided.

Nearby Porthleven is a quintessentially Cornish fishing village, with a beach, independent shops, and good, dog-friendly places to eat. Try The Top Chippy for takeaway fish and chips by the harbour, or the Ship Inn, Atlantic Inn and Amélie, all of which are dog-friendly.

A stone's throw from dramatic Mullion Cove (NT) and the South West Coast Path, Lana's Lodge is set on the edge of Mullion village. With an enclosed garden and generous living space, it's perfect for families and dogs, and even has a warm outside shower for washing off sand at the end of a day on the beach. lanaslodge.co.uk

03. Trelissick Roundwood Quay

Feock
Near Truro
Cornwall
TR3 6QL
01872 862090
trelissick@nationaltrust.org.uk

ABOUT THIS WALK

Distance 4 miles (6.4km)
Difficulty Moderate
Terrain Footpaths and gravel trails through woodland
Stiles No
Interest Wildlife, history

Occupying its own picturesque peninsula, bordered on three sides by water, the Trelissick estate extends across gardens, woodland and parkland with stunning views overlooking the Fal River. It's a haven for waterbirds, with oystercatchers, curlews and lapwings often seen on the foreshore.

Trelissick is renowned for its extensive and diverse gardens, both formal and informal, including an orchard home to a variety of Cornish apple trees. Access to the garden is limited to assistance dogs only, but the wider estate boasts many miles of woodland, waterside walks and open countryside for you and your dog to enjoy.

THINGS TO SEE

Overlooking its sweeping grounds, the façade of Trelissick House, with its grand Neo-classical columns, was erected by Thomas Daniell, of a well-known local mining family, in 1824. The many miles of rides and carriageways that wind through the estate were also laid out at this time. Today, both the interior and exterior of the house reflect a patchwork of the styles and preferences of its various owners over the years.

Above: Trelissick is bordered on three sides by water.
Overleaf: South Wood, on the banks of the River Fal.

Paws for thought

Dogs should be kept on a lead when around the car park, main property and in the parkland. Dogs need to be kept under effective control on the beach, waterside and woodland walks.

Other walkies nearby

King Harry Wood is great for exploring with your dog, especially in the heat of summer when it offers plenty of shady respite from the sun.

Public transport Truro Train
station is 5 miles (8km) away.
Take bus number 493 from
Truro, Lemon Quay to Feock
via Trelissick Garden.
Car Follow the A39 from
Falmouth or Truro; then onto
the B3289 at Playing Place
and follow brown signposts
or signs to the King Harry
Ferry. Satnav: TR3 6QL
OS map Explorer 105
Start/finish Trelissick car park,
TR3 6QL, grid ref: SW835396

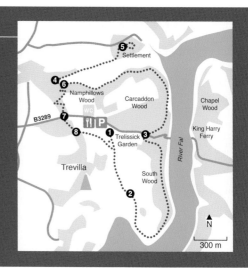

DIRECTIONS

Start/finish: Trelissick car park

1. From the car park, walk past the cattle grid into the parkland, with the sea view in front of you. Walk towards the water to reach the beach.

2. With the beach in front of you, turn left and go through a metal gate, joining the woodland walk.

3. Eventually you'll pass a path down to the ferry pontoon on the right and a small building that leads to the garden. Carefully cross straight over the road to continue on the woodland walk.

4. When you reach a path junction, turn right, following the signed path all the way to Roundwood Quay.

5. At Roundwood Quay retrace your steps back to step 4.

6. From step 4, head uphill, following the zig-zag path through mixed woodland up to the road.

7. Cross the road with care to reach the gate on the opposite side by the Old Lodge, then carry straight on until you reach a tarmac drive.

8. At the drive, go through the gate to the side of the cattle grid and follow the drive until you reach the car park at the start/finish.

DOG-FRIENDLY AMENITIES

Both Trelissick shop and Crofters Café courtyard are dog-friendly. The Old Lodge, built to match the fashionable Neo-classical mansion at Trelissick, is a self-catering cottage that sleeps three and accepts up to two dogs.

04. Great Wood and Parkland Walk, Lanhydrock

Bodmin
Cornwall
PL30 4AB
01208265950
lanhydrock@nationaltrust.org.uk

ABOUT THIS WALK

Distance 3.1 miles (5km)
Difficulty Moderate
Terrain Mostly surfaced paths, with some sections of stony track and pasture. The section along the River Fowey can be muddy
Stiles No
Interest History, wildlife

Nestled in the Cornish countryside near to Bodmin, Lanhydrock's impressive Victorian country house is set within nearly 1,000 acres (405ha) of gardens, parkland and farmland. There's a wealth of walks here, with something perfect for every dog walker at every time of year, from shaded paths through Great Wood to riverside strolling along the Fowey.

Dogs have been important members of Lanhydrock's inhabitants since Victorian times, and today it remains a thoroughly dog-friendly place to visit. This enjoyable circular walk is perfect for dogs, and a great way to explore Lanhydrock's ancient woodland and riverside paths, as well as crossing open parkland and discovering the majestic Beech Avenue.

THINGS TO SEE

Lanhydrock is part of a Cornwall-wide scheme to restore wildlife-rich grassland, 97% of which has been lost in the UK over the past 70 years. The scheme will create over 600 acres (250ha) of species-rich grassland at sites across Cornwall, providing essential habitat for rare and threatened coastal wildlife, such as solitary bees, skylarks and common lizards.

Paws for thought

Dogs aren't permitted in the house or formal gardens. While dogs are welcome on all walking trails, please don't take your dog on the dedicated cycle trails as they may get injured or cause injury to others. Cattle graze the parkland between April and October, followed by sheep till the end of December. The cattle are enclosed by an electric fence but you are welcome to walk through them, just keep dogs on a short lead when in with livestock at all times.

Other walkies nearby

All of Lanhydrock's walking trails are dog-friendly – pick up a trail map at reception and explore them all!

Late autumn at Lanhydrock.

HOW TO GET HERE

Public transport Bodmin
  Parkway station is 1.8 miles
  (2.9km) by cycle or foot; 3
  miles (4.8km) by road.
Car Signed from A30 and A38 as
  well as A390 near Lostwithiel.
  Satnav: PL30 4AB
OS map Explorer 107
Start/finish Lanhydrock main
  car park, PL30 4AB, grid ref:
  SX087643

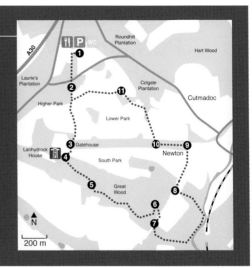

DIRECTIONS

Start/finish: Lanhydrock main car park

1. Leave the main car park, passing the Park Café and play area. Follow the signs for Lanhydrock House, crossing the road.

2. Enter the reception building. You can pick up maps showing the estate trails, dog swimming spots and location of waste bins here. From reception, follow the path down the hill towards Lanhydrock House.

3. Continue past the 17th-century gatehouse, heading towards the woodland.

4. Go through the gate next to the cattle grid and continue straight ahead up Garden Drive. Keep going until the path forks ahead of you. Take the left-hand path into the woodland.

5. Follow the winding path through the woodland, until the path forks again. Take the right-hand fork.

6. Continue along the path as it curves through Great Wood. Eventually, you'll reach a junction with another path. Turn right here and head downhill. Go through the gate and out onto the old Lostwithiel road.

7. Turn right and follow the lane past the Cornish hedge steps, until you see a gate ahead of you. Take the curved path around the corner to your left and follow it downhill towards the river.

8. Cross the little stream and take the gate on the left. Follow the path alongside the river and up the hill until you pass through the gate and reach the crossroads again. Turn right and follow the lane towards Newton Lodge.

9. Continue until you can turn left through the gates by Newton Lodge. Carry on up the hill along the Beech Avenue until you see an unpainted wooden gate in the fence on your right.

10. Enter the gate and head across the field towards the Victorian swimming pool, which is located in a small copse. You can choose to enter through the wooden gate and explore, or you can follow the path as it curves around to the left and head up the field towards the track.

11. Follow the track uphill, past the ranger's yard and office buildings on your right. Continue straight on to the reception building, from where the main path returns you to the Park Café and main car park.

Lanhydrock house and
formal gardens.

DOG-FRIENDLY AMENITIES

Lanhydrock is truly dog-friendly. Well-behaved dogs are welcome inside the Stables tea-rooms and the Park Café. In both locations, you'll find water bowls and even dog biscuits available for a donation. You can also take your dog into the outdoor shopping area of the plant centre.

There are five designated dog bathing areas along the River Fowey. Please keep your dog to these areas to minimise disturbance to wildlife in other parts of the river. Maps showing doggy facilities, including waste bins and bathing areas are available from reception.

05. Coleton Fishacre Peninsula Walk

Brownstone Road
Kingswear
Devon
TQ6 0EQ
01803 843235
coletonfishacre@nationaltrust.org.uk

ABOUT THIS WALK

Distance 5.6 miles (9km); shortcut options
Difficulty Challenging
Terrain Uneven coast path, steep and stepped in places; section of quiet road
Stiles No
Interest History, coastline, wildlife

In a steep-sided valley on the Kingswear Peninsula on Devon's south coast, Coleton Fishacre's exotic garden sweeps downhill from the Arts and Crafts-style house towards the sea. Far-reaching coastal views from the top become an intimate, almost labyrinthine experience as you explore the depths of the valley.

The South West Coast Path passes the lowest point of the garden on its 630-mile (1,014-km) journey from Poole Harbour in Dorset to Minehead in Somerset via the entire coastline of Devon and Cornwall. This walk takes in the dramatic coastal landscape surrounding the house and gardens, starting at Coleton Camp and exploring the inland and coastal paths, and passing intriguing remnants of the area's cultural history.

THINGS TO SEE

Coleton Fishacre's RHS-accredited garden offers regular enticing viewpoints out to sea. Follow inviting paths that weave through the exotic gardens. Here you can admire the collection of tender plants from the Mediterranean, South Africa and New Zealand, which thrive in the damp, sheltered environment of the valley.

Paws for thought

You'll often come across ponies, gentle longhorn cattle, sheep and even seals along the coast path, so always keep your dog under close control and on a short lead around these animals. Some stretches of the path have sheer, unfenced drops. In the garden, where narrow paths are shared with other visitors, keep your dog on a short lead and off the planted areas.

Other walkies nearby
Man Sands and Scabbacombe Sands, two beaches to the north of Coleton Fishacre, are stunning, peaceful, sandy bays edged by dramatic rocky outcrops. Both are dog-friendly all year round. Alternatively, catch the foot ferry over to Dartmouth and explore the historic stretch of the coast path there, including the 600-year-old castle in its spectacular position guarding the entrance to Dartmouth Harbour (not National Trust).

Above: Sea views, across the lower gardens, out to Pudcombe Cove.
Opposite: The South West Coast Path near Coleton Fishacre.

HOW TO GET HERE

Public transport Paignton train station is 6 miles (9.7km) away. Stagecoach bus 120 runs from Paignton (close to train station) to Brixham-Kingswear.
Car Take the A379 and then follow the B3205 towards Kingswear. From here follow signs towards Coleton Fishacre and Coleton Camp car park. Satnav: TQ6 0EQ
OS map Explorer OL20
Start/finish Coleton Camp car park, TQ6 0EQ, grid ref: SX909512

[Map showing the route around Coleton Fishacre, including Scabbacombe Head, Kingswear, Coleton Fishacre, Day Mark Tower, Mill Bay Cove, Newfoundland Cove, Lookout Station, Pudcombe Cove, Kelly's Cove, with numbered waypoints 1-6. Scale 400 m, North arrow.]

DIRECTIONS

Start/finish: Coleton Camp car park, Brownstone Road, Kingswear

1. Follow the track east out of the car park, heading downhill towards the sea and reaching the South West Coast Path at Scabbacombe Head.

2. Turn right onto the coast path to follow it until you reach Pudcombe Cove, near the coastal entrance to Coleton Fishacre garden. If you would like to do the shorter version of this walk, leave the coast path here and walk up through the centre of Coleton Fishacre garden. Normal admission prices to Coleton Fishacre apply, so pop into visitor reception while you're there. When you're ready to continue, follow the driveway and turn right at the top to go back to the start of the route at Coleton Camp.

3. For the full walk, continue on the South West Coast Path round Outer Froward Point and on past Brownstone Battery at Inner Froward Point, a Second World War gun emplacement.

4. The final section of the walk is steeply undulating, so there's another option for a shortcut here, turning right at Inner Froward Point and following the Military Road up to Higher Brownstone Farm (point 6).

5. For the full walk, continue on the South West Coast Path around Newfoundland Cove to reach a track which leads left to Kingswear; don't take this but turn right and climb uphill past Higher Brownstone Farm to join a country lane.

6. Follow the country lane past the entrance to Coleton Fishacre on your right, back to the start at Coleton Camp.

DOG-FRIENDLY AMENITIES

Dogs are welcome throughout the garden, café and shop at Coleton Fishacre, although not in the house.

The pretty, peacefully located twin cottages at Coleton Barton are both dog-friendly with enclosed gardens and make a perfect base from which to explore the area around Coleton Fishacre. Staying here also grants you out-of-hours access to the garden, so you can enjoy its magic in glorious solitude.

06. Baggy Point Headland Walk

Moor Lane
Croyde
Devon
EX33 IPA
01271 891970
northdevon@nationaltrust.org.uk

ABOUT THIS WALK

Distance 4.6 miles (7.4km)
Difficulty Moderate
Terrain Undulating coast path and footpath; can be slippery in the wet
Stiles Yes
Interest Wildlife, coastline

The prominent headland at Baggy Point overlooks the sandy crescent of Croyde Bay to the south, and the vast stretch of Woolacombe Sands that edges Morte Bay to the north. It boasts stunning coastal views, great walks along the South West Coast Path, a dog-friendly tea-room and exciting opportunities for adventure sport, including top quality climbing, surfing and coasteering.

This walk takes in a loop of the headland, making the most of the panoramic views and breathing in the gorse-scented sea air. The tiny island of Lundy can be seen 10 nautical miles (18.5km) off the coast here. Along the way you'll walk through grassland rich in wild flowers and birdlife, and witness some of Croyde and Baggy Point's modern-day draws including climbing and surfing.

THINGS TO SEE

Baggy Point was home to the Hyde family, who lived on this dramatic headland until donating it to the National Trust in 1939. Reminders of their time here can be seen in the handsome farm buildings, freshwater pond – home to many mallard ducks during the Second World War – and the slipway and harbour, where they stored their boats well away from the reach of the stormy sea.

Paws for thought
Croyde beach has a seasonal dog ban in effect from 1 May to 30 September. Sheer drops and grazing animals mean dogs should be kept on leads throughout.

Other walkies nearby
Both Croyde and Woolacombe beaches are fantastic for dogs out of season (October to April). The South West Coast Path also continues either side of Baggy Point on its 630-mile (1,014-km) journey from Poole in Dorset to Minehead in Somerset.

Above: The main trail out towards Baggy Point.

HOW TO GET HERE

Public transport Train to Barnstaple. Regular bus service from Barnstaple to Croyde, then follow brown signs to Baggy Point.
Car A361 to Braunton, take Saunton Road B3231 to Croyde, then follow brown signs. Satnav: EX33 1PA
OS map Explorer 139
Start/finish Baggy Point car park, EX33 1PA, grid ref: SS432397

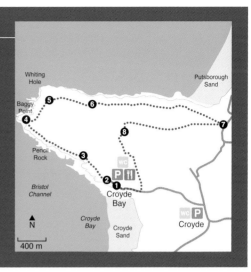

DIRECTIONS

Start/finish: Baggy Point car park

1. Go out of the car park by the kiosk and turn right up the asphalted lane, signed 'Baggy Point 1 mile'. Be careful as there can be traffic on this section. Go through gate posts to the fingerpost at the fork in the path and go left here. On your left at this point is the only dog waste bin in this area. Follow the asphalted track past the houses. Watch out for peregrines flying overhead.

2. Follow this mostly level, graded track along to the end of the headland. Look out to your left across the bays to Hartland in the far distance. We also have downloadable trails for this area – please look on our website for details.

3. As the path curves slightly to your left, look for three steps up to your right where you'll find a pond that's been restored to create a valuable wildlife habitat. The water here is deep so please keep dogs under close supervision. Return to the path, passing through the gorse to the gate. Continue along the South West Coast Path, passing the old harbour on your left. On a clear day there are views out to Lundy Island beyond the headland.

4. At the furthest point of the headland, take some time to stop and admire the views. In dry weather, and when the sea birds aren't nesting, you can often spot rock climbers making their way up the sea cliffs. To continue onwards, follow the coast path as it takes a sharp hairpin turn. Take the grassy path immediately to your left, following it past an old coastguard wreck post. Dogs should be kept on a lead here as the cliff edge is sheer and unfenced.

5. At the trig point, follow the grassy track onto the eastern side of Baggy Point, with great views across Woolacombe Bay. Go through the next gate and at the fingerpost follow the grassy path to your left, passing a concrete bunker, one of several dummy pillboxes on Baggy Point built in the Second World War and used for training for the D-Day Normandy landings.

6. Go through the kissing gate and stay on the grassy track along the top of the cliff along Bloodhills Cliff. Cross through the next kissing gate and follow the winding path through gorse bushes, with their bright yellow, coconut-scented flowers. At the fingerpost, continue straight on, signed 'Woolacombe 3 miles'. Go through the next kissing gate and follow the path downhill alongside a wall. At the next fingerpost, follow the coast path sign along the grassy track off to your right across the field – don't take the path down to the campsite. Cross the field to the fingerpost by the hedgerow.

7. Turn right, leaving the South West Coast Path and following the footpath, keeping the fence and hedgebank to your left. Where the fence turns to your left, follow the yellow footpath arrow diagonally across the field to the far left corner. Go through the gate in the dry-stone wall and follow the narrow path between the hedgerows. At the end of the path, continue straight ahead, along the farm track.

8. Follow the track to the end, then follow the fingerpost down to your left, signed 'Public Footpath'. Continue straight ahead, over the stile and down the hill on a narrow path. Follow the yellow arrow down the farm track, past the farm on your right and down to the road. Turn right, cross the road with care, and follow the path back to the car park.

DOG-FRIENDLY AMENITIES

Dogs are welcome inside and outside at the National Trust Sandleigh Tearooms. Water bowls are provided. Opening times may vary throughout the seasons, so please check before visiting (01271 891230).

Cliffs at Baggy Point.

07. Lorna Doone Valley

**Lorna Doone Farm
Malmsmead
Lynton
Devon
EX35 6NU
01598 741362**

northdevon@nationaltrust.org.uk

ABOUT THIS WALK

**Distance 6.8 miles (11km)
Difficulty Moderate
Terrain Paths, bridleways
and roads. Undulating with
some muddy sections
Stiles No
Interest History, literary,
coastline**

On the northern fringes of Exmoor, where the counties of Devon and Somerset meet, Lorna Doone Valley is set among some of the best walking country you'll find anywhere. The sheer variety and accessibility to the moors, woodlands and coast makes this a top destination for those wanting to explore an unspoilt area rich in wildlife, history and trails.

This circular walk sets out from Lorna Doone Valley, taking you on a wonderful exploration of the landscape that inspired R.D. Blackmore's famous novel of the same name. You'll wander through ancient oak woodlands, over open moorland, and past the medieval village of Badgworthy, as well as the memorial to Blackmore.

THINGS TO SEE

The medieval Doone village is an atmospheric place, hidden in a valley scattered with patches of scree. The traces of stone walls here are thought to be from the 12th century, remnants of the homes of a remote farming community. The houses and field terraces here are some of the best preserved of this type in south-west England.

Paws for thought
This area is home to many creatures, including ponies (many of whom have foals with them in spring and summer), deer, ground nesting birds and grazing animals. Dogs can easily frighten or harm these animals, and should therefore be kept on the lead at all times. The pebble beaches along this stretch of the coast are dog-friendly all year round.

Other walkies nearby
A short distance north from Lorna Doone Valley is County Gate, on the Devon/Somerset border. From here, there are great coastal walks, following footpaths, bridleways and the South West Coast Path west to Countisbury Common, Foreland Point, Watersmeet and Lynmouth, or east through the wooded combes at Culbone towards Porlock. The Tarka Trail and the Coleridge Way also pass very close by.

Above: Badgworthy River near Cloud Farm.
Overleaf: Brendon Common.

Public transport Lorna Doone Valley is 0.7 miles (1.2km) from County Gate car park – a stop on the Exmoor Coaster bus route. From here, follow the footpath heading south down the hill from the car park. This path will briefly join the Coleridge Way, then come to a road. Turning right at the road, The Buttery café can be found around 300 yards along the road.

Car Lorna Doone Valley is 5 miles (8km) east of Lynmouth or 13 miles (21km) west of Minehead. From the A39, turn off to follow New Road to Oare. From here turn right to take Hookway Hill to Lorna Doone Valley. Satnav: EX35 6NU

OS map Explorer OL9

Start/finish Lorna Doone Farm, EX35 6NU, grid ref: SS791478

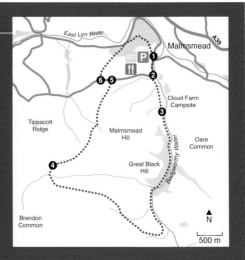

DOG-FRIENDLY AMENITIES

Dog-friendly Cloud Farm campsite is an ideal base from which to explore this part of Exmoor and North Devon. Set in a flat, grassy valley next to Badgworthy Water, it's a peaceful and inspiring place with a range of good facilities and a small shop. The Buttery café is a short walk downstream.

DIRECTIONS

Start/finish: Lorna Doone Farm

1. From the car park walk behind the shop and up the road passing the old stable block to your left and barn on the right. Ignoring the toll gate which leads onto a permissive path, continue up the road until it bends to the right.

2. Go through the gate ahead and take the bridleway marked with a blue arrow. Follow the bridleway passing through the two gates until you reach an open area with a footbridge to the Cloud Farm campsite.

3. Continue along the bridleway following the Badgworthy Water for 3km passing the memorial to R.D. Blackmore and into the ancient woodland. Follow the bridleway through the woodland, which opens into an area of bracken; here, cross a wooden footbridge. Continue along the path until you reach the abandoned medieval village of Badgworthy. The bridleway bends around the hill and up onto Brendon Common.

4. Follow this bridleway onto the moor itself for 2km, passing through a gate in a stone wall field boundary. Finally, through a small ford and up a slope to a crossroad.

5. Turn right at the crossroad signposted towards Malmsmead. Follow the blue bridleway markers as the bridleway turns left off the stone track. Pass through a ford and up a hill and follow the clearly defined path until you reach the road.

6. Cross over the road and through a gate with a signpost. Follow the middle path signposted for Southern Wood looping around the wood. The path then descends downhill to a road. Cross the road back to the Lorna Doone car park.

08. Cott Brake at Arlington Court

Arlington
Near Barnstaple
Devon
EX31 4LP
01271 850296
arlingtoncourt@nationaltrust.org.uk

ABOUT THIS WALK

Distance 5 miles (8km)
Difficulty Moderate
Terrain Footpaths across parkland and through woodland; some sections can be muddy. One steep hill
Stiles Yes
Interest Wildlife, history

Arlington Court is a great place to enjoy the great outdoors surrounded by beautiful, rolling Devon countryside. You'll find more than 20 miles (32.2km) of footpaths here, with something to suit everyone, from easy lakeside strolls to more challenging hikes across the wider estate.

This walk takes you through ancient woodland and up onto steep grassland, with spectacular views of Cott Brake. Along the way, look out for the ornamental Wilderness Pond, the obelisk monument, examples of historic architecture and the estate's herd of majestic red deer.

THINGS TO SEE

Set in the historic stables, the collection at the Carriage Museum has been amassed over the past 60 years. You're welcome to bring your dog into the museum to browse the wide range of vehicles, including some used for grand state occasions and others that would have been servants' carts.

Arlington Court Estate.

Paws for thought

Dogs must be kept on a lead in the pleasure grounds around the house and in the Carriage Museum. On the wider estate, different rules apply at different times of the year:

1 February–31 July: dogs must be kept on a lead everywhere to protect lambs and ground-nesting birds.

1 August–31 January: dogs may be let off the lead on the Lake Walk and the wider estate.

Other walkies nearby

There are over 20 miles (32.2km) of paths to explore at Arlington, all of which are dog-friendly. Try the easy Lake Walk, which visits the bird hide and heronry and takes in some of the estate's historic carriage drives. The longer Deer Park walk, waymarked with green arrows, explores the expansive parkland and nature reserve.

HOW TO GET HERE

Public transport Nearest train
  station is Barnstaple 8 miles
  (12.9km) away. Infrequent bus
  service Barnstaple to Lynton.
Car From South Molton/east stay on
  A399 until turning for A39
  (Arlington is signposted). Don't
  turn left into an unmarked lane: this
  leads to 'deliveries and residents'
  entrance only. Satnav: EX31 4LP
OS Map Explorer OL9
Start/finish Arlington Court car
  park, EX31 4LP, grid ref: SS611407

DIRECTIONS

Start/finish: Arlington Court car park

1. From the car park, cross the road and follow
   the main path to Arlington Court. You'll find
   the reception and Old Kitchen tea-room here.
   From the tea-room, follow signs to the
   Carriage Museum, bearing right before the
   church and passing the Wilderness Pond. From
   here, head down into the Wilderness, taking
   the track down the hill and then bearing left at
   the fork to reach a gate.

2. Once through the gate, follow the track to
   Smallacombe Bridge. Cross the bridge and
   turn left, following signs for Loxhore and
   Deerpark Wood.

3. Just before Tucker's Bridge, take the right-hand
   fork, signed 'Shirwell via Cott Wood'. Follow
   the track alongside the river, going through a
   gate into a wooded meadow.

4. Follow the track through two gates. After the
   second gate, turn left and walk up a steep hill
   with woodland on your left. At the top of the
   hill turn left over a stile onto Cott Brake.

5. Turn right and follow the collapsed hedge bank
   on your right, keeping to the brow of the hill
   until you reach the end of the field. Climb over
   the stile into Cott Wood and follow the narrow
   woodland track until you reach another stile.

6. Go over the stile at the end of the track and turn left. Take the next left down a main track, which is steep and rocky in places. At the bottom you'll join a tarmac road. Cross Cott Bridge then follow the road uphill, bearing left. At the top of the next hill, you'll see Loxhore Lodge, with large gates topped by herons.

7. Go through the gates and onto the wide track, following this to a junction at Tucker's Bridge. Don't cross the bridge but take the track uphill signed 'Arlington Court and Loxhore' via Deerpark Wood.

8. Continue along this track through the woodland alongside a stream. At a crossroad of paths, keep left and cross the bridge. Follow the rocky path uphill and through a gate, following the path around to the right and through any gates.

9. Continue on the path through a small copse.

10. At the end of the path, go through the farm gate and turn right, keeping left along the field edge until you come to a gate on your left. Go through this gate and follow a small track into woodland.

11. When you reach the Sawmill at the edge of the wood, turn left down a concrete slope, then left again along a rough track. From here, you can walk down the slope and back to your starting point at the main gardens and tea-room, with the car park across the road.

DOG-FRIENDLY AMENITIES

The Chichester family, who owned Arlington Court for 11 generations, were a family of dog lovers. Today, dogs are welcome in most areas of the estate, although they do need to be kept on leads on the wider estate at certain times of the year to protect wildlife. You can take your dog into the Carriage Museum and the gardens, although they're not allowed in the main house.

Opposite: Bridge over the River Yeo.
Left: A visitor with her dogs at Arlington Court.

09. Around Killerton Park

Broadclyst
Exeter
Devon
EX5 3LE
01392 881345
killerton@nationaltrust.org.uk

ABOUT THIS WALK

Distance 2.3 miles (3.7km)
Difficulty Easy/Moderate
**Terrain Tracks and
woodland paths which can
become muddy. Steep uphill
at the start**
Stiles No
Interest Wildlife, history

Killerton was home to the Acland family, from the late 17th century until 1944. Over the centuries, the house and its grounds evolved from its late Tudor roots into a grand Georgian, and then Victorian, estate. There are still Tudor elements to be found inside the house, while the gardens boast Georgian landscaping.

Designed specifically to give dogs the best time at Killerton, this circular walk offers plenty of safe open space for dogs to be exercised on and off the lead, along with far-reaching views and rolling Devon countryside. You'll find signs on the gates as you go, telling you where dogs can be let off their leads.

THINGS TO SEE

Killerton's fascinating gardens combine far-reaching views, formal terraces, rolling lawns, ancient trees, a hut with a knucklebone floor (the Bear's Hut) and even an extinct volcano known as The Clump, which was also the site of a Roman hill fort.

Paws for thought
Dogs must be kept on a lead between visitor reception and the house, along the drive, and in the area shaded amber on the map, which can be picked up at visitor reception. Other than assistance dogs, dogs are not allowed in the house, garden or chapel grounds, including the Kitchen Café. Please ensure that your dog is under close control at all times, even in areas where it is allowed off the lead, and look out for seasonal signs advising where livestock is present.

Other walkies nearby
The Deodar Glen walk is another great dog-friendly walk at Killerton. Along the way, you'll discover Park Wood, Deodar Glen and The Plains before finishing with a close-up view of the old quarry and The Clump, all with glorious views out across the Killerton estate. Maps are available detailing the best places at Killerton to walk with your dog. Ashclyst Forest, adjoining Killerton, is another wonderful place to walk your dog and a great place to spot butterflies over the summer months.

Above: Killerton House.
Opposite: Killerton Park.

Public transport Trains to Exeter Central or St David's 7 miles (11.3km) away. Bus services from Exeter to Tiverton. Alight at Killerton Turn.
Car M5 southbound: leave at J28, follow brown signs for Killerton on B3181 towards Broadclyst. M5 northbound: exit J29. Follow signs for B3181 Pinhoe/Broadclyst. Follow brown Killerton signs. Killerton is shortly after leaving the village of Broadclyst. Satnav: EX5 3LE
OS map Explorer 114
Start/finish Killerton car park, EX5 3LE, grid ref: SS976001

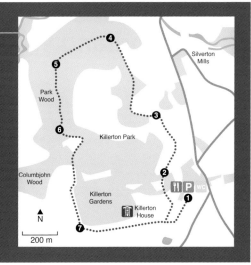

DIRECTIONS

Start/finish: Killerton car park

1. Starting from the visitor car park, head towards the stable block, beyond which you'll find visitor reception. Exiting the reception area, turn right onto the main path towards the house, then first right, in the direction of the chapel. Stay on the main path and head up the hill.

2. Follow the well-trodden path around the top of the valley, then go through a wooden gate leading into a wood, following the path that continues straight ahead to reach a crossroads.

3. Go straight over the crossroads, then, at the top of the hill, leave the path and carry on straight ahead to a metal gate. Go through the gate and continue straight on, crossing over a rutted track. Dogs may be let off the lead in this area, but there are sometimes cattle grazing, so please keep your dog in sight and under control. Follow the path round to the left.

4. After a short distance, the path splits into two. Bear right here, taking in the views over the River Culm.

5. At the next fork, bear left up the hill, then take the next path on the right.

6. At the clearing and path junction, take the middle path up the hill. Carry straight on to reach two wooden gates; going through the one on the right. Once through, turn left down the hill through the field, being aware of cattle, which sometimes graze here.

7. At the bottom of the hill on the left go through a wooden kissing gate. Carry straight on, eventually passing Killerton House. The wooden gate on the left will take you back to the stable block and café, with the car park beyond.

DOG-FRIENDLY AMENITIES

Dogs are welcomed in the reception area, Stables Café and the wider estate, parkland and woodland areas.

There are dog-friendly self-catering cottages on the Killerton estate, including the magical Forest Cottage, hidden in leafy Ashclyst Forest, and Killerton Park Cottage.

10. Tyntesfield Woodland Walk

View towards Tyntesfield house from the parkland in spring.

Wraxall
Bristol
North Somerset
BS48 1PA
01275 461900
tyntesfield@nationaltrust.org.uk

ABOUT THIS WALK

Distance Approx 2.2 miles (3.6km)
Difficulty Moderate
Terrain Unsurfaced woodland paths, steps, gravelled surfaces and steep gradients
Stiles No
Interest History, wildlife

The Grade I-listed Victorian Gothic-Revival mansion at Tyntesfield stands grandly amidst over 540 acres of rolling countryside. Within easy reach of Bristol, this is a perfect place to escape the pavements and explore woodland trails and open grassland with your dog.

Starting and finishing at Home Farm, this route takes in a loop of the grounds with plenty of hills. This varied walk explores the many different aspects of the estate, including the extensive areas of woodland, the gardens and the intriguing Orangery.

THINGS TO SEE

The woodland is a brilliant place to spot fungi. Over 1,000 species have been spotted here, by a team of volunteer fungi hunters. These include the toxic deadly fibrecap, so don't touch and keep dogs and children well away. Later in the walk, you'll promenade along the Holly Walk. Tyntesfield's hollies are considered to be one of the most important features of the garden collection. Each holly on the walk is a different variety.

Paws for thought
When approaching the Kitchen Garden area, please be aware that dogs are not allowed into the Walled Garden. Dogs always need to be kept on a short lead at Tyntesfield. Be aware that livestock graze on the estate.

Other walkies nearby
You'll find a number of other walks on the estate, including the Tyntesfield House route.

DIRECTIONS

Start/finish: Tyntesfield car park

1. Start at the Visitor welcome building. Walk along the concrete path with the Cow Barn Restaurant on your left, continue up the hill until you reach a junction with two large open barns on your left.

2. At the top of the drive, turn left and walk along the grass verge alongside the main drive, keeping the fields on your right and the woodland on your left. Please be mindful of cars on this part of the route, and keep dogs on a short lead. Continue up this road and take the first right, signposted Summerhouse.

HOW TO GET HERE

Public transport The closest train stations are Nailsea and Backwell (4 miles/6.5km) or Bristol Temple Meads (7.4 miles/12km). The X6 bus (Bristol to Clevedon) stops at the main entrance to Tyntesfield.

Car Tyntesfield is located on the B3128, between Long Ashton and Nailsea. Please follow brown signs to the main entrance. From Bristol City centre follow the A370 toward Weston Super Mare, then the B3128. From M5 southbound, use J19. From M5 northbound, take J20. Satnav: BS48 1PA.

OS map Explorer 154

Start/finish Tyntesfield car park, BS48 1PA, grid ref: ST500716

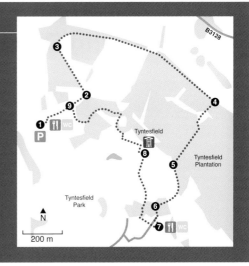

3. Continue until the Summerhouse Cottage is on your left, then keep along the top path past the map sign. Walk on for around 10 minutes until you see a marker post with an arrow right. Turn right and walk through the woods into an open grove.

4. Continue down the hill walking past the poetry board until you arrive at a small set of steps. Head down these steps, turn left and walk along the track, taking the next right down a grass slope onto the main drive.

5. At the tarmac drive, take the second path to the left, down the slope with the field on your right. Continue down until you come to a left-hand turn, signposted to the Kitchen Garden and Pavilion.

6. Take the first left just ahead of the small fenced-off pond and then right through the main gates into the Kitchen Garden; continue until the Orangery is on your left.

7. With the Orangery at your back, walk through the Dial Garden, past the end of the glasshouses and up the steps into the loggia, and then into the Old Orange Garden (courtyard area). Exit through the green metal gate and follow the path over the crossroads and through the gate. Walk across the park on the cobblestone path. Continue through the next gate and up to the terraces in front of the house.

8. Go up the steps in front of the house and turn left at the top. At the end of the terraces, turn right and go up the steps ahead of you. Take the path left up the Broad Walk (holly-lined walk). Half-way up the Holly Walk, take a right-hand turn signposted to the Rose Garden. Follow the path to the left and continue along this route until you meet the main path again.

9. Take a right hand turn to exit through a gate into Top Field. Walk through the field and the next gate then turn left and follow the path back to the Visitor welcome building.

DOG-FRIENDLY AMENITIES

Dogs are welcome in the shop and the dog-friendly section of the Cow Barn Restaurant. The Pavillion Café by the Kitchen Garden is also dog-friendly, serving doggy ice cream year-round and with water bowls outside for a hydrating pit-stop. There's also a dog-friendly holiday cottage on the Tyntesfield estate, offering access to the walks from your doorstep. Sleeping two people and a dog, Summerhouse Cottage is a former hunting lodge with a private patio, intriguing octagonal summerhouse and farmland views.

11. Crook Peak and Wavering Down

Webbington Road car park
BH26 2HN
somerset.countryside@
nationaltrust.org.uk

ABOUT THIS WALK

Distance 6 miles (9.7km)
Difficulty Challenging
Terrain Moorland paths,
steep climb through Kings
Wood, steep descent from
Crook Peak
Stiles No
Interest Wildlife, geology

At the western end of the limestone escarpment of the Mendip Hills, temptingly visible from the M5, rises the shapely summit of Crook Peak. Its name derives from the Old English *cruc* meaning a pointed hill.

Despite its proximity to the motorway, this long ridge of wildlife-rich grassland with expansive views of the Mendips, the Somerset Levels, and across the Severn Estuary to Wales, feels at least a million miles from the traffic speeding by below.

THINGS TO SEE

The Mendip Hills are most important for their large stretches of calcareous grasslands, ancient wooded ravines, and stunning geology, which are home to threatened species such as adders, dormice, horseshoe bats and skylarks. Nearby Cheddar Gorge is a deep limestone gorge – the largest in England. Cheddar, as well as being where the famous cheese is aged, was where Cheddar Man, Britain's oldest complete human skeleton, was found, estimated to be over 9,000 years old.

DOG-FRIENDLY AMENITIES

The Crown Inn at Churchill is a popular and characterful local pub that welcomes dogs and muddy walkers. Specialising in real ales from the barrel and hearty lunchtime food, there's a pretty beer garden to sit in on sunny days, or a cosy interior for winter walks. Water bowls are provided for thirsty dogs. All dogs must be kept on leads for the comfort of other customers.

Paws for thought

Sheep, ponies and cows can often be found grazing on the hills, so keep dogs on a lead at all times.

Other walkies nearby

Mendip Hills National Landscape has a wealth of excellent walking routes. Some areas, such as Cheddar Gorge and Ebbor Gorge are rocky, slippery in the wet and have unfenced sheer drops, so are less well-suited to dogs. But Beacon Batch – the summit of Black Down and the highest point of the Mendip Hills – is another great place for a dog-friendly walk.

Above: Sunrise over the Mendip Hills, from Crook Peak.
Opposite: Wavering Down from Crook Peak.

HOW TO GET HERE

Public transport From Bridgewater train station link up with the FAL bus north, alighting at Shute Shelve Hill for Cross.

Car Take J22 from the M5 and follow A38 towards Cheddar. Turn left at Cross onto Webbington Road. Satnav: BH26 2HN

OS map Explorer 141 and 153

Start/finish Webbington Road car park, BH26 2HN, grid ref: ST392550

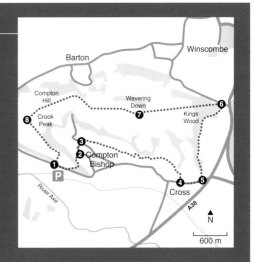

DIRECTIONS

Start/finish: Webbington Road car park

1. Cross Webbington Road and go through the gate opposite, turning right and following the path. Pass the gate and junction with the path up to Crook Peak and continue to the next junction with a bridleway at the edge of the woods. Turn left and then right at the next junction, following the track downhill to Butts Batch in Compton Bishop.

2. Turn left and follow Butts Batch down the hill past the church to the junction with Church Lane. Continue past Coombe Lane and take the next left, signed as a footpath, opposite.

3. Follow this footpath up and right, past a couple of houses and a stable to the end of the track where the path reaches a field. Continue straight ahead, crossing several large fields, to reach a driveway below Bourton Farm. Cross and continue to follow the footpath across some smaller fields to reach the disused limestone quarry above Cross. Turn right in the quarry and follow the footpath downhill to the Old Coach Road in Cross.

4. Turn left and follow the Old Coach Road through the village and past the White Hart to a left turn onto a footpath beside a dog waste bin.

5. Take this footpath and follow it uphill, trending right through Kings Wood to reach the car park. The walk can also be started from this point.

6. Turn left at the car park, joining the West Mendip Way and follow the path uphill to the trig point on Wavering Down.

7. From the trig point, continue on the West Mendip Way, walking downhill. Pass Barton Hill to reach a path junction at a wall corner. Leave the West Mendip Way and head uphill to the rocky summit of Crook Peak.

8. Turn left and follow the path down the main ridge to reach your outward path. Turn right and follow this path back to the start.

12. Burton Bradstock and Hive Beach

Hive Beach Office
Beach Road
Burton Bradstock
Dorset
DT6 4RF
01297 489481
burtonbradstock@nationaltrust.org.uk

ABOUT THIS WALK

Distance 2 miles (3.2km)
Difficulty Easy
Terrain Coast path, some gentle hills and one steep hill, can be slippery in the wet
Stiles Yes
Interest: Coastline, history, wildlife

Hive Beach is popular with walkers, families and dogs alike. With the South West Coast Path passing by, the beach is easy to access and offers a range of walks, from those on the beach itself to spectacular clifftop routes with glorious coastal countryside and sea views.

The shingle beach at Hive is surrounded by spectacular sandstone cliffs. It is a striking section of the Jurassic Coast World Heritage Site and the largest shingle ridge in the world.

THINGS TO SEE

Burton Cliff is one of the finest examples of the distinctive, alternately hard and soft layered geology of the Bridport Sands area, which makes it appear to glow bright gold in the sunlight. Regular rock falls from the unstable cliffs on this stretch of the coastline sometimes expose fascinating fossils, such as ammonites with their spiral shells.

Other walkies nearby
Other enjoyable dog-friendly walks along the Jurassic Coast include the 2.2-mile (3.5-km) Cogden Circular from Cogden, and walks on the Golden Cap estate, including the 1.4-mile (2.3-km) loop around Langdon Woods, always spectacular in later spring when bluebells carpet the woodland floor.

Paws for thought
The cliffs along this stretch of the coast can be unstable, so keep away from the edges and don't walk under the cliffs in areas where there are warning signs. Dogs should be kept on a short lead when the beach or coast path is busy, and around grazing animals. Please also keep your dog on a lead between 1 March and 31 July when ground-nesting birds are vulnerable. From 1 June to 30 September, dogs (other than assistance dogs) are not permitted on the beach directly in front of the café. Dogs are allowed east of the beach, past the wooden chalet towards Cogden and Portland Island.

Above and opposite: Burton Beach.

Public transport The Jurassic Coast X53 bus operates a daily service, linking Hive Beach with Bridport, Weymouth train station and Axminster train station.

Car Hive Beach is located roughly 2 miles (3.2km) east of Bridport, just off the B3157 Bridport to Weymouth road.
Satnav: DT6 4RF
OS map Explorer 116
Start/finish Hive beach car park, DT6 4RF, grid ref: SY491888

DIRECTIONS

Start/finish: Hive Beach car park

1. Follow the South West Coast Path out of the top left of the car park. Walk diagonally across the next field to a path junction. Turn left and follow the coast path across another field towards the sea to the cliff top path. Bear right and follow Burton Cliff until you reach the mouth of the River Bride.

2. Follow the coast path inland around the headland, tracing the course of the river inland to reach the end of Southover Road.

3. Follow Southover Road until you reach Cliff Road. Cross over and go up the steps and over the stile. For a village detour, turn left along the main road. Burton Bradstock is an idyllic village, well worth exploring, with many of the buildings made in a traditional style from local stone.

4. Follow the path diagonally across a large field. Go through the kissing gate at the other end of the field and across the next field and gate. Go through this and straight down to return to the car park.

DOG-FRIENDLY AMENITIES

Hive Beach Café, just minutes from the beach, is very dog-friendly and a great place for a pre-walk breakfast, post-walk cake or a celebratory meal.

The National Trust has a selection of cosy, dog-friendly cottages near Burton Bradstock, including Oak Cottage, on the Golden Cap estate and Chesil Cottage at West Bexington.

13. Bath Skyline

South-east of the city of Bath
Bath and NE Somerset
01225 833977

bathskyline@nationaltrust.org.uk

ABOUT THIS WALK

Distance 5.9 miles (9.5km)
Difficulty Moderate
Terrain Very varied, grassy, rocky, gravel and surfaced trails. Some steps and steep up and down hills
Stiles Yes
Interest: Wildlife, history

Tracing the high ground above the World Heritage Site of Bath, the views from this circular walk offer new perspectives of the city, bird's-eye views of the Royal Crescent, Circus and abbey surrounded by Bath's seven hills.

There's a real feeling of escape on the Skyline, whether you're following clear trails over open grassland with far-reaching vistas, winding through lush woodland, or enjoying the tranquillity of fields and wildflower meadows, there's a fantastic variety of localities and terrains to experience. Please ensure you follow directions in a clockwise direction.

THINGS TO SEE

Standing high on Claverton Down, commanding far-reaching views across Bath and the Avon valley, the Grade II-listed folly at Sham Castle can be reached via a short detour off the Bath Skyline at point 2 of the walk.

Paws for thought
Bath Skyline takes you through places where animals may be grazing and also past children's play areas and sports fields. Please keep your dog on a short lead at these points, and under close control at all times. There are several road crossings on the route, some of which cross busy roads with poor visibility. Take extra care here, ensuring your dog is under close control on the approach to roads.

Other walkies nearby
Bathampton Meadows is the National Trust's first 'green corridor', linking the world heritage city of Bath to the countryside beyond. The route runs from Kensington Meadows along the River Avon to Bathampton Meadows, taking in the villages of Bathampton, Bathford and Batheaston. Abundant with wild flowers over the spring and summer months, this is a great place to spot butterflies and other pollinators. Visit in the evening to see bug-hunting bats, or early in the morning for the chance to see beavers along the river.

Above: Bath Skyline meadows, overlooking Bath.
Opposite: Bushey Norwood fields.

Public transport Bath Spa
station is 0.8 miles (1.3km)
from the start of the walk.
Car Bath is just off the A4
Bath to Bristol road, and
the A36 from Warminster;
10 miles (16km) from J18
on the M4. Satnav: BA2 6JP
OS map Explorer 155
Start/finish Bathwick Hill at
Cleveland Walk, BA2 6JP,
grid ref: ST760647

DIRECTIONS

Start/finish: Bathwick Hill at Cleveland Walk

1. From Bathwick Hill, follow Cleveland Walk for about 400 yards
   until you can turn right onto a narrow footpath opposite Sham
   Castle Lane. Follow this path to North Road, turning right here
   and crossing the road to reach a kissing gate on your left.

2. Go through the kissing gate, up the steep steps and follow the
   path up through a field. At the top go through a kissing gate onto
   a small road with a bench on the left. Take the path left, down
   some steps and through the woodland. Continue on the path,
   bearing right and heading uphill to reach a kissing gate at the top.

3. At the radio masts, where the main track turns right, continue
   straight ahead on a smaller grassy path across two fields and down a short slope.

4. When the path descends towards the trees, go through the gate on the right into
   the woods and follow the winding path until you reach a path junction. Go straight
   across, passing some large rocks on both sides and walking up a short slope
   between two trees where the path splits. Take the wider path in the middle, passing
   a large rocky cliff on the right. Keep to the higher path ascending to a path junction.
   Bear left here and continue to a kissing gate.

5. Go through the kissing gate into a field. Cross the field to reach a gate in the wall.
   Go through the gate and bear right. Cross the next field, go through a gate and
   turn left along a track. Turn right before the metal gates and go through a wooden
   gate (University land). Go over a stone stile in the wall on the left and turn right
   onto a road. After 100 yards, turn left onto a public footpath just before Bath Cats
   and Dogs Home. Follow the footpath to reach Claverton Down Road.

6. Cross the road with care, bearing left to a layby with a gate onto a footpath. Go
   through the gate and follow the path for 800 yards, through two wooden gates
   until you reach a clear path into the woodland on the right.

7. Turn right into woodland, and follow the woodland path for 0.6 mile (1km), passing a play area on your right and staying right at the next junction, continue with woodland on your left and fields on your right to reach a wooden gate.

8. Go through the gate onto a gravel track. Turn left and immediately right, following the footpath with a playing field on your right. Bear right around the corner of the playing field and then left down a rocky slope.

9. Turn right and follow the path with the fence and views down the valley on the left. Go past a pond and kissing gate on the left then bear right up steps. Continue straight ahead through trees to reach a gravel track. Turn left and follow the track for 150 yards until you reach a metal kissing gate on the left.

10. Go through the kissing gate and follow the steep, uneven path down to reach the road (Widcombe Hill) at the bottom. Cross the road with care, and continue down the road to a kissing gate on your right. Go through this and immediately left through a second kissing gate into a field with views to Bath straight ahead. Walk downhill, bearing right to reach a gate next to a water trough. Continue steeply down the steps and hill to reach a gate onto a lane at the bottom.

11. Go through the gate, cross the lane, and continue through the gate opposite. Follow the steep, winding path and steps uphill to a kissing gate. Go through the gate and continue on the path up the hill. Bear right at the top, heading for the gap in the hedge. The official route descends left into Richens Orchard here, where dogs are not permitted. Instead, go through the gap in the hedge and turn left, continuing straight ahead to a gate. Go through this and bear slightly right, following the path across the field to a pedestrian gate next to a larger gate. Go through the gate and follow the path to return to Bathwick Hill.

DOG-FRIENDLY AMENITIES

Dexter's cafe on Bathwick Hill – a few minutes' walk downhill from the start – is very dog-friendly, and was even named after a dog. The Bath Brew House on James St West welcomes dogs in all areas.

Many hotels and self-catering accommodation options in Bath accept dogs, including Homewood Park in Freshford, a few miles outside Bath, which recently won 'Best in Show' at the PetsPyjamas Travel Awards.

Claverton Down path.

14. Secret Stourhead

**Stourhead
Stourton
Warminster
Wiltshire
BA12 6QD
01747 841152**
stourhead@nationaltrust.org.uk

ABOUT THIS WALK

Distance 3.4 miles (5.4km)
Difficulty Moderate
Terrain Gravel and surfaced
paths, grass and woodland.
Some sections can be
muddy after rain
Stiles Yes
Interest History, accessible
alternative trail

Best-known for its world-renowned landscaped gardens, picturesque lakeside trail and intriguing follies, **Stourhead** also has a hidden wild side that's perfect for exploring with dogs. Taking you deep into the Wiltshire countryside surrounding the estate, this scenic walk visits the Iron Age hill fort at Park Hill Camp, wanders through leafy woodland and returns along peaceful Six Wells Valley.

This is a glorious escape from the summer crowds, with plenty of welcome shade along the way. Keep an eye out for birds such as nuthatches, tree creepers and long-tailed tits, and enjoy colourful displays of bluebells in the woods and wildflowers across the grassland over the spring and summer months.

THINGS TO SEE

There's so much to see at Stourhead – make sure you allow plenty of time to explore it all. Here are some highlights:
• One of the first grand Palladian-style villas to be built in England.
• World-famous landscape garden, a scenic lake with an accessible waterside trail.

• The Temple of Flora, the Temple of Apollo and the Pantheon, which was inspired by the Pantheon in Rome.

Paws for thought

Dogs are welcome across the garden and wider estate at Stourhead, including in the shop, restaurant, visitor reception and the Spread Eagle courtyard, but only assistance dogs are permitted inside the house and the garden buildings. Your dog will need to be kept on a lead throughout this walk.

Other walkies nearby

There are three more great, dog-friendly walks around the Stourhead estate, ideal for exploring all year round. Maps and information are available from visitor reception.

The Temple of Flora, the
Bristol High Cross and the
Palladian Bridge.

Public transport Gillingham is
the closest train station 6.5
miles (10.5km) away. The 58
bus goes from Gillingham
station, alight at Zeals (1.2
miles/2km) away.

Car Please arrive at Stourhead
via the main road network,
following brown signs off A303
or the B3092 from Frome.
Satnav: BA12 6QD
OS Map Explorer 142
Start/finish Stourhead car park,
BA12 6QD, grid ref: ST778339

DIRECTIONS

Start/finish: Stourhead visitor reception

1. From visitor reception, follow the zig-zag path down to the Spread Eagle Inn. Walk
   through the courtyard to reach a road. Be aware of passing traffic as you turn left
   here and walk down the road, passing St Peter's Church on your left. Continue
   along the road, go under the Rock Arch, then take the first right.

2. Follow the main track with Turner's Paddock lake and the waterwheel on your left.
   Continue past a cattle grid and Beech Cottage on your right, then go over a stile. A
   little further on the main track forks: bear right here and go through a gate. Follow
   the track along the top of the field and over the stile. To your left you can spot the
   ruins of Tucking Mill.

3. Follow the track for about 250 yards, until you reach a red waymarker. Turn right here, following the steep path to the top of the hill. Continue straight on until you come to a T-junction; turn left here to reach Park Hill Iron Age hill fort. This area is grazed by a small flock of Wiltshire Horn sheep, so take extra care with your dog.

4. At the information panel, turn right and follow the fence on a narrow path that skirts the edge of the hillfort. Turn right at the next track, then take the next sharp left down into Six Wells Valley. At the end of the track, continue straight on over the stile. To your left is St Peter's Pump, marking the source of the River Stour, from which Stourhead takes its name.

5. Turn right and follow the path diagonally through the valley. Once you reach the medieval fishponds, bear left, following the path up the side of the valley. Go through the gate at the top and follow the obvious track through the woodland, through a second gate and then left up a short slope to reach Great Oar Meadow and the Obelisk. The original was erected in 1746 as a focal point at the end of Fir Walk, but the structure has since been replaced and restored after deterioration and lightning damage.

6. From the Obelisk, with your back to the inscription, head left across the meadow to join the main track, an 18th-century carriage ride. Turn right onto the track and follow it towards Stourhead House. Follow the driveway in front of the house, turning right just before the Clock Arch into the walled garden. Cross through the garden and over the bridge, then take the zig-zag path back up to the visitor reception area to finish.

DOG-FRIENDLY AMENITIES

Stourhead Estate Motorhome Site accommodates five pitches in a peaceful corner of the Stourhead estate, all with water and electric hook-up. One dog is permitted per pitch. Guests have free entry to explore the estate during opening hours, including the Palladian house, landscape garden, King Alfred's Tower and miles of countryside walks through chalk downland, ancient woodland, Iron Age hillforts and farmland.

Opposite: The Obelisk in Stourhead Park.
Left: Evening light at Stourhead.

15. Corfe Castle and Common

The Square
Corfe Castle
Wareham
Dorset
BH20 5EZ
01929 481294
corfecastle@nationaltrust.org.uk

ABOUT THIS WALK

Distance 3.1 miles (5km)
Difficulty Easy
Terrain Footpaths and a short section of road. Can be muddy on the common
Stiles No
Interest History, wildlife, coastline

One of Britain's best-known survivors of the English Civil War, Corfe Castle was partially demolished in 1646 by the Parliamentary forces. Today, the atmospheric ruins tower over the pretty Dorset village of the same name, commanding spectacular views out across the Isle of Purbeck, the rolling countryside and the coast.

The castle is a fantastic place to learn about history in an engaging and interactive way. Showcasing 1,000 years as a royal palace and fortress, it's exciting to visit, with fallen walls and secret nooks, 'murder holes' and arrow loops.

THINGS TO SEE

You can't go for a walk here without visiting the imposing fortress at Corfe Castle. Fortunately, dogs on leads are welcome in the castle, tea-room, shop and welcome centre, as well as on the walking trails exploring the surrounding countryside.

Above: Corfe Castle from Corfe Common.
Opposite: The castle and sea from Corfe Common.

DOG-FRIENDLY AMENITIES

Situated in the heart of the village, the Corfe Castle Tea-room is perfectly placed for enjoying a post-walk cuppa, snacks or lunch with your dog.

Paws for thought

You are in one of the most wildlife-rich areas of the UK, so please keep paws on paths. Dogs should be kept on leads in all areas of Corfe Castle. On the common dogs should be kept on a short lead all year round as grazing animals are likely to be present.

Other walkies nearby

The Purbeck Ridgeway, from Corfe Castle to the coast, offers superb high-level walking with glorious views over the Isle of Purbeck. The full route is 9.5 miles (15.3km) or there's a shorter option at 8.7 miles (14km), both of which are dog-friendly, although dogs do need to be kept on leads. Studland Bay, only a few miles away from Corfe Castle is great for a dog-friendly beach walk, but dogs should be kept on leads from 1 May to 30 September.

DIRECTIONS

Start/finish: National Trust car park on A351

1. Cross the A351 with care, using the traffic island, and turn left, crossing the minor road and then turning right onto the footpath along the base of Corfe Castle. Follow this around the castle to reach the National Trust ticket office.

HOW TO GET HERE

Public transport The nearest mainline train station is Wareham, after which you can take the Purbeck Breezer 40 bus to Corfe Castle. Swanage Railway runs a seasonal service that stops at Corfe Castle Station.

Car Follow the A351 Wareham to Swanage road. National Trust parking on A351 opposite the castle mound on the left when approaching from Wareham. Satnav: BH20 5DR

OS map Explorer OL15

Start/finish National Trust car park on A351, BH20 5EZ, grid ref: SY959824

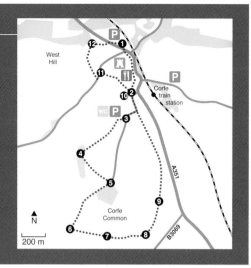

2. Turn left and walk along West Street through Corfe Castle village.

3. Turn right towards West Street car park. At the far end of the car park, turn right through a kissing gate. Once through the gate, follow a path along the edge of the field.

4. Go through the kissing gate to reach Copper Bridge. Don't cross the bridge, but instead turn left and walk up the slope, following the hedge. When you get to the top of the slope, bear right at the cattle grid to join an unclassified road.

5. Turn right and follow the road down the dip and up the other side onto Corfe Common.

6. At the top, leave the road and follow the path left to the top of the ridge.

7. Continue along the ridge, where you'll find a series of low humps – the remains of 4,000-year-old Bronze Age burial mounds. Take a moment here to explore and enjoy the views.

8. Turn left at the large, low burial mound at the end of the ridge and make your way to the bottom of the slope, following the sunken tracks – once quarry tracks – towards the lower common.

9. Follow the path towards the gate at the top corner of the common, along the path between the houses and onto Middle Halves. Signposts then mark the way back to Corfe Castle.

10. Turn left outside the ticket office and follow the footpath around the base of the castle to reach the road.

11. Turn left onto the road, crossing the bridge and then turning right onto a footpath. Follow this between West Hill and Corfe Castle to the next path junction.

12. Turn right and follow the path back to the A351, crossing with care to return to the car park.

South
East

16. White Horse Hill

**Uffington
Oxfordshire
SN7 7UK
01793 762209**
whitehorsehill@nationaltrust.org.uk

ABOUT THIS WALK

Distance 8 miles (12.9km)
Difficulty Challenging
Terrain Grassy and
surfaced trails, some
sections can be muddy.
Undulating but no big hills
Stiles No
Interest History, wildlife

The 87-mile (140-km) Ridgeway National Trail runs between Ivinghoe Beacon in the Chiltern Hills in Buckinghamshire, and the World Heritage Site of Avebury in Wiltshire. It is part of an ancient route that once ran from Dorset to the Wash and still crosses the chalk ridges of the Berkshire, Oxfordshire and Wiltshire Downs.

This enjoyable and varied walk following inviting trails across Oxfordshire's chalk downland is a perfect way to explore this fascinating area and its long human history. Along the way, you'll discover the Uffington White Horse and Castle, and a delightful stretch of the Ridgeway National Trail, one of England's oldest routes.

THINGS TO SEE

At the summit of White Horse Hill, Oxfordshire's highest point from where you can see over six counties on a clear day, the well-preserved earthworks of Uffington Castle are an outstanding example of a large Iron Age hill fort, dating back around 2,500 years. The White Horse itself, measuring 360 feet (110m) from nose to tail and carved deeply into the hillside, is the oldest chalk-cut hill figure in Britain, thought to be over 3,000 years old.

Paws for thought
Dogs should be kept under close control, and on leads around grazing animals. Between 1 March and 31 July, please keep to the mown pathways to help protect skylarks, which nest on the ground and are easily harmed by trampling.

Other walkies nearby
There's a wonderful selection of dog-friendly waymarked walks on the Buscot and Coleshill estates, 20 minutes from White Horse Hill. Try the 3-mile (4.8-km) Red Walk, which

follows a stunning stretch of the Thames Path National Trail to the lock at Buscot Weir – the smallest on the River Thames.

DOG-FRIENDLY AMENITIES

There's plenty of space for dogs to run free at White Horse Hill, and you'll find dog waste bins at the car park.

Pubs and cafés, including the dog-friendly Fox & Hounds, can be found in nearby Uffington and Woolstone villages. In Coleshill, 20 minutes away, the farm shop at Coleshill Organics is a great place to pick up local organic supplies. Based on a National Trust estate, you can also rent The Wagon – a cosy, dog-friendly glamping hut that sleeps two people. www.coleshillorganics.co.uk

The bronze-age horse at White Horse Hill.

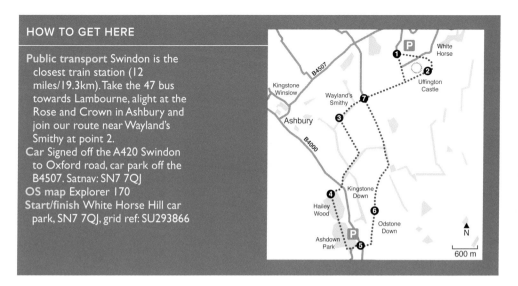

HOW TO GET HERE

Public transport Swindon is the closest train station (12 miles/19.3km). Take the 47 bus towards Lambourne, alight at the Rose and Crown in Ashbury and join our route near Wayland's Smithy at point 2.
Car Signed off the A420 Swindon to Oxford road, car park off the B4507. Satnav: SN7 7QJ
OS map Explorer 170
Start/finish White Horse Hill car park, SN7 7QJ, grid ref: SU293866

DIRECTIONS

Start/finish: White Horse Hill car park

1. From the car park, take the middle staircase by the pay-and-display machine and head across the field to the White Horse. Leave the horse and walk uphill, passing the old earthworks of Uffington Castle on your right and reaching a gate onto the Ridgeway National Trail.

2. Turn right and walk up the Ridgeway Trail, over the hill and down to a cross roads. Walk straight ahead, following the obvious Ridgeway Trail across the next crossroads. Pass Wayland's Smithy on the right and continue to the next path junction.

3. Leave the Ridgeway Trail here, turning left and following the track past a barn on your right. Continue to a path junction at a tree line, turn right and follow the path to the B4000. Cross and follow the path opposite to the end of the avenue that heads through Ashdown estate.

4. Turn left and follow the grassy path down the avenue towards Ashdown House. Shortly before reaching the house, turn left, following signs to the car park. Walk through the car park and back to the B4000.

5. Cross and go through the gate onto Weather Cock Hill and head straight up the slope with the fence line on your left until you reach a kissing gate in the corner of the field. Go through and follow the footpath as it drops down across large fields.

6. Continue on the path, heading downhill to reach the byway in Compton Bottom. Turn left onto this and follow it back to the Ridgeway at one of the junctions you walked past earlier.

7. Turn right and follow the Ridgeway back to the next crossroads. Take a left here and follow the track back to the car park and the start.

Near Romsey
Hampshire
SO51 0LP
01794 340757
mottisfont@nationaltrust.org.uk

ABOUT THIS WALK

Distance 5.7 miles (9.2km)
Difficulty Moderate
Terrain Grassy, woodland
and fields as well as some
sections of country road.
Some sections become muddy
Stiles No
Interest History, gardens,
wildlife

Mottisfont Estate, in the heart of the Test Valley, is a mosaic of habitats from woodland, farmland and rivers covering 1,645 acres (665 hectares). You can explore the Estate through a network of public footpaths, including the Test Way and Mottisfont Estate Walk; or by bike, on the cycle routes.

This delightful, waymarked walk takes in an anticlockwise loop of the wider estate, weaving through woodland and along a picturesque section of the Test Way.

THINGS TO SEE

Many areas of woodland on the Mottisfont estate are classified as ancient, thought to be well over 400 years old. The National Trust manages the woods for nature conservation, meaning many species of flora and fauna flourish here.

DOG-FRIENDLY AMENITIES

You'll find water bowls outside visitor reception and a dog-friendly indoor café area in the Stables – either the coffee shop or within the Coach House – as well as outdoor seating.

Paws for thought
Allow nature the space to flourish. Please don't stray from the defined tracks or walk among the flora and fauna. Dog bins are located at both the entrance and exit at Spearywell Wood. Take care to avoid disturbing grazing animals or native wildlife out on the estate – dogs aren't allowed to paddle or swim in the river or streams.

Other walkies nearby
Extend your walk along the Test Way or the Monarch's Way, both of which you'll follow for a short distance on this route.

DIRECTIONS

Start/finish: Spearywell car park

1. If Spearywell car park is busy, alternative parking can be found at Keepers Lane car park, SO51 0LH, grid ref: SU314268.

2. Take the gravel track out of the back of the car park, past the Spearywell information board. Follow this path through the woods to a T-junction. Turn left, following the fingerpost Estate Walk sign to Cadbury Junction.

3. Walk across the junction and take the path next to the map lectern, following the Estate Walk blue waymarkers. Follow this path downhill through woodland, bending to the left to reach a path junction near the edge of the woods.

Public transport Mottisfont & Dunbridge train station is a 1 mile (1.6km) walk across fields.
Car Take J2 from the M27 or J8 off the M3; follow signs to Romsey then Stockbridge. Mottisfont is signed from the A3057 Stockbridge road. Satnav: SO51 0LN
OS map Explorer 131
Start/finish Spearywell car park, SO51 0LS, grid ref: SU316275

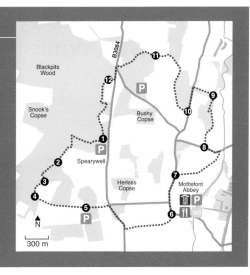

4. Turn right and follow the path close to the edge of the woods. Turn left and follow the path along the edge of the woodland into a grassy avenue and on to the edge of the woods.

5. Follow the path across the field with the hedge to your left, continue along the track across fields and through a small wooded area to a metal gate, this is the start of Keepers Lane.

6. Walk along Keepers Lane, passing the alternative car park, to reach the B3084. Turn right and follow the B3084 downhill. Turn left onto the quieter Hatt Lane, this is signed to Mottisfont Abbey. Follow Hatt Lane to reach a junction with Mottisfont Lane.

7. Turn left and follow Mottisfont Lane out of the village. Bear right onto Oakley Road and continue until you reach a path on the right, signed Estate Walk.

8. Turn right, following the path along the back of the Mottisfont estate parkland to Oakley Lane. Turn left and walk along the lane for a short distance to a field gate on the right.

9. Follow this path around the gate to a small area of woodland. Stay on the path which follows the right-hand edge of the woodland. Follow the path as it turns into the woods and then goes right, walking through the woods to a path junction at the edge of the woodland.

10. Turn left and walk across a field with the hedge to your right; at the far side turn left just before the road, and follow this path along the edge of the field. Take the next right at a waymarker and cross Horsebridge Road.

11. Follow the path with Clapgate Copse on your right and fields to the left. At the junction turn left and follow the footpath to the edge of Great Copse.

12. Continue on this main path through the wood, ignoring several paths which head off left. You'll follow a larger track and gate shortly before reaching the B3084 at the top of Jerram's Hill. Turn left and walk down the road until you can turn right onto a path into Spearywell Wood. Follow the path into the wood, turning left and then right at the next fork. Take the next left and then walk right at the crossroads, and back to the Spearywell car park.

Above: The River Test and the front lawn at Mottisfont.
Opposite: The meadow and surrounding estate in summer at Mottisfont.

18. Compton Bay and Downs Walk

Compton
Isle of Wight
PO30 4HB
01983 741020
comptonbay@nationaltrust.org.uk

ABOUT THIS WALK

Distance 7.8 miles (12.6km)
Difficulty Challenging
Terrain Beach or coast path, grassy downs footpaths and short sections of road. Steep sections; can be slippery
Stiles Yes
Interest: Wildlife, coast, history

Home to one of the Isle of Wight's most beautiful beaches and backed by cliffs rich in fossils that tell the story of the area over millions of years, Compton Bay is a great spot for walking, playing, or simply enjoying the view.

This walk heads out along the Tennyson Trail, crossing Afton Down and Compton Down, which together make up one of the most extensive areas of chalk grassland in Britain, and have remained largely unchanged since the end of the last Ice Age.

THINGS TO SEE

If you enjoy fossil-hunting you're in for a treat at Hanover Point, where you'll find some incredible 120-million-year-old (from the Cretaceous period) dinosaur footcasts that have fallen from the cliffs. At the western end of the beach, the rocks are younger and indicate that the sea level was gradually rising. Fossils found in the chalk at Tennyson Down are 'only' 65 million years old.

DOG-FRIENDLY AMENITIES

Dogs are welcome on the beach, east of Shippards Chine, all year round.

For post walk refreshments, the Red Lion is a friendly, gabled and chimneyed red-brick pub by the church in Freshwater, near to the start/finish of this walk. www.redlion-freshwater.co.uk

Above: Dinosaur fossils can be found around the cliffs at Hanover Point.
Opposite: Aerial view of Compton Bay.

Paws for thought
Be aware of unfenced cliffs and erosion along the coast. There's a seasonal dog ban on the beach west of Compton Bay car park from 15 May–15 September each year. Dogs are welcome elsewhere but must be kept on a short lead around grazing animals and under close control at all other times.

Other walkies nearby
There's an almost endless selection of great walks on the Isle of Wight, covering downland, woodland, coastal trails and quiet roads. One of our favourites is the Mottistone Common Walk, a 4-mile (6.4km) trail with amazing views of the coastal scenery and some fascinating ancient historical features along the way, including the mysterious Longstone.

DIRECTIONS

Start/finish: Freshwater Cliffs car park

1. Join the Tennyson Trail behind the car park and turn right, following it up onto Compton Down and through the golf course. Follow the path through a gate and continue, deviating left and up to the trig point if you wish. Continue on the Tennyson Trail downhill, through a gate and to the B3399.

2. Turn right and follow the road for a short distance, then turn left up a tarmacked drive towards Brook Hill House. When the private drive bends right, stay left and follow the footpath through a gap in the fence. Take this path and turn right just before the kissing gate, walking down through woodland and out through another kissing gate into a field. Follow the path across the fields and through three kissing gates to reach the B3399 at Hulverstone.

3. Follow the road left, then take the next right onto the byway called Hulverstone Lane. After walking a short distance down this, turn right, over the wall onto a footpath signed 'BS47 Brook'. Follow this towards the sea, passing to the right of the pond and crossing four stiles. At the path junction bear right and reach the road in Brook village.

4. Turn left, following the road with houses to your right until you reach the busy A3055 Military Road. Cross carefully and follow the track opposite towards the sea. Turn right and follow the path parallel to the road to reach the Brook Chine National Trust car park.

5. At high tide or in bad weather follow the coast path right to the National Trust Compton Bay car park. At low tide, you can descend the steps to the beach and walk this next section to Hanover Point car park on the sand.

6. Continue to follow the coast path with the sea to your left. Walk along above Compton Bay and towards Compton Chine following the coast path signs. Go through a gate, a footbridge over the chine and two more gates to reach the A3055 Military Road.

7. Follow the path which stays to the left of the road and follows the coast back towards Freshwater Bay and the start. Once you reach the E.L.M. memorial obelisk, turn right and cross the road to return to the car park.

19. Hindhead and the Devil's Punch Bowl

London Road
Hindhead
Surrey
GU26 6AB
01428 681050
Hindhead@nationaltrust.org.uk

ABOUT THIS WALK

Distance 6.8 miles (10.9km)
Difficulty Challenging
Terrain Gravel and dirt tracks, short sections of road, some sections are rocky. One long climb
Stiles No
Interest Wildlife, history

The Devil's Punch Bowl is a deep hollow set within the heaths and commons of the Surrey Hills, forming a steep-sided nature reserve – a microcosm of flora and fauna. This route traces the rim of the bowl, following clear, inviting trails with glorious views out across the surrounding countryside and exploring the intriguing landscape of this fascinating natural amphitheatre.

The first section along the western edge is followed by a descent into the heart of the valley, crossing the brook that runs along its central line before a zig-zag ascent up to the eastern ridge is rewarded with further fine views. The return trip takes you alongside the former A3, its route still clearly visible though now a gently winding track, passing the outstanding viewpoint at Gibbet Hill before returning to the start.

THINGS TO SEE

Until the Hindhead Tunnel opened in 2011, the busy A3 London to Portsmouth road ran around the south-east edge of the Devil's Punch Bowl. The area is now a designated Site of Special Scientific Interest, where extensive work has been undertaken to restore the fragile heathland habitat and, as a result, it has seen the return of an abundance of wildlife, including rare breeding birds such as woodlarks and nightjars.

Paws for thought
Dogs should be kept on leads between March and September to protect wildlife, as well as at all times when near grazing animals. Assistance dogs only in the café.

Other walkies nearby
The waymarked Greensand Way runs for 108 miles (174km) across Surrey and Kent, starting in the nearby town of Haslemere and skirting around the Devil's Punchbowl. Nearby Frensham Common also has a fantastic variety of walks and is only a few miles away.

Above: Devil's Punch Bowl trail.
Opposite: The viewing point at Hindhead Common.

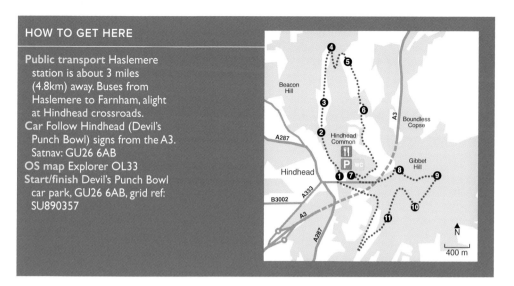

HOW TO GET HERE

Public transport Haslemere station is about 3 miles (4.8km) away. Buses from Haslemere to Farnham, alight at Hindhead crossroads.
Car Follow Hindhead (Devil's Punch Bowl) signs from the A3.
Satnav: GU26 6AB
OS map Explorer OL33
Start/finish Devil's Punch Bowl car park, GU26 6AB, grid ref: SU890357

DIRECTIONS

Start/finish: Devil's Punch Bowl car park

1. Walk out of the car park towards the viewpoint overlooking the Punch Bowl. Turn left here and follow the bridleway through the trees, signed by white Roam 639 discs. This path follows the rim of the Punch Bowl.

2. On reaching a path junction with an electricity substation to the left. Turn right through the gate by the cattle grid, and walk onto Highcombe Edge. Don't take the next right, which heads downhill. Carry on along the larger path, following the rim of the Punch Bowl to reach a path junction.

3. Take the smaller path to the right and walk past the Robertson Memorial. Continue on this path, re-joining the main gravel path and following it gently downhill to a major path junction.

4. Turn sharp right and follow the trail downhill, turn left at the next path and walk more steeply downhill passing Keepers Cottage on the right. Follow the path down to the ford and then up the hill on the other side, through a gate and onto a rough track at the edge of the woodland. Turn right and follow this up across moorland to reach a byway.

5. Bear right onto this and walk downhill to a gate and cattle grid at the edge of the moor. Go through and walk along the gravel roadway, past Gnome Cottage, and continue slightly uphill to the next junction. Turn left and follow the road uphill, with Highcombe Farm to your right.

6. Turn right onto a footpath, walk through a gate and through an area of trees, then out onto Hindhead Common. Follow the sandy path, bearing left at the fork and walking slightly uphill to reach a spring. Follow the path right and up the steep side of the Punch Bowl, through a gate and onto a good path close to the viewpoint and the start.

7. You can finish here after about 3.4 miles (5.5km). To carry on, turn left and follow this path across the grass track which was the former course of the A3. Bear left onto the paved road and follow it to the left. Pass the Sailor's Stone and then take the smaller path, right and uphill to the trig point on Gibbet Hill.

8. Bear right and follow a narrow and sometimes muddy path downhill to a path junction with a bigger track. Cross and follow the wide path opposite through trees to the Temple of the Four Winds.

9. Turn right and follow the sometimes muddy path downhill to a path junction with a small lake to the right.

10. Turn right and follow the path through a gateway and across some open land. Walk uphill to a path junction where you turn left and walk back downhill to a galvanised metal gate. Walk through to the unpaved road.

11. Follow this roadway to the right, walking up to the top of the hill to reach a galvanised metal gate on the right, signed onto Hindhead Common. Go through and follow this track gradually uphill across the common. Curve left near the top and follow the Greensand Way back to the start.

DOG-FRIENDLY AMENITIES

The Devil's Punch Bowl Café serves hot and cold drinks and snacks and has an outdoor seating area where you can sit with your dog, although only assistance dogs are allowed inside. There's also a kiosk for drinks and snacks to go, which is open seasonally.

A 20 minute drive from the Punch Bowl, the Swan at Chiddingfold is well regarded for food and is one of the most dog-friendly establishments we've come across. As well as dog-friendly rooms, complete with dog beds, bowls and treats, the pub has teamed up with Sir Woofchester's Canine Hospitality to provide a full doggy menu, including full dinner bowls for hungry dogs, treats, dog-friendly ice cream and even alcohol-free dog beer. www. theswaninnchiddingfold.com

20. Runnymede Countryside Walk from Egham

Windsor Road
Near Old Windsor
Surrey
SL4 2JL
01784 432891
runnymede@nationaltrust.org.uk

ABOUT THIS WALK

Distance 3.2 miles (5.1km)
Difficulty Moderate
Terrain Pavement, well surfaced paths and grassy meadow. Sections can be wet, muddy and prone to flooding in winter. There is some uneven ground
Stiles Yes
Interest History, wildlife

The meadows at Runnymede, beside the River Thames, are steeped in history. Its name comes from the Anglo-Saxon 'Runemede', meaning 'meeting meadow', and it was where, in 1215, King John sealed the Magna Carta – the first document to state that the king and his government were not above the law, establishing the foundations of modern democracy.

Today, this is a place to discover wildlife-rich pockets and welcome open green space within the busy Home Counties. You'll pass a monument to the Magna Carta, Coopers Hill Woods and Langham Pond (both SSSIs), and a number of thought-provoking art installations.

THINGS TO SEE

On the other side of the Thames from Runnymede, Ankerwycke is a fascinating site to explore, with many millennia of history dotted among the woods and fields. Nestled in a bend of the river, you'll find the Ankerwycke Yew, which, at 2,500 years old, is the oldest tree in the National Trust's care and is said to be where Henry VIII courted Anne Boleyn.

Above: The Magna Carta memorial.

Paws for thought

Dogs should be kept under close control, and on leads around grazing animals and the memorials.

Other walkies nearby

Simon's Wood is an area of wet woodland and lowland heath, providing rare habitat for many birds and invertebrates. The Simon's Wood Trail (1.3 miles/2.1km) discovers far-reaching views and the flora and fauna of the mixed woodlands, Heath Pond and open heathland.

DOG-FRIENDLY AMENITIES

Dogs are more than welcome in the National Trust Magna Carta Tearoom. It serves a range of hot and cold drinks, light meals and snacks. They have a dog station with water bowls and biscuits.

HOW TO GET HERE

Public transport The route starts at Egham railway station.
Car Either park in one of the Egham town car parks and join the route at the station or use the National Trust Runnymede car park and join the route at point 6. Satnav: Runnymede car park TW20 0AE
OS Map Explorer 160
Start/finish Egham train station, TW20 9LB, grid ref: TQ011710

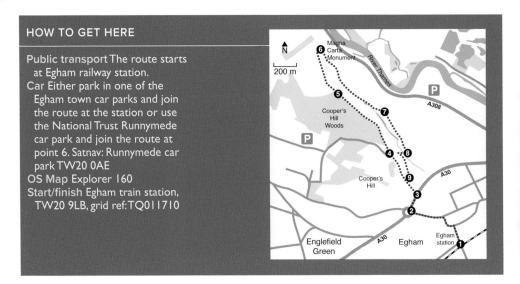

DIRECTIONS

Start/finish: Egham train station

1. Exit the station from the London-bound (ticket office) side and turn right onto Station Road. Follow Station Road, then turn left at the traffic lights, walking along High Street to a roundabout.

2. Cross the roundabout to the right, using the staggered pedestrian crossing. Walk up the pavement in the direction of the traffic until you can turn left onto Cooper's Hill Lane.

3. Follow Cooper's Hill up to the gate on the right, with paths heading sharp right onto Runnymede Meadows, or slightly right into Cooper's Hill Woods.

4. Follow the path all the way through Cooper's Hill Woods to reach a gate at the corner of the woods, and a meadow ahead.

5. Walk through the gate and past Writ in Water by Mark Wallinger along the path towards the Magna Carta Memorial.

6. With the Magna Carta Memorial to your left, go through the kissing gate to your right to enter a grazed meadow along an ancient field boundary of pollarded willow. If you start at Runnymede, join the walk from this point. At the end of the meadow you'll reach Langham Pond (on the right) and a boardwalk with a stile in the hedge ahead.

7. Walk along the boardwalk and cross the stile to walk across the small meadow to the edge of the trees and reeds. Follow the boardwalk through the reed bed. On leaving the reed bed, take the diagonal path to your left and go through the kissing gate on the opposite side of the meadow.

8. Turn left and follow the hedge line. When you've passed through the hedge line in front of you, walk diagonally right towards the farm buildings and then through the kissing gate.

9. Retrace your outbound route by turning left onto Cooper's Hill Lane, right along the main road, and left across the roundabout. Walk left down High Street and right along Station Road.

21. Ham House and Richmond Park

**Ham Street
Ham
Richmond
Surrey
TW10 7RS
0208 940 1950**
hamhouse@nationaltrust.org.uk

ABOUT THIS WALK

Distance 2.9 miles (4.7km)
Difficulty Easy
Terrain Paths can get muddy; steep hill up to King Henry's Mound, but it's not very long. High tide causes the tow path to flood occasionally
Stiles No
Interest Wildlife, history, urban escape

Set on the banks of the River Thames in Richmond, Ham House stands surrounded by its own formal and kitchen gardens and a patchwork of green fields edged with mature trees and criss-crossed with footpaths and bridleways. A delightful escape from the city, the start of this walk is easy to reach by public transport.

Starting along the Thames Path National Trail, you'll soon head into Richmond Park, one of London's Royal Parks. With 2,500 acres (1,012ha) to explore, the expansive grasslands and woodland offer vast scope for extending your walk should you wish. A short climb takes you to the top of King Henry's Mound, with Pembroke Lodge, a Grade II-listed Georgian mansion a little further on.

THINGS TO SEE

At 184ft (56m), the steep-sided prominence of King Henry's Mound in Pembroke Lodge Gardens is one of the highest points in London. The view on a clear day from here to St Paul's Cathedral, some 10 miles (16km) away, is protected by law from being obscured by development, one of eight such sites around the capital.

Paws for thought
Only assistance dogs are welcome in the house itself. To keep the lawns perfect for picnics and playing, please keep to the gravel paths where possible. Dogs are not allowed in Petersham Meadows between April and October when the cows are grazing.

Other walkies nearby
Explore the extensive network of paths and trails through Richmond Park – be aware of the deer that graze here. Alternatively, arrive by train and enjoy the stunning riverside stroll from Kingston Station to Ham House and Garden – 4.5 miles (7.2km) each way.

Tulips and muscari on the south front of Ham House.

HOW TO GET HERE

Public transport Richmond underground, overground and mainline stations are about two-thirds of a mile (1km) from our route. Walk along the river and join the route between points 5 and 6. Additionally, Hammertons Ferry runs seasonally between Ham and Marble Hill Park.

Car Ham Street car park is on the banks of the Thames off the A307 between Richmond and Kingston.

Satnav: TW10 7HF

OS map Explorer 161

Start/finish Ham Street car park, TW10 7HF, grid ref: TQ169731

DOG-FRIENDLY AMENITIES

Dogs on leads are very welcome in all outside areas, inside the gift shop, and in the Orangery Café.

The New Inn on Ham Common is a popular local pub for dog walkers. To book a table call 020 8940 9444.

DIRECTIONS

Start/finish: Ham Street car park

1. Walk out of the car park to the River Thames and turn right. Follow the Thames path along the river towards Richmond, passing Ham House. Continue until you reach a paved road which heads towards Petersham.

2. Turn right and walk along River Lane away from the Thames. The National Trust-managed Petersham Meadows are to the left. Follow River Lane to Petersham Road, turn left and follow this until you can cross using the pedestrian crossing at the Dysart. Turn left and continue along the road, then turn right through a large kissing gate into Richmond Park. Turn left and bear right up the steep hill to the viewpoint on King Henry's Mound in Pembroke Lodge grounds.

3. Exit the grounds and turn left to join the paved footpath. Head towards Richmond Gate and exit the park.

4. Walk along Richmond Hill, using two zebra crossings to pass the Richmond Hill Hotel. Turn left to take a path down the Terrace Fields.

5. At the bottom of the path, exit through a gate onto Petersham Road and use the pedestrian crossing.

6. Head back towards the river to re-join the Thames Path, following the signs for Ham House.

22. Claremont and West End Common

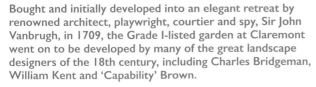

**Portsmouth Road
Esher
Surrey
KT10 9JG
01372 467806**
claremont@nationaltrust.org.uk

ABOUT THIS WALK

Distance 3 miles (4.8km)
Difficulty Moderate
Terrain Grassy and
surfaced trails which can
become muddy. Short
sections of pavement.
Undulating but no long hills
Stiles No
Interest History, gardens,
wildlife

Bought and initially developed into an elegant retreat by
renowned architect, playwright, courtier and spy, Sir John
Vanbrugh, in 1709, the Grade I-listed garden at Claremont
went on to be developed by many of the great landscape
designers of the 18th century, including Charles Bridgeman,
William Kent and 'Capability' Brown.

Each designer's distinctive vision can be seen here in the pleasure
grounds, charting the evolution of the English Landscape Garden. In
1866, Queen Victoria bought the estate for her youngest son Prince
Leopold, Duke of Albany, to save it from development. This walk has
two distinct halves, starting out with an anticlockwise loop around
the lake and gardens at Claremont, before crossing the road and
heading out for a clockwise loop around West End Common. This
open area of heathland is a 174-acre (70.4-ha) Local Nature Reserve
and Site of Special Scientific Interest (SSSI).

THINGS TO SEE

Today, as you wander around
Claremont, there are still many
of the original historical features
to admire in the garden, including
the turf amphitheatre –
constructed as a viewpoint over
the Surrey Hills rather than as a
theatre – the serpentine lake,
grotto, Camellia Terrace and
Belvedere Tower.

Paws for thought
Dogs should be kept on short
fixed leads throughout the
garden. West End Common is
open access land, so dogs
should be kept under close
control here, and on leads
around other animals and
during the nesting season
(1 March–31 July).

Other walkies nearby
Esher Common, which lies to
the south of Claremont, is an
open area of mixed woodland,
heathland and scrub, and a
designated SSSI for its range of
habitats, including areas of
marsh, bog and open water. A
loop of the common, following
the network of paths, is 2–3 miles
(3.2–4.8km), and thoroughly
enjoyable walking.

The amphitheatre at
Claremont was created around
1722 by Charles Bridgeman.

67

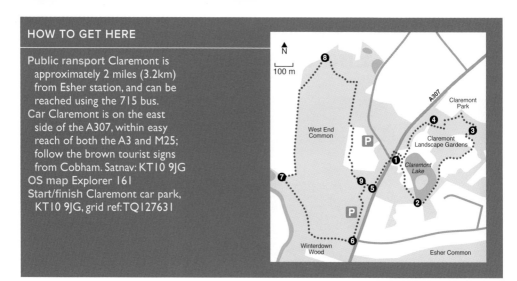

HOW TO GET HERE

Public ransport Claremont is
  approximately 2 miles (3.2km)
  from Esher station, and can be
  reached using the 715 bus.
Car Claremont is on the east
  side of the A307, within easy
  reach of both the A3 and M25;
  follow the brown tourist signs
  from Cobham. Satnav: KT10 9JG
OS map Explorer 161
Start/finish Claremont car park,
  KT10 9JG, grid ref: TQ127631

DIRECTIONS

Start/finish: Claremont car park

1. The first section of this walk loops around the Claremont Landscape Garden. Start by following the Lake Walk from the Welcome Kiosk and through the garden to the Grotto at the southern end of the lake.

2. Continue on the lakeside path and then branch right, following the ha-ha and leaving the lake behind. Join the Views Walk and follow this path uphill, turn right onto Camellia Terrace and head through the hedge to the long avenue with views of the Belvedere Tower to your right.

3. Cross the avenue and follow the Views Walk path along the North Terrace. Cross the avenue, turn right and follow the path, passing the steps to the Amphitheatre Viewpoint.

4. Follow the path down the hill back to the car park and start. The next section of the route leaves the National Trust property and extends the walk by completing a loop of West End Common. To continue, walk out of the car park to the A307. Use the crossing on the right to cross the road, continue on past West End Lane then follow the pavement on the other side until you can turn right on an often muddy path into the woodland.

5. Follow the path into the woods and turn left, walking parallel to the A307 until you reach the Horseshoe Clump car park.

6. Turn right and follow the path out of the back of the car park and across the wooded common, into Winterdown Wood and continue in the same direction to a path junction at the top of a steep slope. Turn right and follow this path along the edge of the slope to the corner of the woodland above a meander in the River Ember.

7. Follow the path right and then to the left keeping to the edge of West End Common; bear right at the fork near the far end and follow this to the northern edge of the wood where you'll reach a path junction with fields in front of you.

8. Turn right and follow the smaller path through the trees, passing Margy Pond (which often dries out in the summer) on the right. Continue to a path junction with a long, straight path cutting across you. Turn right and follow this through the woods, bear left into the open area where you can see the West End Road car park to the left. Follow this path across the common and curve left into the trees opposite.

9. You'll soon reach the path you used to enter the woods. Carry on back to the A307, turn left and cross to return to the start.

DOG-FRIENDLY AMENITIES

Dogs on short fixed leads are welcome everywhere at Claremont Landscape Garden, including in the Gardener's Bothy café. You'll find a water bowl and jar of dog biscuits near the kiosk and a dog waste bin outside the toilet block in the lower car park. Dog waste bags are available at the kiosk.

31 Rowan Road, a lovely B&B in Hammersmith, offers two dog-friendly suites, each sleeping two people. www.abetterwaytostay.co.uk

The Woodland Walk at Claremont Landscape Garden.

23. Polesden Lacey Parkland and Commons Walk

**Great Bookham
Near Dorking
Surrey
RH5 6BD
01372 452048**
polesdenlacey@nationaltrust.org.uk

ABOUT THIS WALK

Distance 5 miles (8km)
Difficulty Challenging
Terrain Tracks, grassy and
surfaced paths, can be
muddy. Not steep but fairly
long up and down hills
Stiles No
Interest Wildlife, gardens,
history

Set within the rolling North Downs, and the Surrey Hills Area of Outstanding Natural Beauty, the wisteria-clad Edwardian house, elegant gardens and open spaces of the 1,600-acre (648-ha) Polesden Lacey estate offer a wonderful escape from the bustle of the nearby towns and cities. And all within easy reach of London by train.

You'll find no less than four waymarked walks here, ranging between 1.5 and 4 miles (2.4–6.4km). You can walk any of them individually, or link them up, as we have with this walk.

THINGS TO SEE

The wider Polesden Lacey estate comprises two working farms, ancient woodlands, commons, former farmsteads and downland, providing a diverse range of habitats. Lying on the chalk escarpment of the North Downs, there's a wonderful variety of wildlife here, with chalk grassland being one of the most species-rich habitats in the world, supporting rare wild flowers such as the orchid, and the chalkhill blue butterfly.

DOG-FRIENDLY AMENITIES

Dogs are welcome inside the Coffee Shop, as well as at the outdoor seating by the Café. You can stay on the Polesden Lacey estate with your dog. Yew Tree Barn is a beautiful, secluded holiday let nestled in a quiet area of the estate near to Yew Tree Farm.

Paws for thought

Dogs aren't allowed in the formal gardens, house, shop or indoors at the main café. There are working farms and grazing animals on the estate, so dogs should be kept under close control at all times and on leads when near to other animals.

Other walkies nearby

As well as the waymarked walks on Polesden Lacey estate, the potential for walking in the North Downs and Surrey Hills is vast. Box Hill, Denbies Hillside and Leith Hill (all National Trust) are nearby.

The parkland at Polesden Lacey.

HOW TO GET HERE

Public transport Boxhill &
Westhumble train station 3 miles
(4.8km) away – from there you can
walk mostly on footpaths; Bookham
train station 2.6 miles (4.2km). 478
bus Guildford–Leatherhead stops in
Great Bookham.
Car From J9 of the M25: follow the
A243, before picking up the A24 and
then the A246, follow brown signs
from there. Satnav: KT23 4PZ
OS map Explorer 146
Start/finish Polesden Lacey car park,
KT23 4PZ, grid ref: TQ133524

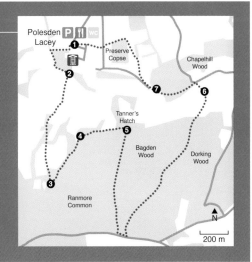

DIRECTIONS

Start/finish: Polesden Lacey car park

1. Walk out of the back of the car park following the Blue Butterfly trail left and then right following the field edge, then turn left with the Blue trail through a strip of woodland. Turn left through a gate and left along the top of a field to a gate onto a larger track known as the Causeway.

2. Turn right onto the Causeway and follow the Blue Butterfly trail down and uphill. Bear right to join a larger track and pass Yew Tree Farm on your left. Bear left after the farm, walking uphill on a broad track past the orchard and continue straight past a metal gate.

3. Continue to follow the Blue Butterfly trail by turning a sharp left off the wide track through a barway gate, walking straight ahead through an open glade and onto a woodland edge path. Continue to follow this path to the junction by a cottage known as Prospect Lodge.

4. Turn right following the Blue Butterfly trail downhill; following the path along the medieval boundary ditch along the woodland edge. Pass the viewpoint back to Polesden, to reach a path junction near Tanner's Hatch YHA.

5. Following the Blue walking trail turn right, up a wide track through woodland to reach the track next to the cottages by Ranmore Common Road. Turn left in front of the cottages and left again after the last cottage, following the bridleway and Blue trail down past a metal gate. Walk down through the woodland, bear right at the bottom to keep on the wide track and out, through a gate into fields. Continue towards Bagden Farm buildings ahead.

6. Bear left in the field and continue through a gate, up the slope beside the converted barns towards Bagden Lodge. Go through the gate turning left uphill on a wide track. Go past the charcoal kiln and switching to the Purple Dragonfly trail bear left over the Italianate bridge.

7. At the head of the track where there is a timber gate turn right into Nursery Field on the Purple trail and follow the path through the middle of the field to a gate in the top corner. Go ahead following the Purple trail through another gate into Golf Course Field. Walk across this, following the boundary of Preserve Copse on the left. Turn left on the corner, following the copse and through a gate to reach the driveway. Follow this straight ahead back to the start.

24. Winkworth Arboretum

Hascombe Road
Godalming
Surrey
GU8 4AD
01483 208477
winkwortharboretum@
nationaltrust.org.uk

ABOUT THIS WALK

Distance 2.2 miles (3.6km)
Difficulty Moderate
Terrain Surfaced and
unsurfaced woodland and
lake side paths. Steep slopes
and can be muddy
Stiles No
Interest Wildlife, history

Covering 121 acres (49ha) in the Surrey Hills, Winkworth Arboretum is home to over 1,000 different species of trees and shrubs, set in a wooded valley around the peaceful Rowe's Flashe Lake. The arboretum was originally created in the early 1900s by local doctor Wilfrid Fox, who was passionate about preserving the natural landscape close to his home.

Today, Winkworth shines throughout the year as a place to visit, admire the incredible trees, walk the many trails that explore the estate or, if you're lucky with the weather, picnic on the grass while taking in the views. Spring, when the first flowers come into bloom, and autumn, when the trees blaze with fiery colours, are particularly spectacular. Following the red waymarkers, you'll wander through planted areas, woodland and alongside the lake with its old boathouse.

THINGS TO SEE

If you're visiting with children, the natural playground at Winkworth is particularly special. Split into two halves, it's not far from the entrance, where there are toilets and baby-changing facilities. The Tree Adventure play area is made using oak trees from the arboretum and complete with a climbing wall, firefighter's pole, rope tunnel and ladders.

Paws for thought
Winkworth is home to many native animals, from deer to dormice. Dogs should be kept on leads throughout the estate.

Other walkies nearby
The Access for All route (approx. 0.6 miles/1km) follows the blue waymarkers on a level, step-free walk around the top of the arboretum.

The Taste of Winkworth route (approx. 1mile/1.6km) follows the yellow waymarkers, taking in Winkworth's key features. You'll encounter some steep paths and steps along the way, but the beautiful views out across the lake are well worth it.

Above: Autumn colours in
the arboretum.
Opposite: Morning mist
above the lake.

Public transport Godalming train station is 2 miles (3.2km) away but the roads are narrow and it's not a safe walk. The 42 bus (Mon–Sat only), from Godalming, stops outside the entrance.

Car The arboretum is located between Godalming and Hascombe, on the east side of the B2130. Satnav: GU8 4AD

OS map Explorer 145

Start/finish Winkworth Arboretum car park, GU8 4AD, grid ref: SU989411

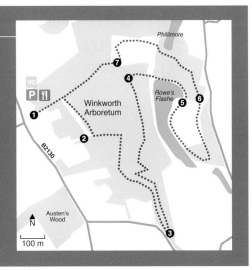

DIRECTIONS

Start/finish: Winkworth Arboretum car park

1. Walk through the visitor reception – where you can collect a map – into Winkworth Arboretum. Turn right, following the red waymarkers along the edge of the arboretum to location post 2, a path junction at the corner of Holly Wood.

2. Turn left following the path to the next junction at location post 4, then turn right. Follow this path slightly downhill, straight across the next junction and down to a sharp left corner at the southern end of the arboretum.

3. Follow the path around to the left, walking back the way you came, but further down the hill. Take the next right to reach a path junction with the yellow trail at location post 10. Turn left, then bear right and follow the path slightly uphill to a junction at location post 7.

4. Turn right, walking down the Azalea Steps and past the boathouse. Follow the path, with the lake to your right, to a path junction with Rowe's Flash Meadow in front of you.

5. Stay right, walking along the lakeside path to the southern tip of the lake, then curve left, walking back up the other side of the meadow and back to a junction with a larger track.

6. Cross and follow the path opposite downhill on the wetland walk. Cross the stream and then start walking uphill, through a clearer area in the bluebell woods and left to a path junction.

7. Turn left and walk to the top of the hill, then continue on the same path, downhill to the car park and start.

DOG-FRIENDLY AMENITIES

Dogs are welcome to join you in the large seating area outside the tea-room. You'll also find a water bowl here.

73

25. Morden Hall North and South Parks Walk

Morden Hall Road
Morden
London
SM4 5JD
0208 545 6850
mordenhallpark@nationaltrust.org.uk

ABOUT THIS WALK

Distance 2.5 miles (4km)
Difficulty Easy
Terrain Flat, mostly well surfaced paths but some sections can still get muddy in wet weather
Stiles No
Interest Wildlife, urban escape

One of the few remaining estates that once lined the River Wandle, Morden Hall Park is a secret and peaceful escape in the heart of busy south London. Passing under the archway, through the gates in the high wall that encircles the park, feels like stepping into a different world where a meandering river, veteran trees, grassy meadows, parkland and a sublimely scented rose garden await discovery.

There's a friendly, community-feel here, centred around the renovated Stableyard with its second-hand bookshop, and the café. Local craftspeople use some of the former estate buildings as workshops, while the western mill is home for the new Children & Young People Hub. This walk loops the park either side of Morden Hall (private venue not open to visitors), passing the Snuff Mill, where tobacco was dried and ground by watermills into snuff. You can see the original waterwheel that once powered the huge millstones to crush the tobacco.

THINGS TO SEE

The wetlands, with their sedge beds, are home to a rich variety of species, including the closest heronry to central London. You might spot a kingfisher or a little egret if you're lucky, as well as the resident mallard ducks, while the 2,000 roses in the rose garden are popular with pollinators. The park is also an important refuge for city dwellers, for whom it's a place to escape to, and be in nature, within a friendly, inclusive setting.

You'll also find the National Trust's only garden centre here.

Paws for thought
The car park isn't very big, so please arrive on foot or by public transport if possible. To protect the wildlife at Morden Hall Park, please keep your dog on a lead in the Rose Garden; around the buildings, including the Stableyard, Snuff Mill, cafés and Garden Centre; the Adventure Play Area; on the Wetland Boardwalk; and in the Garden Centre.

Other walkies nearby
There's a wealth of great walks in London, with its many parks, gardens and riverside trails. Visit Osterley Park, Ham House and the Royal Parks. You can find lots more inspiration on London walks on the National Trust website: www.nationaltrust.org. uk/visit/london/walking

Above: The boardwalk gives access to the wetlands area at Morden Hall Park.
Opposite: Entrance to the Stableyard Café.

Public transport Morden Underground station is a short walk along the Aberconway Road from Morden Hall Park. Tramlink to Phipps Bridge. The following bus routes stop on the boundary of the park: 80, 118, 157, 164, 201, 470, 93, and the K5 route terminates at Morden Station.
Car Morden Hall Park is off the A24 and A297, south of Wimbledon, north of Sutton. Satnav: SM4 5JD
OS map Explorer 161
Start/finish Morden Hall car park, SM4 5JD, grid ref: TQ260684

DIRECTIONS

Start/finish: Morden Hall car park

1. Walk through the gate between the Potting Shed Café and the Garden Centre, turn right and walk past the stables on the left to a junction with the Snuff Mill to your right. Turn left here, following the path to a crossroads with Morden Hall visible to the left.

2. Continue in the same direction, crossing a bridge and following the path left around Willow Wood. This path loops the edge of the wood and returns to the bigger track; turn left and cross the bridge into North Park. Bear right at the next two junctions, and walk along the edge of the park to the path junction at the northern end of the park.

3. Turn right and follow the path around the edge of the parkland, crossing a trail and walking through an area of wetland. Follow the path right to reach Kingfisher Bridge.

4. Cross and turn left, joining the outbound route and recrossing the bridge to arrive at the junction in front of Morden Hall. Turn left and walk across White Bridge, then bear left following the path and river to a footbridge close to the edge of the park.

5. Turn right and follow the path around the edge of South Park. Keep the boundary close on the left, walking around the park until you reach the River Wandle.

6. Turn right and follow the path with the river to your left. After passing the island, the path bears right, away from the river and through the arboretum, to a path junction with a bridge to your left.

7. Cross the bridge and follow the path back, over the White Bridge and left to return to the start.

DOG-FRIENDLY AMENITIES

Dogs are welcome in all parts of the grounds of Morden Hall Park, but should be kept on a lead in some areas – see 'Paws for thought' for details. You'll find dog water bowls outside the dog-friendly Potting Shed and Stableyard Café, which serve dog-friendly ice cream in summer, and in the plant area of the Garden Centre.

26. Chartwell and Emmetts Garden Walk

Mapleton Road
Westerham
Kent
TN16 1PS
01732 868381
chartwell@nationaltrust.org.uk

ABOUT THIS WALK

Distance 5.3 miles (8.5km)
Difficulty Moderate
Terrain Woodland, farm and estate paths and tracks, with sections of rougher ground, some areas can get muddy. Some steep but not particularly long hills
Stiles Yes
Interest: Wildlife, history

This lovely walk through the High Weald of Kent visits two National Trust properties, each one special in its own way. Starting at Chartwell, Winston and Clementine Churchill's family home for 40 years, you'll make your way across rolling fields and through areas of woodland as far as Emmetts Garden.

Set at one of the highest points in the county of Kent, this Edwardian estate was owned by banker and plantsman, Frederic Lubbock, and the gardens were laid out in the early 1900s. From Emmetts, you'll continue the loop, walking past the former Tudor mansion at Weardale Manor and over Toy's Hill, joining the Greensand Way for a stretch before returning to Chartwell. Both properties occupy high positions, offering far-reaching views out across the Weald.

THINGS TO SEE

In Emmetts Garden you'll encounter the Italianate Rose Garden with its pink-and-white theme; the Rock Garden with its hardy species and pretty lily pond; the North Garden with its highly unusual Wedding Cake tree; and the South Garden with its varied collection of shrubs and plants from around the world, including handkerchief (or dove) trees, one of which is an original specimen, imported by Frederic Lubbock from China, and is over 100 years old.

Paws for thought
Dogs should be kept on leads in the gardens, main visitor areas and around grazing or other animals.

Other walkies nearby
The Westerham to Chartwell trail starts in the village of Westerham and wanders the 2 miles (3.2km) through beautiful Weald countryside to reach Chartwell. After a cup of tea at the Landemare Café, it will be time for the return journey to Westerham.

Above: Investigating the flowerbed at Chartwell.
Opposite: View of Chartwell House across the lake.

Public transport Trains to Edenbridge (4 miles/6.4km) or Oxted (6 miles/9.7km), then 236 bus along the B2026 road. Alight at Mapleton Road junction and walk from there. It's about half a mile (0.8km) along a country road to Chartwell.

Car From M25 join the A25 and follow the brown National Trust signs. The entrance is off the B2026 between Westerham and Crockham Hill. Satnav: TN16 1PS

OS map Explorer 147

Start/finish Chartwell car park, TN16 1PS grid ref: TQ454513

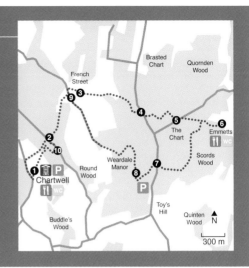

DIRECTIONS

Start/finish: Chartwell car park

1. With your back to the café, go left until reaching the main entrance gate to the car park. Exit and turn immediately right onto an enclosed path. Follow uphill until reaching Hosey Common Lane.

2. Cross the road to the bridleway opposite. Remain on this track keeping to the right whenever it forks. At the road (French Street hamlet) turn left. Shortly opposite a 'GR' red post box in the hedge, turn right onto a footpath taking the right fork. This enclosed path descends via steps and a couple of stiles to a footbridge.

3. Continue straight ahead uphill to a pedestrian kissing gate in the top-right-hand corner of the field. Once through the kissing gate, cross the track and take the path opposite. Over the next pedestrian kissing gate bear diagonally right heading towards a further kissing gate in the corner of the field. Walk through the pedestrian kissing gate and continue straight on with the fence on your left. Where the fence ends, bear right and follow this path for a short way to a crossing track. Turn left soon, ignoring a path to the right and continue to a road – Chart Lane.

4. Cross the road and take the path opposite. Follow it through the glade for some distance to emerge by a fence onto Emmetts Lane. Turn left ignoring the bridleway opposite.

5. Opposite the entrance to Ide Hill House turn right onto a footpath. Eventually you will come to a crossing track and waymark post.

6. Leave Emmetts along the footpath by which you entered the garden (immediately next to the tea-room). Go over the stile, ignoring a minor path to the left and continue on to a crossroads of paths. Turn left downhill, over crossroads then uphill on a sunken path through Scords Wood.

7. At the next crossroads of paths, go straight ahead and continue on this path for some distance. At the next crossroads, turn right and go steadily uphill. On reaching a junction of 5 paths, maintain direction uphill. At the top, go straight over a crossing track to Chart Lane. Cross the road and take the path opposite to the left of the house. At a T-junction turn left onto a wide path. Very soon you will go over a crossing track and continue on this path, ignoring two paths to the left, until you reach the site of Weardale Manor on the left.

8. Maintain direction on the wide stony track between the information panel and the monument; later pass two paths on the right and go through a wooden barrier. Go straight over a crossing track, ignore two paths on the right and continue downhill to exit Toys Hill through posts by a gate. Continue down the lane for some distance.

9. Pass a farm and continue uphill to French Street hamlet. After passing the first few cottages turn left on a sign-posted bridleway and keep left whenever the path forks until reaching a road – Hosey Common Lane.

10. Turn left onto the road and after a short distance turn right by a National Trust sign for Chartwell. Almost immediately turn right at a T-junction. Follow this wide path down to a gate leading back to the car park. From here you have magnificent views over the estate and the Weald of Kent.

DOG-FRIENDLY AMENITIES

Chartwell: Dogs are welcome in all outdoor areas at Chartwell. They can be off the lead under close control across the wider estate, including the fields and woods outside the formal gardens, when there are no grazing animals. Your dog can join you in the Lady Soames Room adjoining the Landemare Café, accessed via a side door. There's also plenty of outside seating, where dogs are welcome.

Emmetts Garden: Dogs are welcome on leads in all outdoor areas. You'll find water bowls at the main visitor areas. Only assistance dogs are allowed inside the Old Stables Tea Room, but there's plenty of outdoor seating where your dog can join you for refreshments.

The meadow at Emmetts Garden.

27. Ightham Mote to Wilmot Hill

Ightham Mote
Mote Road
Ivy Hatch
Sevenoaks
Kent
TN15 0NT
01732 810378
ighthammote@nationaltrust.org.uk

ABOUT THIS WALK

Distance 3.5 miles (5.6km)
Difficulty Moderate
Terrain A mixture of woodland, footpaths and some steep inclines
Stiles Yes
Interest Wildlife, history

The delightful 14th-century moated manor house at Ightham Mote nestles in a secluded Kent valley, surrounded by peaceful gardens and 500 acres of wider estate extending into the Kent Downs Area of Outstanding Natural Beauty. Built from Kentish ragstone and great Wealden oaks, its architecture and interiors showcase the development of the quintessential English country house

This walk explores the periphery of the estate, taking in Scathes Wood, a section of the Greensand Way, Wilmot Hill and Broadhoath Wood along the way.

THINGS TO SEE

Stroll around the tranquil gardens, enjoying the natural streams and spring-fed lakes, as well as an orchard, flowering plants and a cutting garden. Dogs are welcome on short leads in the garden between September and February. The wider estate offers a wealth of wonderful walks with secret glades and surprise views awaiting discovery.
If you're visiting with children, they can let off steam in the wild play area, with a natural stream to paddle in, and chimes, balance beams and stepping stones to play on. No dogs in the play area.

Paws for thought
Ightham Mote and its surrounding countryside is home to lots of wildlife and livestock, so dogs must be on a lead and kept away from the play area. From March to August, assistance dogs only are welcome in the garden. In the indoor spaces, including the house, shop and indoor catering, only assistance dogs are allowed. More information can be found at visitor reception.

Other walkies nearby
For a longer walk, there are three other routes which start at Ightham and head out into the Kentish countryside, visiting other historical landmarks and country estates, including Oldbury Hill, Old Soar Manor and Knole. The routes vary from 5 to 9 miles (8 to 14km) in length and are all dog-friendly.

Sunset over the snowy grounds at Ightham Mote.

HOW TO GET HERE

Public transport There are three rail stations within easy reach of Ightham Mote: Hildenborough (4 miles/6.4km) Sevenoaks (7 miles/11km) and Borough Green and Wrotham (3½ miles/5.6km). Taxi ranks / public phones are available at all stations.

Car Follow the brown signs to Ightham Mote along the A227 from Tonbridge, the A25 from Sevenoaks, or the A20/A25 from Maidstone. Satnav: TN15 0NU

OS map Explorer 147

Start/finish Ightham Mote car park, TN15 0NU, grid ref: TQ585535

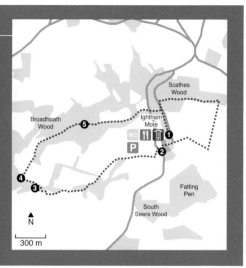

DOG-FRIENDLY AMENITIES

After a good walk, head for the Mote Café, where you'll find outdoor seating on the patio with water bowls as well as doggy treats. There are also water bowls outside visitor reception.

To the west of Ightham, over the border into Surrey, the National Trust's Bagden Farm cottages 1 & 2, set within the Polesden Lacey estate in the nearby Surrey Hills Area of Outstanding Natural Beauty, sleep up to six people and a dog each, with fabulous walks right from the doorstep.

DIRECTIONS

Start/finish: Ightham Mote car park

1. Walk away from Ightham Mote house up the driveway until you can turn right, over a stile into Scathes Wood. Follow this path through the woodland to a path junction. Turn right and follow this bridleway downhill along the edge of a field to a T-junction. Turn right, following the National Trust sign and the track along the edge of a field and behind Ightham Mote house to Mote Road.

2. Follow Mote Road right for a short distance, then turn left onto the track to Mote Farm – this is the Greensand Way trail. Walk up the track, past the farmyard and continue on the Greensand Way; stay left at the fork and walk past Wilmot Cottage and an old brick filter house. Continue to a footpath on the right.

3. Turn sharp right, leaving the Greensand Way and walking up some steps; follow the path as it turns sharp left and continue uphill to the National Trust signed stile at the top.

4. Cross the stile and turn right, passing a permissive footpath barrier and heading downhill to a path junction below Wilmot Hill. Cross and continue on the path opposite, walking downhill into Broadhoath Wood. Follow the path as it bears right and passes another timber barrier to join a bridleway which comes down from the left.

5. Join this bridleway and follow it downhill through the woodland. Pass the hopper huts and silt trap before reaching Mote Road. Cross the road and walk up the footpath opposite to the top of the Ightham Mote garden. Continue up a few steps to the drive, turn right and follow this back to the car park.

28. Scotney Castle Woodland and Parkland Walk

Lamberhurst
Tunbridge Wells
Kent
TN3 8JN
01892 893820
scotneycastle@nationaltrust.org.uk

ABOUT THIS WALK

Distance 2.8 miles (4.5km)
Difficulty Moderate
Terrain Surfaced, grassy and woodland trails plus a bit of tarmac. Hilly but not very steep
Stiles No
Interest Wildlife, history

Set within Kent's Bewl Valley, Scotney Castle and its surrounding estate combines the romantic ruins of a part-ruined, 14th-century moated castle with a grand Victorian country mansion and a fascinating history. The wider grounds comprise 780 acres (316ha) of ancient, Grade I-listed parkland, including 300 acres (121ha) of Wealden woodlands, criss-crossed by waymarked trails and perfect for exploring with your dog.

This walk commences with the enjoyable, waymarked Parkland Trail, exploring the park and visiting the many viewpoints offering picturesque scenes of the estate. Starting at the house you'll trace the path around the old castle and moat before heading out across open grassland and crossing the River Bewl. Here you'll detour from the main route, following sheltered trails through Kilndown Wood. Emerging from the trees, you'll recross the river, from where the final stretch winds its way pleasantly back along quiet lanes and through fields to return to the house.

THINGS TO SEE

Be sure to visit the romantic ruined medieval castle while you're at Scotney. Standing on its own moated island, it forms the centrepiece of Edward Hussey III's visionary Picturesque garden and is a delight to explore for visitors of all ages.

Paws for thought

Only assistance dogs are allowed in the house, old castle and the walled garden. Occasionally, dogs may not be allowed in the tea-room because of an event, but this will be clearly signed. You'll find grazing animals and wildlife across the estate, so dogs must be kept on leads. There are two off-lead areas close to this walk, see below for details.

Other walkies nearby

Starting at pretty Kilndown village, this route and many others in the Scotney area can be walked entirely on public footpaths, in which case payment/NT membership is not required.

Scotney Castle estate.

Public transport Wadhurst is the closest train station (5.5 miles/8.9km). The 256 Tunbridge Wells–Wadhurst bus service runs via Lamberhurst Monday to Friday. You can walk via footpaths to Scotney Castle (1 mile/1.6km).

Car Follow brown Scotney Castle signs from the A21. Satnav: TN3 8JN. All visitors should book their parking in advance via the Scotney website or the NT app.

OS map Explorer 136

Start/finish Scotney Castle car park, TN3 8JN, grid ref: TQ686354

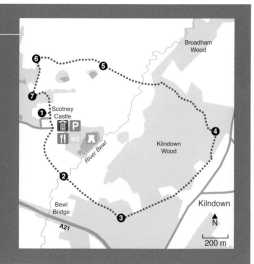

Frosty morning on the estate at Scotney Castle.

DIRECTIONS

Start/finish: Scotney Castle car park

1. Turn right out of the car park and follow the drive to and through Salvin Gate. Follow the old carriageway right across the parkland, then curve to the left, crossing Sweetbourne Bridge and walking through the next gate. Continue to Bewl Bridge.

2. Follow the trail in front of you, walking uphill across the parkland towards the woods. Pass a turning where the Parkland Trail goes left and continue uphill on the Woodland Trail. Walk into the woods and up to a path junction.

3. Turn left, following the footpath towards the village of Kilndown. The path runs along the back of some gardens (on your right) and then bears left, away from the village, and back into Kilndown Wood.

4. When you reach a path junction, turn left, walking downhill through the woodland and back into the parkland which surrounds Scotney Castle. The Parkland Walk joins your path from the left, and then you cross the River Bewl. Continue on the trail across the next field and through a gate. Follow the path along the edge of the next field and go through the gate onto a road and information post.

5. Follow the road left for a short distance, then bear right, through a gate into a field. Follow the path along the edge of the field, through a gate into the next field and continue on the path to the edge of the field at the top of the hill.

6. Walk left and downhill along the footpath through a gate to reach a forestry track at the edge of some woodland. Turn left onto the road.

7. Follow the forestry track for a short distance, and then turn right at some cottages and walk through the old barn and back to the start.

DOG-FRIENDLY AMENITIES

Scotney is a very dog-friendly property and dogs are welcome on short leads in the main Picturesque garden, the shop and tea-room, as well as across the wider estate.

While dogs must be kept on leads on this walk, if your dog would like to run free, there are off-lead areas in the woodland at Sprivers and Nap Wood. Please take extra care during bird-nesting season (1 March–31 July) to prevent the disturbance of ground-nesting birds; when there are lambs and sheep at Sprivers, dogs should be on leads. Nap Wood is just off the A267 Tunbridge Wells to Eastbourne road, and the postcode for Sprivers Wood is TN12 8DN.

Scotney West Lodge is a pretty former gatehouse, tucked away on the estate, with hundreds of acres to explore on your doorstep. With an enclosed, private garden, this cosy house sleeps up to four people and a dog (NT Holidays).

Birling Gap from East Dean

**East Dean
Near Eastbourne
East Sussex
BN20 0AB
01323 423197**

birlinggap@nationaltrust.org.uk

ABOUT THIS WALK

Distance 3.7 miles (5.9km)
Difficulty Moderate
Terrain Mostly short,
grazed chalk grassland
which doesn't tend to get
muddy; some gravel track
and tarmac. Steep but not
very long hills
Stiles No
Interest: History, coast,
wildlife

The towering chalk cliffs of the Seven Sisters rise from the sea on the East Sussex coast. Above the cliffs, the South Downs Way runs along the top, an undulating trail that mirrors the waves below.

This circular walk makes the most of the glorious views. Following old drovers' and smuggling routes from the downland village of East Dean to Birling Gap, perfectly placed for mid-walk refreshments.

THINGS TO SEE

Nestled between the better-known Beachy Head and Seven Sisters, the hamlet of Birling Gap, visited at the half-way point on this walk, houses a National Trust café, shop and visitor centre along with a row of former coastguard cottages. Some of the buildings have already been claimed by coastal erosion, which is reducing this stretch of coastline at a rate of around 3ft (1m) a year, while others remain inhabited.

Paws for thought
You'll find grazing animals and sheer, unfenced cliffs in this area. Please keep dogs on leads.

Other walkies nearby
The South Downs Way National Trail runs for 100 miles (161km) between Winchester and Eastbourne, right across the South Downs National Park. Friston Forest, just to the north of this route, has an excellent network of trails for exploring on foot or bike.

DIRECTIONS

Start/finish: East Dean village car park

1. Turn right out of the car park and walk past the Tiger Inn to the village green. Walk left across the green and then right onto Upper Street. Follow Upper Street and go around the right-hand corner to reach a track on the left.

2. Follow this track between houses and out into the field. Walk through the gate and follow the path uphill across the field known as Hobbes Eares, continue to Friston church, and then Crowlink Lane.

3. Turn left and follow the lane through the National Trust car park. Just after the cattle

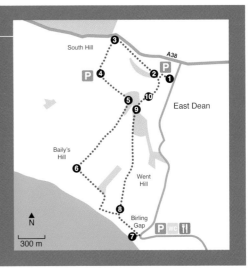

Public transport Eastbourne is
the closest train station (5.5
miles/8.9km). Buses between
Eastbourne and Brighton
regularly call at East Dean.
Car East Dean is off the A259
between Seaford and Eastbourne.
Park in the village hall car park.
Satnav: BN20 0DR
OS map Explorer OL25
Start/finish East Dean village hall
car park, BN20 0AB, grid ref:
TV557977

grid, turn left and follow the fence line.

4. Follow the fence and the edge of the large field until you reach
the far corner, where the path turns right next to an area of
woodland.

5. Continue to follow the fence line to the corner where there is
some woodland and turn right following the edge of the field.

6. Turn left and follow the path downhill, and then the zig-zag path
up Went Hill. Once at the top turn right and walk towards a
small gate in the electric fence. Go through the gate and turn
left – you are now on the South Downs Way and coast path.
Follow the path to a gate at the edge of Birling Gap hamlet. Go
through the gate and follow the track to the National Trust car
park and café.

7. Return on the outbound route up the track through the houses
at Birling Gap, this time stay on the track as it curves right; you
will pass Seven Sisters Cottage and reach a gate.

8. Walk through the gate and follow the bridleway up Went Hill,
with the field boundary to your right. Cross the next field and
pass a red barn on your right. At a marker post which indicates a
bridleway, bear right and follow it down through the woods.

9. Follow the track, through a gate and curving right out of the
wood; go across a field and behind a house to reach another
gate and the end of Went Way road.

10. Walk along Went Way until you get back to the village green.
Walk across the green towards the Tiger Inn and turn right to
get back to the car park.

DOG-FRIENDLY AMENITIES

The café at Birling Gap offers
welcome half-way refreshments
and has a dog-friendly seating area.

The Star & Garter in East Dean
is close to the start/finish.
Welcoming well-behaved dogs
and children, it offers a
comprehensive breakfast and
sandwich menu.
www.thestarandgarter.co.uk

Opposite: The beach at Birling Gap.

30. Royal Military Canal and Saxon Shore Way

**Royal Military Canal
From Appledore Bridge to
Warehorne Bridge
Kent
0344 800 1895**

lse.customerenquiries@
nationaltrust.org.uk

ABOUT THIS WALK

**Distance 5.2 miles (8.4km)
Difficulty Moderate
Terrain Canal path, field
paths and short sections of
road. The fields can be muddy
and there is a small hill
Stiles Yes
Interest History, wildlife**

The Kent village of Appledore has a history that dates back to Roman times. It was once a busy port on the estuary of the River Rother – a hub for trading luxury goods such as silk, wine and lace as well as an important centre for the ship-building industry. In the 14th century, however, fierce storms caused the river to change its course, while reclamation of Romney Marsh caused the sea to retreat, following which the village lost its strategic importance.

Today, Appledore is an attractive village with medieval houses, a shop and pubs, and a 14th-century church, St Peter and St Paul. But the Royal Military Canal remains as an echo of its tumultuous past, from the Vikings who arrived with 250 longships, to the Hundred Years' War, when French troops raided the coastline, sacked the village and burned down the church. This walk heads out along a scenic stretch of the canal, returning along the Saxon Shore Way.

THINGS TO SEE

This walk takes you through the graveyard of St Mary's Church, Kenardington. The church stands on an old Saxon fort, as well as on the site of battle, when the Vikings brought their longships to Appledore in the 9th century.

Paws for thought
You'll encounter lots of wildlife and often grazing animals on this walk. Please keep dogs on leads.

Other walkies nearby
The 160-mile (257-km) Saxon Shore Way, part of which is followed on this walk, is a long-distance footpath from Gravesend in Kent, tracing the coast as it was in Roman times as far as Hastings, East Sussex. Based on the shoreline prior to the reclamation of Romney Marsh, the route runs significantly inland from the modern coastline.

Above: The Royal Military Canal, near Appledore.

Public transport Appledore train
station is about 1.3 miles (2km)
away, connected by footpaths
across the fields.
Car Off the B2080 in Appledore,
between Tenterden and New
Romney. Satnav: TN26 2AE
OS map Explorer 125
Start/finish Appledore Village car
park, TN26 2AE, grid ref:
TQ955296

DIRECTIONS

Start/finish: Appledore Village car park

1. Turn right out of the car park and follow The Street through
   Appledore to a gate on the left, just before the bridge over the
   canal. Turn left through this onto the canal path.

2. Walk along the canal path, with the canal to your right, until you
   reach the bridge at Higham. Go through the gate onto the road.

3. Turn left and follow the road for a short distance, then take the
   signed footpath right, over a plank bridge and across two large
   fields, divided by a stile, to reach St Mary's Church.

4. The Saxon Shore Way long distance footpath crosses in front of
   you and our walk will follow it back to Appledore. Turn left and
   follow the path along the field boundary to Church Road. Turn
   left onto the road then right, through a gate and follow the path
   across three fields and through a couple of gates to reach a
   sunken lane near Smith's Farm.

5. Cross the lane and walk up a few steps, then follow the path
   across the vineyard to another road. Cross and follow the
   footpath opposite across a field, a footbridge and three more
   fields to reach Mill Mound, a Bronze Age burial site.

6. Bear left here and follow the Saxon Shore Way across several
   more fields until you reach a track at the corner of the
   recreation ground in Appledore. Cross the track and the
   recreation ground to reach The Street. Turn left to return to the
   car park and the start.

DOG-FRIENDLY AMENITIES

Quirky Miss Mollett's High Class
Tea Room in Appledore is
dog-friendly and has plenty of
outdoor seating, perfect for
sitting out on a sunny day. www.
missmollettstearoom.co.uk
Just north of the canal, near to
Rye, self-catering Boxwood is a
stunning, contemporary space
surrounded by ancient mixed
woodland. Sleeping up to seven,
and dog-friendly, it's the perfect
retreat and a great base for
exploring this part of Kent.
www.boxwood-retreat.co.uk

East

Lyveden
Near Oundle
Northamptonshire
PE8 5AT
01832 205259
lyveden@nationaltrust.org.uk

ABOUT THIS WALK

Distance 8.2 miles (13.2km)
Difficulty Moderate
Terrain Woodland, fields
and footpaths. Some
sections can get muddy, but
it's fairly flat
Stiles No
Interest History,
archaeology, wildlife

A remarkable survivor of its time, Lyveden is an unfinished Elizabethan lodge and moated garden, standing amidst rolling Northamptonshire countryside. Started as an ambitious project by Sir Thomas Tresham, a prominent Elizabethan Catholic landowner, the lodge stands intriguingly suspended in time, abandoned following Tresham's death in 1605.

This walk follows the waymarked Lyveden Way, a circular path through beautiful Northamptonshire meadows, woodland and villages. The full loop starts at nearby Fermyn Woods Country Park, extending the walk distance to 9.9 miles (16km).

THINGS TO SEE

A short distance from Lyveden New Bield stands the Grade I-listed Lyveden Manor, sometimes called Lyveden Old Bield. Built by the Tresham family in 1570, it was in private ownership until acquired by the National Trust in 2013.

Restoration work has been carried out on the rare Elizabethan garden with its 390-ft (119-m) concentric design for visitors to fully experience Tresham's vision for Lyveden.

Paws for thought
Dogs must be kept on short leads throughout the buildings and grounds at Lyveden. You'll often find animals grazing here, so take extra care if you encounter them on your walk.

Other walkies nearby
The Nene Way runs through Wadenhoe, at the furthest point of the Lyveden Way from Lyveden New Bield. This long-distance path follows the course of the river Nene from Badby in Northamptonshire to Sutton Bridge in Lincolnshire, a distance of 114 miles (183km), linking up with many other paths along the way.

Above and opposite: Dogs on leads
are welcome throughout Lyveden.

HOW TO GET HERE

Public transport The closest train station is Corby. Take the No. 14 bus from there to Brigstock and walk the Lyveden Way from there.
Car Lyveden is off A6116. From Oundle take A427. Satnav: PE8 5AT
OS map Explorer 224
Start/finish Lyveden New Bield car park, PE8 5AT, grid ref: SP979858

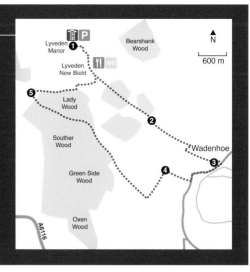

DIRECTIONS

Start/finish: Lyveden New Bield car park

1. Exit the car park and follow the path past Lyveden Manor to a track; turn right and follow this past the orchard to the visitor centre. Follow the accessible path towards the unfinished garden lodge, pass this on your right to reach a path junction with the Lyveden Way. Bear left and follow the bridleway into Lilford Wood. Continue following the bridleway, emerging from the wood, crossing a stream, and joining a main track to reach a track junction just before Wadenhoe Lodge.

2. Turn left, following Lyveden Way waymarkers past the lodge to reach a lane. Turn right onto the lane and then left, following the Lyveden Way into the village of Wadenhoe.

3. Turn right onto Main Street and follow the Lyveden Way through Wadenhoe. Bear right onto Mill Lane, then right again onto Church Street. Walk past The King's Head pub and bear right onto a footpath past the church to reach Wadenhoe Road. Turn left onto the road, then right onto a footpath, following this to a junction.

4. Turn left onto a byway and follow this to the next path junction. Turn right off the byway onto a footpath following the Lyveden Way across fields. Follow this path along the edge of the woods, eventually bearing left and walking through woodland to reach a path junction where the Lyveden Way heads left to Fermyn Wood and right to Lyveden.

5. Turn right and follow the Lyveden Way back to the path junction beside the unfinished garden lodge. Turn left and re-trace your outbound steps back to the finish.

DOG-FRIENDLY AMENITIES

Dogs on leads are welcome throughout Lyveden, including the ground floor of the manor, the gardens and courtyard areas, and within the lodge. There's a water bowl outside the dog-friendly café. Further afield on the Lyveden Way, dogs can be off the lead but, due to roads and grazing animals, under close control at all times. The King's Head pub in Wadenhoe is dog-friendly and has plentiful outdoor seating in its beer garden. www.kingsheadwadenhoe.com

**Whipsnade Road
Dunstable
Bedfordshire
LU6 2GY
01582 500920**
dunstabledowns@nationaltrust.org.uk

ABOUT THIS WALK

Distance 4.6 miles (7.4km)
Difficulty Moderate
Terrain Chalk downlands,
woodland and farmland. The
footpaths can get muddy
and slippery
Stiles No
Interest Wildlife, history

Lying just a few miles north-west of London, the Chilterns are a beautiful, peaceful corner of southern England. With gently rolling hills and swathed in woodland, open downland and pretty red brick and flint villages. The highest point of the Chilterns AONB, Dunstable Downs, is networked with footpaths to explore.

Dunstable Downs boasts a landscape of sculpted chalk hills, wildlife-rich grassland and glorious views, as well as several Sites of Special Scientific Interest (SSSIs). This circular walk follows the Icknield Way along the edge of the downs, visiting Whipsnade with its Tree Cathedral and safari park. After a pleasantly shaded stretch of woodland at Whipsnade Heath, you'll descend to the chalk quarries at Kensworth, before returning to the visitor centre and café back at the downs.

THINGS TO SEE

Five Knolls is a cluster of seven round barrows, comprising two bowl barrows, three bell barrows and two pond barrows. Excavated in the 1850s and 1920s, the burial ground is thought to have been used for kings or chiefs. Originating in the late Neolithic and Bronze ages, they were re-used for burial in the Roman period.

Paws for thought

Dogs must be kept on a lead around the visitor centre and car parks. You may also encounter grazing animals and areas important for ground-nesting birds – please keep dogs on a lead in these areas.

Other walkies nearby

There are three waymarked walks to enjoy on Dunstable Downs – the Stone Age Walk (red waymarkers), Wildflower Walk (blue waymarkers) and Tree Cathedral Walk (purple waymarkers). All start and finish at the Chilterns Gateway Centre.

Above: Views across the landscape at Dunstable Downs and Whipsnade Estate.

HOW TO GET HERE

Public transport Luton station 7 miles (11.3km), from here take Arriva 61 bus service. From Dunstable, Centrebus 40 passes Dunstable Downs Mon–Sat.
Car On B4541 west of Dunstable and Whipsnade. Satnav: LU6 2GY Parking charges apply (free for National Trust members).
OS map Explorer 181 and 193
Start/finish Chilterns Gateway Centre car park, LU6 2GY, grid ref: TL008195

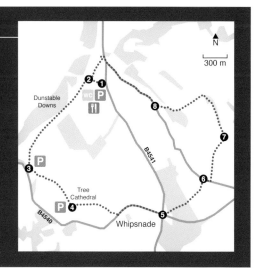

DIRECTIONS

Start/finish: Chilterns Gateway Centre car park

1. From the car park, head downhill past the Chilterns Gateway Centre towards the modern sculpture of the Windcatcher, then turn left at the waymarker onto the bridleway that runs alongside the hedgerow.

2. Continue along the bridleway (also the Icknield Way) into grassland and onwards towards Bison Hill car park.

3. Before you reach Bison Hill car park, turn left and continue along the bridleway, where it becomes an ancient, sunken hollow-way, with hedgerows on both sides. Continue along the bridleway as it opens out, passing the Whipsnade Zoo car park on your right. Continue past some houses until you reach a footpath sign on your left.

4. Turn left and follow the footpath through a kissing gate and then another gate, which leads to the Whipsnade Tree Cathedral. Continue along the footpath with the Tree Cathedral on your left, heading through the car park and keeping left as you approach the B4540. Cross the road with care and proceed past the church, continuing downhill past the Old Hunters Lodge pub to reach a roundabout.

5. Cross the roundabout with care and head towards Whipsnade Heath car park on your left. Follow the tarmac path until you can take the footpath straight up through the woodland. Continue following the footpath through the woodland to reach a kissing gate. Go through this and follow the path to reach a quiet road opposite Green End Farm.

6. Take the road to the right, cross and then turn left onto the footpath to the right of Green End Farm. Follow the footpath around the edge of the field, then downhill and through a kissing gate on your left.

7. Walk diagonally uphill across Codling Bank to the kissing gate in the chain link fence. Go through this and then turn left, following the footpath down through the wooded area, past a small brick shed and onto a footpath by the quarry fence. Continue along the footpath, bearing right to join the path along the left-hand field edge – you'll see a tall aerial on the skyline ahead. Follow the path into the copse and out onto the roadside.

8. Turn right to join Isle of Wight Lane, following this to the junction with the B4541 at Robertson Corner. Cross the road with care and return to the Chilterns Gateway Centre.

DOG-FRIENDLY AMENITIES

Dogs are welcome in most areas of Dunstable Downs – dogs should be kept under close control at all times and on leads in the visitor centre, car park and around livestock. You'll find water bowls outside the visitor centre, and three dog bins on site at the visitor centre, car park and Chute Wood. The View Café, located in the Chilterns Gateway Centre, is also dog-friendly, with plenty of outdoor seating and, as its name suggests, fantastic views from the escarpment.

May view of Whipsnade Tree Cathedral.

33. Hughenden Boundary Walk

Hughenden Manor,
High Wycombe,
Buckinghamshire
HP14 4LA
01494755565
hughenden@nationaltrust.org.uk

ABOUT THIS WALK

Distance 4 miles (6.4km)
Difficulty Moderate
Terrain Mostly footpaths with one short road section and two road crossings. Some of the route can be muddy and slippery after wet weather. Some steep uphill and downhill slopes
Stiles No
Interest Wildlife, history

The grand, red-brick mansion and former home of Victorian prime minister, Benjamin Disraeli, Hughenden feels a world away from the bustling south-east.

This walk traces the outer boundary of the Hughenden estate, marked in places with red waymarkers. These can be a little sporadic, however, so be prepared to do some gentle navigating as you go. As well as the house itself, you'll discover woodland alive with the sound of birdsong, open parkland, farmland and a rare, crystal-clear chalk stream, typical of this area.

THINGS TO SEE

Beech trees dominate the woodlands, which is typical of the Chilterns. Look out for chalk pits and sawpits, evidence of industry long before Disraeli bought the estate. Along the trail, you'll see the 50ft-high Disraeli Monument. It commemorates Disraeli's father Isaac, a literary critic and historian.

Other walkies nearby
There are three other waymarked walks at Hughenden if you'd like to continue exploring the estate.

DOG-FRIENDLY BENEFITS

Dogs are very welcome in the stable yard area and the café. Water bowls are provided here and at the visitor welcome kiosk.

The Disraeli monument.

Paws for thought
At Hughenden, you can enjoy the formal gardens, drop by for a snack in the café or take one of the estate walks with your four-legged friend. The only place dogs aren't allowed is inside the house itself.

Dogs are welcome to be off lead around the woodland and parkland. Please return them to a lead when walking in areas with cattle and sheep.

DIRECTIONS

Start/finish: Hughenden car park

1. From the car park, head towards the Visitor Centre. Bear left at the first fork by the dew pond. Go downhill and into the woodland. Turn left at a crossing and walk through Woodcock Wood, past the sawpit, to the edge of the wood.

HOW TO GET HERE

Public transport The nearest station is
High Wycombe 2 miles (3km) away. The
Arriva 300 is a regular bus service
between High Wycombe and Aylesbury,
stopping at the estate entrance.
Car Hughenden is a short distance north
of High Wycombe off the A4128 towards
Great Missenden. Exit 4 from M40, then
A404 towards High Wycombe, then
follow signs to Eden Shopping Centre,
then A4128 towards Great Missenden.
Satnav: HP14 4LA
OS map Explorer 172
Start/finish Hughenden car park,
HP14 4LA, grid ref: SU859957

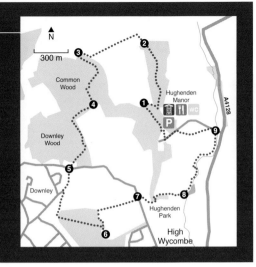

2. Go through the gate and walk left, across the field and through another gate. Follow the path left along the field edge to reach Flagmore Wood. Turn right and follow the woodland edge to a metal gate.

3. Go through the gate into Flagmore Wood. Follow the path Left, past the chalk pits to a fork. Bear right and follow the path downhill, ignoring the trails turning off either side. At the bottom of the hill at a bridleway, turn left and continue to meet a gate.

4. Don't go through the gate. Turn right and follow the path uphill into Common Wood (signposted to Downley). At the boundary ditch, walk left, following the path downhill with the ditch on your right. At the bottom of the hill, cross a track and go up the other side of the valley. Follow the path to meet Coates Lane in Downley.

5. Carefully cross Coates Lane and follow Littleworth Road (stick to the pavement on the left) to meet a footpath on the left, just after no.78. Follow the path along the back of some gardens to reach a path junction at the edge of Little Tinkers Wood. Bear left and continue to the next junction. Ignoring the larger path to the left, continue on the smaller path through Little Tinkers Wood to a metal gate at the far edge. Go through the gate and turn right to reach the Disraeli Monument.

6. Leave the monument by the same gate but stay right, following the woodland edge downhill and through a gate into a field. Turn right, following the path along with the fence on your right. Continue to Coates Lane Carefully cross and turn left, following the road a short distance, then take a sharp right through a metal gate onto a track.

7. Follow this track uphill to a gate signposted Middle Lodge. Turn left and walk through a set of gates into Hughenden Park. Turn right and follow the path downhill, to reach a path along the bank of Hughenden stream.

8. Turn left and follow the path along the Stream, past an ornamental lake, until you reach the main drive to Hughenden Manor.

9. Turn left and follow the drive uphill. Bear left and walk through the church car park. To avoid the churchyard, walk uphill across the meadow with the church hedge on your right. Walk uphill towards the manor, re-joining the driveway through a gate next to the cattle grid. Follow the drive to reach the Stable yard and Walled Garden entrances on your right. Turn right and follow the signs back to the car park.

34. Hatfield Forest

Bush End Road
Takeley
Bishop's Stortford
Essex
CM22 6NE
01279 870678
hatfieldforest@nationaltrust.org.uk

ABOUT THIS WALK

Distance 4 miles (6.4km)
Difficulty Moderate
Terrain Flat, but the woodland trails can be muddy in wet weather
Stiles No
Interest History, wildlife

Once a royal hunting forest, the Hatfield Forest of today is a National Nature Reserve, a SSSI with rare wildlife of national importance, and a peaceful place to walk. With a long history of different owners, from kings to commoners, this managed forest has been created by centuries of human intervention. Traditional woodland management techniques continue to be used, including coppicing, pollarding and grazing.

This family-friendly walk offers an enjoyable anti-clockwise loop of the forest, taking in sections of the Flitch Way and Forest Way paths. As you go, you'll pass the site of the Doodle Oak, the Iron Age settlement at Portingbury Hills, the Shell House and the lake.

THINGS TO SEE

Nature thrives in Hatfield Forest, which is home to over 3,500 species of wildlife. Insects, lichens and fungi live in and around the ancient trees, some of which are over 1,000 years old. Look out for the site of the Doodle Oak, which died in 1858, but was believed to have been one of the biggest trees in history by circumference.

Hatfield Forest National
Nature Reserve.

Paws for thought
In the winter, to reduce damage to the forest, car parking is limited to the hard standing area only. The car parks will be closed when they reach capacity. Dogs must be kept on leads near livestock, around the lake and wherever temporarily signed. Dogs are not permitted in the fenced sheep enclosures and the dog-free zone between the Shell House and the Decoy Lake. These are all clearly signposted. The walk is not totally accessible between the months of late October to early April due to seasonal route closures. This is the case between point 6 and point 8.

Other walkies nearby
The Flitch Way, which is open to both pedestrians and cyclists, follows 15 miles (24km) of the route of the former Bishop's Stortford to Braintree railway.

HOW TO GET HERE

Public transport The nearest railway stations are Bishop's Stortford (5 miles/8km) and Stansted Airport station (3 miles/4.8km). From there, take a bus, Arriva service 508, to the Green Man, Takeley Street.
Car From the west: from M11 exit 8 roundabout, take B1256 towards Takeley. From the east: from the A120, take the junction for Takeley. Once in Takeley, turn into the road opposite the Green Man pub (at the brown sign). Follow this straight road for 0.7 miles (1.2km) to the entrance car park on your right. Satnav: CM22 6NE
OS map Explorer 195 and 183
Start/finish Hatfield Forest car park, CM22 6NE, grid ref: TL547203

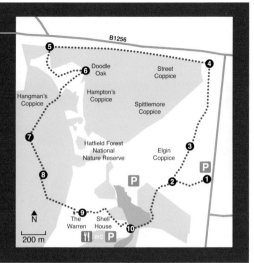

DIRECTIONS

Start/finish: Hatfield Forest car park

1. From the car park, head along the entrance road until you reach a boardwalk path to your left. Turn right opposite the boardwalk and head across the plain.

2. Continue straight ahead, with the trees on your left, until you reach the exit road from the forest. Cross the road with care and continue straight on, heading slightly to the right.

3. Head across the plain and uphill to reach the top of Takeley Hill. Continue straight ahead, with Hatfield Forest Estate Office on your right. Take the exit through the metal gate and turn left onto the Flitch Way.

4. Follow the Flitch Way for about 1 mile (1.6km), going through three gates to reach Elman's Green, the last one labelled 'Gate 16'.

5. After the third gate, turn left into Hatfield Forest, onto the Forest Way. Keep left of the open pasture, alongside the trees, until you can bear left at the fork, leaving the Forest Way. Go diagonally left across the pasture to the far side.

6. The site of the Doodle Oak is to your right here. Enter and return the same way from the trees, then, to continue, turn left to rejoin the Forest Way. Turn left and immediately right, once again leaving the Forest Way. Continue along this path, then take the third path on your left at Six Wantz Ways – where six paths meet.

7. Continue to the crossroads, where you'll find Portingbury Hills Iron Age settlement on your left, at Beggar's Hall coppice. From here, rejoin the path and go straight over the crossroads to a T-junction with a yellow signpost marked number 13.

8. Turn right, then almost immediately left onto a smaller path to Round Coppice, bearing left when you reach the crossroads. Walk straight across the open plain to reach a gravel track at the far side. Paws for thought that cattle and deer often graze in this area, so dogs should be kept on short leads.

9. At the gravel track, turn left and follow the track round to the right past Warren Cottage, then round to the left to reach a road junction. Cross the road and continue straight over the grass. Turn right over a small bridge, then bear left to a boundary gate into the lake area. Go through the gate, keeping the lake to your left, to reach the Shell House and Discovery Room, where you'll find toilets and a café. Please keep dogs on leads in this area.

10. From The Shell House, turn right onto the path and follow it over the dam. Join a boardwalk path and stay on this through the woods, going through one gate then across open ground until you reach a road. Turn right and follow the road back to the car park.

DOG-FRIENDLY AMENITIES

You'll find water and drinking bowls in the lakeside area and dog waste bins in all car parks, at key gateways and along the internal road. The café is dog-friendly with plenty of outdoor seating. You'll find route maps showing dog-friendly walks and areas where dogs can and can't go.

Down Hall Country House Hotel offers dog-friendly accommodation with a dog bed, bowl and treats plus access directly onto 100 acres (40.5ha) of grounds perfect for dog walks. Dogs are also allowed to accompany their owners to the lounges and outdoor restaurant terrace.

35. Brancaster Beach

Brancaster Beach
Beach Road
Brancaster
Norfolk
PE31 8BW
01263 740241
norfolkcoast@nationaltrust.org.uk

ABOUT THIS WALK

Distance 8.7 miles (14km)
Difficulty Moderate
Terrain Beach, common land, farmland and country lanes. Some areas can be wet and muddy
Stiles No
Interest: Coast, wildlife, history

The wide expanse of Brancaster beach with its golden crescent of sands is perfect for dog walks all year round – you'll find calm and freedom here even on the busiest of summer days.

This relaxing walk starts with a loop of the beach before exploring Brancaster Staithe. You'll have non-stop coastal views and opportunities for wildlife spotting – look out for the Brent geese, oystercatchers and many other bird species that either visit or make their homes here. Along the way, you'll visit The Downs, cross Barrow Common, discover the fascinating Roman site of Branodunum Fort, and spot the mysterious wreckage of *SS Vina*.

THINGS TO SEE

History is a key feature at Brancaster, going back to Branodunum Fort, an intriguing Scheduled Ancient Monument that was once the home of the Roman army. Today, it's a grassy meadow and essential habitat for skylarks and invertebrates.

If you're visiting Brancaster in winter, the awe-inspiring sight and sound of vast flocks of over-wintering pink-footed geese flying over the estate to roost is one not to be missed.

Paws for thought
Between May and September, there is a fenced-off dog-free zone at the eastern end of the beach. Please follow the signs and keep your dogs on a lead as protected nesting birds can be found here and it is a criminal offence to disturb them. You may also encounter people horse riding on the beach – please keep your dog on the lead around horses. Also be aware that the beach road at Brancaster can flood during high spring tides.

Other walkies nearby
The Norfolk Coast Path affords enjoyable exploration of the coastline in either direction, offering panoramic views of the saltmarshes, over to Brancaster Harbour and Scolt Head Island, a National Nature Reserve managed by Natural England. The full long-distance trail runs for 83 miles (134km) between Hunstanton and Hopton-on-Sea.

Above: Sand dunes at Brancaster Beach.
Opposite: The beach is perfect for you and your pooch to get some exercise.

HOW TO GET HERE

Public transport Coasthopper buses run all year round between King's Lynn, Hunstanton, Wells, Fakenham, Sheringham and Cromer. Coastliner 36 passes through Brancaster.
Car Beach Road car park off the A149 (not National Trust), charges apply. Satnav: PE31 8AX
OS map Explorer 250
Start/finish Beach Road car park, PE31 8AX, grid ref: TF771450

DIRECTIONS

Start/finish: Beach Road car park

1. From the car park, head out onto the beach to enjoy some off-lead time, taking care to avoid any fenced-off or signed areas. Return to the car park to continue the walk.

2. Follow the footpath to the right of the road heading inland towards Brancaster village. At the end, turn left onto a track and follow it to the road.

3. Cross the road, turn left and then right onto the coast path. Follow the coast path between Brancaster village and the marsh. Pass Brancaster Staithe Quay car park and take the next right at a path junction.

4. Follow the byway inland to the White Horse pub on the A149 coastal road. Turn right onto the road then take the next left onto Delgate Lane. Follow Delgate Lane to the sharp right in Downs Woods.

5. Turn right and follow the road to the next junction. Cross and join the footpath opposite, which runs along the edge of Barrow Common. Follow the path along the edge of the common around to the right and back towards the sea.

6. Following the footpath off the common, join Green Common Lane and follow this left, then right and back to the A149 coastal road. Cross the road and follow the path across the site of Branodunum Fort and through a gate back onto the coast path.

7. Turn left and follow the outbound route back to the start.

DOG-FRIENDLY AMENITIES

Apart from the dog-free zone, dogs are welcome on the whole of Brancaster beach all year round. Brancaster Beach Kiosk serves snacks and hot and cold drinks as well as a range of beach essentials. Alternatively, follow the coast path west across Holme Dunes Nature Reserve to Old Hunstanton, where you'll find the Old Town Beach Café, a lovely, dog-friendly café with outdoor seating that serves a range of hot food as well as snacks and drinks.

36. Blickling Estate walk

Blickling Estate
Aylsham
Norfolk
NR11 6NF
01263 738030
blickling@nationaltrust.org.uk

ABOUT THIS WALK

Distance 4 miles (6.4km)
Difficulty Moderate
Terrain Mostly grassy or woodland paths with some rooty sections
Stiles Yes
Interest Wildlife, history

Blickling's magnificent Jacobean mansion, built in the 1620s, is surrounded by 55 acres of formal garden including parterre, lake, kitchen garden and the unforgettable front drive, framed by ancient yew hedges. Explore the surrounding woodland, parkland and winding country roads within the beautiful River Bure landscape. With many miles of waymarked walks through varied landscapes dotted with interesting features, adorned with views and buzzing with wildlife, it's a perfect escape with your dog.

Henry and Dorothy Hobart created Blickling Hall. They built on the important history of this corner of Norfolk – King Harold owned the Estate and it is widely believed to have been the birthplace of Anne Boleyn.

THINGS TO SEE

This walk takes in a wide loop of the Blickling Estate's parkland, visiting points of interest including the Great Wood, the Tower and the iconic Mausoleum along the way. Blickling is home to about 1,000 mature, veteran and ancient trees, including ancient small-leaved limes, some of which can be seen in the Great Wood. During April and early May, the wood is carpeted with native bluebells.

Paws for thought

Dogs must be kept under close control at all times, and on leads in signed areas, including around grazing animals and bluebells. Dogs on short leads are welcome in the farmyard, the bookshop, on the front drive, in the estate barn and in Muddy Boots café. Please note that dogs are not permitted in the main house, east wing or formal garden.

Other walkies nearby

Blickling's multi-use, all-weather family-friendly trail is ideal for walkers and cyclists. Mobility scooters and all-terrain wheelchairs are available to hire from visitor reception. Covering about 4 miles (6.4km), it takes you through leafy woods and across open parkland, visiting the Tower, Great Wood and the Mausoleum.

Above: Blickling Hall from across The Lake.

Public transport Sanders Coaches
  Services 43, 44, 44A, X44 from
  Norwich to Aylsham, 2 miles
  (3.2km) from Blickling Estate.
Car On Blickling Road (old B1354,
  reclassified to C593), signposted
  off A140 Norwich/Cromer.
  Satnav: NR11 6NF
OS map Explorer 238
Start/finish Blickling main car park,
  NR11 6NF, grid ref: TG178286

DIRECTIONS

Start/finish: Blickling main car park

1. From the car park and facing the visitor centre, walk to the left of the building and follow the path to the road. Turn left and walk along the road past the driveway to the main house.

2. Follow the road past the church, then turn right onto Silvergate Lane.

3. Follow Silvergate Lane to the right onto a path marked with an orange arrow. Follow this trail over a stile and through two small areas of woodland to the edge of a large field.

4. Turn left and follow the path along the field boundary to the lane at Hall Farm. Turn right onto the lane and follow it for about 100 yards to a track on the left.

5. Take the track left and follow it until you can turn left onto a footpath that runs between the road and Hercules Wood. Keep on this path to the end, where you turn right and cross the road into Long Plantation.

6. Turn left in Long Plantation just before the gate and follow the path through the woodland to reach the Tower (on your right).

7. Leaving the Tower, continue through the woods until you reach the path junction close to the road. Turn sharp right here and follow the path along the edge of Buck's Common woodland to a gate. Go through the gate and continue on the path across Hyde Park.

8. Continue across the park to Bunker's Hill Plantation. Go through the gate, turn right and follow the path downhill along the edge of the woodland. At the bottom of the hill turn right and take the path uphill along the edge of Great Wood. Turn left and follow the path into Great Wood to reach the open area with the Mausoleum to your left.

9. Cross the open area and take the right-hand trail; bear right again to reach the edge of the wood and a large field. Follow the path along the edge of the field and then left through the small area of woodland called the Beeches.

10. Turn right at this path junction and follow the path across the parkland towards Blickling House. Go through the park gates and after a short distance turn left, the car park and start will be on your right.

Below and previous page:
Blickling Park walking trails.

DOG-FRIENDLY
AMENITIES

Head to the dog-friendly Muddy Boots café, where you can purchase hot and cold drinks as well as light snacks. You'll also find a variety of doggy treats and ice cream, and water bowls available outside visitor reception. Dog bins are provided in the car parks and the farmyard.

Sleeping up to four people and two dogs, Bureside (National Trust Holidays) is a cosy, characterful, semi-detached cottage on the Blickling Estate. The garden has a grassed lawn leading down to a private stretch of the meandering River Bure.

37. Felbrigg Church and Ice House Walk

**Felbrigg Hall
Gardens and Estate**
Norwich
Norfolk
NR11 8PP
01263 837444
felbrigg@nationaltrust.org.uk

ABOUT THIS WALK

Distance 2.8 miles (4.5km)
Difficulty Easy
Terrain Undulating but no big hills, footpaths and woodland trails. Can be muddy around the lake
Stiles No
Interest History, gardens, wildlife

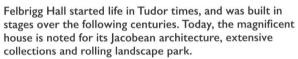

Felbrigg Hall started life in Tudor times, and was built in stages over the following centuries. Today, the magnificent house is noted for its Jacobean architecture, extensive collections and rolling landscape park.

This family-friendly walk visits St Margaret's Church, home to one of the few remaining brasses of a 15th-century Knight of the Garter. You'll wander through open fields and woodland – ideal for staying cool on warm summer days – and pass both the lake and the historic ice house.

THINGS TO SEE

Just after the lake, you'll pass Great Felbrigg Sessile Oak. Thought to be around 500 years old, this statuesque tree marks the boundary between Felbrigg and Aylmerton parishes.

Paws for thought
Dogs aren't allowed in the house or formal gardens, including the West Garden and the Walled Garden. Dogs should be kept under close control throughout the estate, and on leads between 1 March and 31

July to protect ground-nesting birds. You may also encounter animals grazing on the estate – these areas will be signed.

Other walkies nearby
Norfolk isn't known for its hills, let alone mountains. But on the Mountain Walk, you'll accumulate a total of 1,140ft (348m) of ascent over a distance of 16 miles (25.7km). Taking a circular route through countryside and parkland, the walk starts and finishes at Felbrigg Hall, visiting Sheringham and Weybourne along the way.

DOG-FRIENDLY AMENITIES

Dogs are allowed across the estate, including in the Squire's Pantry, which has both indoor and outdoor seating, and into the shop while you have a browse. You'll find water bowls in the main visitor areas and dog bins in the car parks and at the beginning of the Victory 'V' walk.

Sleeping up to five people and two dogs, Sexton's Lodge on the Felbrigg Estate is a perfect base from which to explore the surrounding parkland, woodland and the extensive Norfolk coast. It also has a fully enclosed garden, perfect for dogs.

Above: Frosty morning in the park at Felbrigg Hall.
Overleaf: Felbrigg Pond.

HOW TO GET HERE

Public transport Train stations at Cromer or Roughton Road, both 2.5 miles (4km) away.
Car 2 miles (3.2km) from Cromer; off B1436, signposted from A148 and A140. Satnav: NR11 8PP
OS map Explorer 252
Start/finish Felbrigg Hall main car park, NR11 8PP, grid ref: TG193394

DIRECTIONS

Start/finish: Felbrigg Hall main car park

1. Walking from the main car park towards Felbrigg Hall, take the first left, following the blue way marker. Go through the iron gate and onto a surfaced track. Follow this to the church.

2. Go through the small gate at the end of the church wall and follow the path to the right, signed with a blue arrow. At the far side of the field, follow the path to the right of the line of trees to a kissing gate.

3. Go through the gate and turn left, through another gate and then turn right. Now follow the edge of the field down the hill to Felbrigg Lake. Go through the gate and keep along the path round the pond, at the end of the pond turn right following the blue way marker.

4. Go through the gate following the blue way markers straight ahead. At the third blue way marker turn right along the path to a gate. Go through the gate and up the steps; at the top turn left and follow the path to the Great Felbrigg Sessile Oak. The sessile is on the right of the board walk. Continue and go through the next gate.

5. Follow the fence line to the left, turn left and go through the gate. Continue straight on when the path forks and go through the gate. Bear right and follow the path, through the woodland and parallel to the road. Pass through a small car park to reach a road.

6. Turn left and walk towards the painted house, turning right before the house onto a path into the woods next to the Corstorphine Sycamore. At the footpath junction walk right following the all-weather path to the ice house.

7. After passing the ice house, turn right and continue along the path until you reach the apex of the 'V' for Victory clearing.

8. Take the left arm of the 'V' down the hill and back to Felbrigg Hall and the start.

38. Ickworth Estate

**The Rotunda
Horringer
Bury St Edmunds
Suffolk
IP29 5QE
01284 735270**
ickworth@nationaltrust.org.uk

ABOUT THIS WALK

**Distance 2.2 miles (3.5km)
Difficulty Easy
Terrain** Well maintained
trails with some tree roots
in sections. The Trim Trail
section can become muddy
in the winter
**Stiles No
Interest** Wildlife, history

Stretching across more than 1,800 acres (728ha) of gardens, parkland and woodland, Ickworth combines peaceful, restorative natural surroundings with easy-to-follow walks, including a new accessible all-weather trail.

Recently named by *The Times* as one of the best dog-walking spots in the country, Ickworth Estate has a range of waymarked walks, all of which are dog-friendly. This shorter walk links up the woodland trails at the heart of the estate, ideal for hot summer days, or for seeing the autumnal colours at their best.

THINGS TO SEE

Ickworth House, with its distinctive and highly unusual Rotunda, was the vision of the 4th Earl of Bristol, an art collector known as the Earl Bishop. Upon inheriting the estate in 1779, he aspired to build a house that would, in his own words, unite 'magnificence with convenience', providing a family home, a gallery for his collection and a showpiece with which to impress visitors.

Paws for thought
Dogs aren't permitted in the house or formal gardens – these areas are clearly marked both on the ground and on the map. Grazing animals are often present on the estate, so take extra care around these, especially ewes and lambs during the lambing season.

Other walkies nearby
The Monument Trail (5.9 miles/9.6km) is surfaced for all-weather use, and is suitable for buggies, wheelchairs and bikes.

Above: Walking trails near Ickworth House.

HOW TO GET HERE

Public transport Ickworth is between Bury St Edmunds and Clare/Haverhill. A regular bus service runs from Bury St Edmunds, including the No. 14 and 15 buses. The bus stop is in the village of Horringer; it's about a 15-minute walk from the bus stop to Ickworth's visitor centre.

Car From A14 take J42 towards Westley; on west side of A143. For all other routes, head towards Horringer. Satnav: Please don't use our postcode for Satnav; the main entrance to the Ickworth Estate is via Horringer Village on the A143 and follow the brown signs. Please avoid routes through Chevington (this is a no-through road).

OS map Explorer 211

Start/finish Ickworth main car park, IP29 5QE, grid ref: TL814615

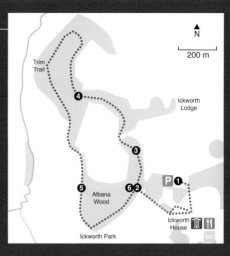

DIRECTIONS

Start/finish: Ickworth main car park

1. Turn right out of the car park, walking towards Ickworth House. Turn right before you reach the house, heading for the Albana Walk by taking the path through the laurel hedge, opposite the Porters Lodge café – it's well worth a stop here to enjoy some treats for you and your dog. Continue through Walnut Paddock and then through two gates.

2. Take the right fork in the path, signposted 'Albana Walk'. Follow this path past the old summerhouse to reach a path junction. You can turn left here to view Round Hill, an old deer enclosure.

3. Continue on the trail through Albana Wood, curving to the right then the left until you reach a sign for a path on the right for the Trim Trail. The Trim Trail tends to be muddier than the Albana Walk, and you can shorten the walk by missing it out if you'd prefer. To avoid the Trim Trail continue straight on.

Left: View towards the Rotunda and gardens in spring.

4. Otherwise, turn right and follow the Trim Trail as it loops around the edge of the woodland. You'll find some exercise machines here if you fancy an extra workout! Continue on the path as it curves to the left and brings you back to the Albana Walk. Turn right and follow the Albana Walk past a rare old box tree, to the edge of the deer park on your right.

5. Continue on the Albana Walk around the edge of the woodland, with the deer park to your right. The paths curve to the left until you get back to the fork signed 'Albana Walk' at point 2 in this walk.

6. Turn right and retrace your steps, through the two gates, past the café and back to the start.

DOG-FRIENDLY AMENITIES

Ickworth is very dog-friendly, with dogs welcome on leads in the parkland, on woodland walks and at the Porters Lodge café, where you'll find water bowls and doggy treats (including muffins and ice cream), as well as dog beds and blankets. You'll also find dog bowls and bins around the estate. Dog training and dog parkour sessions are also available at Ickworth – contact the property or ask at visitor reception for more details. The Ickworth Hotel, which occupies the East Wing of the house, has dog-friendly rooms.

Below: Ickworth Park in winter.

39. Dunwich Heath Woof Walk

Coastguard Cottages
Minsmere Road
Dunwich
Suffolk
IP17 3DJ
01728 648501
dunwichheath@nationaltrust.org.uk

ABOUT THIS WALK

Distance 2.5 miles (4km)
Difficulty Easy
Terrain Heathland trails, some rooty sections but fairly flat. Can be muddy in the winter
Stiles No
Interest Wildlife, history, coast

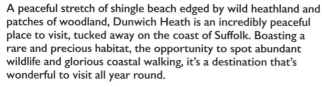

A peaceful stretch of shingle beach edged by wild heathland and patches of woodland, Dunwich Heath is an incredibly peaceful place to visit, tucked away on the coast of Suffolk. Boasting a rare and precious habitat, the opportunity to spot abundant wildlife and glorious coastal walking, it's a destination that's wonderful to visit all year round.

This walk follows Dunwich Heath's specific dogs-off-leads trail, known as the Woof Walk which starts at point 3 on the map (part of the purple trail). You can let your dog off the lead on this trail knowing you can enjoy the walk without worrying about your dog escaping onto the road or disturbing the wildlife.

THINGS TO SEE

Dunwich Heath is famous for its birds, some of which are resident species, while others are summer or winter visitors. Keep an eye – and an ear – out for the rare Dartford warbler and the skylark, which both appear on the UK's Red List for Birds of Conservation Concern, both have distinctive and beautiful songs.

Other walkies nearby

For a longer walk, your dog is also welcome to be off the lead on the beach. You will need to use the lead between this trail and the beach.

Dogs are welcome on the other walks at Dunwich, but must be kept on leads. Ickworth (see page 107) and Sutton Hoo (see page 112) offer other fantastic dog-friendly walks in Suffolk.

Paws for thought

Dogs can be off the lead throughout this walk, but note there are sections that are open to the road. Between 1 March and 31 August, for the protection of birds, dogs will need to be on the lead on all trails except for the Woof Walk and the beach. You'll find dog waste bins at the start, one-third and two-thirds of the way round. For extra dog safety, all entrances/exits to the road are gated, except the public bridleway.

Dogs can be let off their lead on the beach all year, but please prevent them from chasing birds or approaching seals.

Above: Views of Dunwich Beach and the sea.
Opposite: The lawn near Coastguard Cottages.

HOW TO GET HERE

Public transport The nearest
train station is Darsham 6
miles (9.7km) away.
Car Signposted from A12. From
Westleton/Dunwich road, turn
right 1 mile (1.6km) before
Dunwich village into Minsmere
road, then 1 mile (1.6km) to
Dunwich Heath. Satnav: IP17
3DJ
OS map Explorer 231
Start/finish Coastguard
Cottages, IP17 3DJ, grid ref:
TM476677

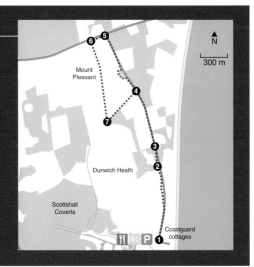

DIRECTIONS

Start/finish: Coastguard Cottages

1. Dogs should be on leads until point 3. From the car park, walk past Coastguard Cottages and cross the access road onto Dunwich Heath and follow the heath path which runs to the left of the access road heading north.

2. Continue straight along the path through the trees and when you pass the dog bin you will see the beginning of the Woof Walk as signed.

3. Once past the Woof Walk sign, dogs may be taken off the lead.

4. At the junction with the bridleway continue straight on the fenced path. Please note the bridleway entrance is not fenced and is open to the road.

5. Turn left along the boundary hedge.

6. Turn left and follow the track south past Mount Pleasant farm.

7. At the crossroads with the bridleway turn left (east) and follow the bridleway back towards point 4. Retrace your steps 4 to 1 with dogs back on leads at point 3.

DOG-FRIENDLY AMENITIES

The National Trust Coastguard Tearoom is dog-friendly, with indoor and outdoor seating. Alternatively, Flora Tearooms at the opposite end of the beach is a traditional fish and chip café that also welcomes dogs. Both open seasonally, so check opening times before visiting. Water bowls and taps are provided around the buildings, while spare leads, treats and dog waste bags are available from the visitor information centre. There are even tennis balls so that you can enjoy a game with your dog.

No.1 Church Cottages (dunwichcottage.co.uk) offers dog-friendly accommodation for up to eight people within easy reach of the beach, heath and woodland. A former stable block, the cottage is set within the village, close to amenities, and offers comfortable year-round accommodation with enclosed front and back gardens.

40. Sutton Hoo

Tranmer House
Sutton Hoo
Woodbridge
Suffolk
IP12 3DJ
01394 389700
suttonhoo@nationaltrust.org.uk

ABOUT THIS WALK

Distance 4 miles (6.5km)
Difficulty Moderate
Terrain Woodland and field footpaths, some are rooty. A short steep hill
Stiles No, but crossing over the river wall can be tricky.
Interest History, wildlife

Sutton Hoo, set amidst 245 acres (99ha) of beautiful Suffolk countryside with far-reaching views over the River Deben, is home to one of the greatest archaeological discoveries of all time.

While you're here, be sure to explore the extraordinary Royal Burial Ground, and climb the 56-ft (17-m) viewing tower to discover the history of the ship burial of an Anglo-Saxon king and his treasured possessions.

Paws for thought

Please keep your dog on a short lead at all times to protect the wildlife on site as well as grazing sheep and lambs. Only assistance dogs are allowed inside the High Hall Exhibition, Tranmer House and the second-hand bookshop.

THINGS TO SEE

Visit Tranmer House, the former home of Edith Pretty, who hired Basil Brown, a local excavator and amateur archaeologist, to find out if anything lay beneath the mysterious mounds on her estate. You can also visit the High Hall Exhibition to see replica and original objects discovered at Sutton Hoo.

DOG-FRIENDLY AMENITIES

Dogs are welcome on all the estate walks at Sutton Hoo, but they do need to be kept on a short lead. Dogs are allowed inside the shop and café, which has designated seating for those with dogs. You'll find water bowls in the courtyard, outside the High Hall Exhibition, behind the café, near Tranmer House and close to the bookshop.

Other walkies nearby

There's a great selection of waymarked walks at Sutton Hoo, with something to suit everyone. There is an accessible yellow route out to the Royal Burial Ground which takes about 20 minutes. There's also steeper terrain on the red waymarked Valley Walk and the blue waymarked Pinewood Walk, both of which take about 50 minutes.

Above and Opposite:
Sutton Hoo walking trails.

HOW TO GET HERE

Public transport The nearest train stations are Melton (1.2 miles/2km) and Woodbridge (3 miles/4.8km). The 71 service operated by First Buses from Woodbridge stops outside the entrance to Sutton Hoo.

Car On B1083 Melton to Bawdsey, follow signs from A12. Satnav: IP12 3DJ. Please be aware that the postcode will sometimes direct to the neighbouring farm. When turning off the B1083 follow the driveway all the way to the main car park.

OS map Explorer 212

Start/finish Sutton Hoo reception and car park, IP12 3DJ, grid ref: TM290493

DIRECTIONS

Start/finish: Sutton Hoo reception and car park

1. After entering Sutton Hoo, walk past the sculpture of the great ship burial and follow the path down the valley to a T-junction.

2. Turn left and follow the track past the dairy farm to a path junction.

3. Take the right turn, which is just after the farm, and follow the signed footpath between gardens and up to the river wall.

4. When you reach the river, turn left and follow the path along the river wall to the end of Ferry Cliff Woods.

5. Turn away from the river and climb the steps to the top of the cliff. Turn left here, following the bridleway along the edge of the woodland. Stay on the path until you can turn right then left to reach the second sharp right corner.

6. At this corner of the woods, turn right, following the bridleway and ignoring the path ahead which heads into the woodland. Follow the path with Deben Wood to your left. Continue on the path across the field and through a gap in the hedge to a tarmacked bridleway.

7. Follow the bridleway left to the estate track. Turn left and follow this to the road.

8. Turn left and follow the road for about 200 yards to the next left onto a track.

9. Follow this track to the top of a field, where you'll find a National Trust sign.

10. Walk past the sign and take a sharp right through a gate, then follow the path back to Tranmer House and the start.

Midlands

41. Boathouse Walk at Woodchester Park

**Tinkley Lane
near Nailsworth
Gloucestershire
GL10 3UH
01453 860037**
woodchesterpark@nationaltrust.org.uk

ABOUT THIS WALK

Distance 2 miles (3.5k)
Difficulty Moderate
Terrain Some steep hills
and very muddy in wet
weather
Stiles Yes
Interest Wildlife, history,
viewpoints

A stone's throw from Bristol, the imposing, unfinished Gothic Revival mansion at Woodchester stands in a hidden valley surrounded by tranquil woodland. This 'lost landscape' is the remains of an 18th- and 19th-century landscape park, complete with a chain of five lakes. Park Mill Pond, the last of these lakes, boasts a population of enormous carp and a man-made island that's now a heronry.

On this walk you'll also discover the restored, 19th-century boathouse, home to clouds of bats that roost in the roof space, emerging at dusk to hunt over the lake.

The restoration of this varied and fascinating landscape is an ongoing project. While the estate is cared for by the National Trust, the mansion is not and is open seasonally – check www. woodchestermansion.org.uk before visiting.

Paws for thought

Dogs must be on a short lead and under close control along the more sensitive areas at Woodchester, such as the play trail and on the tracks through fields of grazing sheep and cows. Long leads are perfect on the woodland tracks, where there are no grazing animals. Make sure to keep dogs out of the lakes to protect the local wildlife.

Other walkies nearby

A few miles away is Newark Park, which has a long history of welcoming dogs into the garden and estate. Previous residents, Bob Parsons and Michael Claydon, who restored Newark in the 1970s, were known for their love of Great Danes.

THINGS TO SEE

The boathouse was used by the Leigh and Ducie families and their guests for outings. It was restored in 1998 when the roof, windows and floor timbers were replaced.

Woodchester is a wonderful place to spot wildlife. At the lake you might see herons, kingfishers, mandarin and tufted ducks. At the boathouse and mansion, close to dusk on a warm summer's day, you'll see bats bug-hunting. You may even spot rare greater horseshoe bats as there's a breeding roost near the mansion. On sunny days in spring and summer, the wildflowers in the valley teem with colourful insects, including scarlet tiger moths, and butterflies such as the peacock, painted lady and silver-washed fritillary.

Exploring Woodchester Park.

HOW TO GET HERE

Public transport Stroud train station is 5 miles (8 km) away. The number 65 bus operates between Stroud and Gloucester, alight at Nympsfield Cross. Or use the 165 bus from Stroud, alighting at Tinkley Farm.
Car From Stroud follow the A46 into Nailsworth. At the roundabout, take the third exit onto Nympsfield Road. From Bath, follow the A46 into Nailsworth. At the roundabout, take the first exit onto Nympsfield Road. Continue up the hill and follow Tinkley Lane for half a mile. The entrance to Tinkley Gate is on your right. Sat nav: GL10 3UH
OS map Explorer 168
Start/finish Tinkley Gate car park, GL10 3UH, grid ref: 8048400852

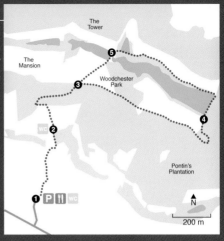

DIRECTIONS

Start/finish: Tinkley gate car park

1. From the car park, walks towards the café. At the information board, turn left and follow the path through the fields, heading downhill until you get to the toilet hut.

2. At the fingerpost, continue straight ahead, following the blue waymarkers. Follow the path as it zig-zags on a steep downhill through the woods. Take extra care here, as the path can get extremely muddy and slippery after rain.

3. As you emerge from the woods and the path levels out, ignore the stile on your left. Continue straight ahead, with the trees on your right and views over the valley to your left. The path then bears left downhill and past the Kennels to join Middle Pond.

4. At Middle Pond, cross over the dam and turn left. These deep lakes were created through the damming of a small stream. Continue along the path, keeping the lakeside on your left.

5. At the end of the lake, you'll reach the boathouse. Turn left and walk over the dam between Middle Pond and Old Pond. Go through the gate into the field and climb the path uphill. At the top of the hill, go over the stile. Turn right into the woodland. Continue on the return path back to Tinkley Gate café.

DOG-FRIENDLY AMENITIES

Most of the waymarked routes around the park are perfect for a walk with your four-legged friend. Dogs are also welcome to join you at Tinkley Gate café in the outdoor seating areas, as well as the dog-friendly area inside. There are water bowls and doggy treats on offer in the café.

The boathouse next to the lake.

42. Sherborne Park

Sherborne Park Estate
Aldsworth
near Cheltenham
Gloucestershire
GL54 3DT
01451 844130
lodgepark@nationaltrust.org.uk

ABOUT THIS WALK

Distance 2.6 miles (4.2 km)
Difficulty Easy
Terrain Some moderate hills and can be muddy in wet weather
Stiles No
Interest Wildlife, history

The peaceful expanse of Cotswolds estate at Sherborne is home to England's last surviving 17th-century grandstand, an ornate building which would have overlooked the surrounding hunting grounds. Originally, the grandstand consisted of two storeys and a basement, with an entrance hall on the ground floor, the Great Room for entertaining on the first floor, and the kitchens in the basement. The grounds could be observed from the flat roof or from the balcony over the entrance portico.

This walk is suitable for the whole family and takes in the estate's rolling farmland, wildlife-rich woodland and picturesque Sherborne village.

THINGS TO SEE

Sherborne has an incredible array of birds and other wildlife to spot along the way. In the fields, look out for skylark, yellowhammer, linnet and hare. In the woodland, you might see goldcrest, chiff chaff, great spotted woodpecker and muntjac deer. On Sherborne Brook there may be snipe, wigeon, teal, swan and kingfisher. Carved wooden nature sculptures line the route. Don't miss the icehouse in Quarry Wood, built in the 19th century for the Dutton family of Sherborne House.

Paws for thought

Sherborne is a working estate with livestock grazing throughout, so please stay on the paths and keep your dog under close control to avoid harm to wildlife or grazing animals. Only assistance dogs are allowed at nearby Lodge Park.

Other walkies nearby

There are two other waymarked walks from Ewe Pen Barn if you wanted to continue exploring the estate. Or head over to the quintessential Cotswold village of Bibury for walks along the River Coln.

HOW TO GET HERE

Public ransport The S2 bus runs between the train stations at Cheltenham and Oxford; alight in Northleach. You will need to take a taxi from there or walk an extra 3 miles (5km) to join the route.
Car Ewe Pen Barn car park is a short distance off the A40, between Cheltenham and Oxford. Turn off the A40, following signs for Sherborne and Clapton (opposite the brown sign for Lodge Park). Satnav: GL54 3DT
OS map Explorer OL45
Start/finish Ewe Pen Barn car park, GL54 3DT, grid ref: SP158143

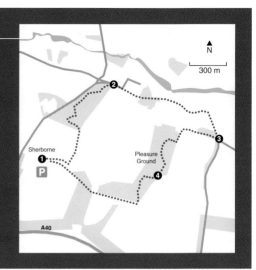

DOG-FRIENDLY AMENITIES

Sherborne Park is rated a one pawprint site, so although dogs are welcome, facilities are limited. Dog waste bins are located near the car parks and along the roads in the village.

Oliver's Coffee House in Sherborne village is dog-friendly and open 7 days a week: www.oliverscoffeehouse.co.uk

Deer Park Lodge is dog-friendly National Trust holiday cottage on site, offering accommodation for 4 people and 2 dogs with access to the walking trails from the door: www.nationaltrust.org.uk/holidays/cotswolds-gloucestershire/deer-park-lodge

DIRECTIONS

Start/finish: Ewe Pen Barn car park

1. Turn right and walk past Ewe Pen Barn, following the pink waymarkers away from the car park. Turn left and follow the fence line along the edge of the field to Ragged Copse wood. Follow the path through the wood to reach the road at the edge of Sherborne village.

2. Turn right, walking along the road through the village. Pass Sherborne House on the right and continue to the war memorial and a doorway next to a red phone box on your right.

3. Turn right and follow the path through the doorway towards the pleasure grounds. The path follows the edge of Sherborne House gardens and turns left beside a tree; follow the iron fence and enter the pleasure grounds. Follow the pink waymarkers through the pleasure grounds to an iron gate.

4. Leave the pleasure grounds through the gate and follow the waymarkers past the icehouse and through another gate into Quarry Wood. Walk through the woodland and past the old quarry works to a gate on the far edge of the wood. Go through this and turn right, following the farm track back to Ewe Pen Barn.

Sherborne Park Estate.

43. Lakes and Valley Walk at Stowe

**Stowe Gardens
Buckingham
Buckinghamshire
MK18 5EQ
01280 817156**
stowe@nationaltrust.org.uk

ABOUT THIS WALK

Distance 3 miles (4.8km)
Difficulty Easy
Terrain Flat and predominantly on well surfaced trails
Stiles No
Interest Gardens, history, wildlife

Said to be celebrated landscape gardener and architect Lancelot 'Capability' Brown's masterpiece, Stowe is considered to be one of the greatest landscape gardens in the world. With its serene lakes and more than 40 temples and monuments dotted across its manicured grounds, it's a fascinating place to visit.

There's a great variety of walks to enjoy here, whether you're taking a gentle amble on the multi-user lakeside path, or heading out into the fields, meadows and groves to explore the surrounding countryside.

THINGS TO SEE

The church at Stowe is all that remains of a medieval village, one of more than 2,000 that were once scattered across England. Your walk will take you close to some of the amazing temples, but there are many more to get distant views of in the garden.

Paws for thought
Dogs should be kept on leads throughout the estate at Stowe. Assistance dogs only inside the café at the New Inn or near the vegetable patches within the Farmhouse Garden.

Other walkies nearby
The wider estate at Stowe is criss-crossed by footpaths and bridleways, including the Ouse Valley Way long-distance path. There's also the alternative, shorter, dog-friendly walk, which loops the lakes but misses out the longer section around the Grecian Valley.

Above: Palladian Bridge at Stowe.
Left: The Temple of Friendship at Stowe.

Public transport Both the Stagecoach X5, Oxford to Cambridge bus and the Arriva X60, Aylesbury to Milton Keynes bus stop in Buckingham town, 1.5 miles (2.4km) from Stowe.

Car Access via Stowe Avenue from Buckingham. Follow brown signs from the A421 between the M40 and Milton Keynes. Satnav: MK18 5EQ

OS map Explorer 192

Start/finish Stowe car park, MK18 5EQ, grid ref: SP682364

DOG-FRIENDLY AMENITIES

Dogs on leads are welcome at Stowe Gardens. At the New Inn your dog is welcome in the shop, Parlour Rooms and bookshop. Dogs are also allowed in all outdoor café seating areas and the indoor seating area in the corridor next to the main café. You'll find waste bins and water bowls here; dog treats and accessories in the shop and a free dog wash within the Farmhouse Garden.

You can also join the group dog walks at Stowe, held on the third Wednesday of every month. These guided walks start at the garden entrance at 10.30am and take approximately an hour and a half – a great opportunity to meet and chat with other dog owners – and their dogs.

DIRECTIONS

Start/finish: Stowe car park

1. Walk out of the car park and turn left, following Bell Gate Drive up to Bell Gate. Enter Stowe Gardens.

2. Turn right and follow the path past the Temple of Friendship, then curve left to the Palladian Bridge.

3. Cross and follow the path past the Gothic Temple and the Saxon Deities to reach Lord Cobham's Pillar on the right.

4. Turn left along Lord Cobham's Walk to reach the far corner of the park at the Fane of Pastoral Poetry.

5. Turn left and follow the path to the Temple of Concord and Victory. You can walk this section on the grassy trails to the right if you prefer.

6. Follow the path left, with an open grassy area to your left and trees to the right. Walk past the Grotto and the end of the lake on your left, and continue to Captain Grenville's Column outside St Mary's Church.

7. Follow the path past the Temple of Ancient Virtue to reach Octagon Lake. Follow the lake shore and look right to see the magnificent Stowe House. Continue to a T-junction.

8. Turn left, and walk to the Ruin on the Cascade. Look left to see the Palladian Bridge you crossed earlier, and look right through the arch across Eleven Acre Lake. Turn left at Lake Pavilion to return to Bell Gate and retrace your steps back to the New Inn.

44. Hanbury Hall Estate Walk

**School Road
Hanbury
Droitwich Spa
Worcestershire
WR9 7EA
01527 821214**
hanburyhall@nationaltrust.org.uk

ABOUT THIS WALK

Distance 2.4 miles (3.9km)
Difficulty Easy
Terrain Grassy paths and surfaced trails. A small hill up to the church, but this is avoidable
Stiles No
Interest Wildlife, history

A country retreat, nestled in the heart of Worcestershire's countryside yet within easy reach of Birmingham, Hanbury Hall offers an enjoyable day out for everyone. The house and garden, originally a stage set for summer parties, allow you to imagine what life must have been like here in the 18th century.

There are three wonderful waymarked walks to guide you around the estate at Hanbury. This is the longest, following the orange route over 2.2 miles (3.5km). You'll wander along majestic tree-lined avenues, passing cedars, limes and rare black poplars; visit a 600-year-old oak tree, and climb to the top of a hill to visit the church of St Mary the Virgin and take in the views.

THINGS TO SEE

Also known as Hanbury Woods, Piper's Hill, which lies just on the edge of the Hanbury estate, is one of the Wildlife Trust's flagship nature reserves. Look out for an abundance of flora and fauna in the woods, including over 200 species of fungi such as chanterelle, beefsteak and bracket fungi.

Paws for thought

The estate at Hanbury is home to many wild creatures as well as grazing animals, so dogs must be kept on leads at all times. Assistance dogs only in the formal gardens, the Courtyard Kitchen and the Hall.

Other walkies nearby

Two further enjoyable waymarked walks loop the estate – the 1-mile (1.6-km) blue route and the 1.2-mile (1.9-km) grey route. The orange route, described above, can also be extended to visit Piper's Wood, by continuing a short distance past the church.

Above: Hanbury Hall from the Lime Tree Walk.
Overleaf: You'll find plenty of facilities in the stableyard to help keep your dog refreshed.

HOW TO GET HERE

Public transport Droitwich Spa is the
closest train station (4 miles/6.4km).
Buses run from Droitwich Spa to
Wychbold, but you then need to walk
3.3 miles (5.3km) to Hanbury Hall.
Car Exit at J5 on the M5 and follow
A38 to Droitwich; Hanbury Hall is 4
miles (6.4km) along the B4090. Satnav:
WR9 7EA
OS map Explorer 204
Start/finish Hanbury Hall car park,
WR9 7EA, grid ref: SO946637

DOG-FRIENDLY AMENITIES

Dogs are welcome on leads in the forecourt,
stableyard, courtyard, parkland and inside the
Stables Café. You'll find water bowls, taps and
waste bins at convenient locations.

The Vernon pub in Hanbury is dog-friendly and it's
also the birthplace of *The Archers*, as Godfrey
Baseley, the original creator and editor of the show
drank in the bar; it's suggested that many of his
characters were based on local residents. www.
vernonhanbury.co.uk

DIRECTIONS

Start/finish: Hanbury Hall car park

1. Walk out of the car park and turn right,
   following the drive up to the formal gardens in
   front of the house.

2. Turn right and follow the path around the
   house to the stableyard, where there is a café.
   Continue past the café and follow the path
   with the parkland to your right. Continue to a
   path junction by a small pond.

3. Turn right and follow the footpath across the
   estate. Pass Brick Kiln Pool on your right and
   walk across the lines of two impressive
   avenues. Continue to a gate in the far corner
   at the edge of the estate. Go through the gate
   and walk across the field and up the hill to
   the church.

4. Turn around and retrace your steps to the
   gate into Hanbury Hall estate.

5. Stay left and follow the path along the edge of
   the estate to return to the drive in front of the
   house. Turn left to return to the start.

45. Berrington Hall

**Near Leominster
Herefordshire
HR6 0DW
01568 615721**
berrington@nationaltrust.org.uk

ABOUT THIS WALK

Distance 3.2 miles (5.1km)
Difficulty Moderate
Terrain Parkland, wood and
paths, grassy and
occasionally muddy
Stiles No
Interest Wildlife, history,
gardens

The Neo-classical Georgian mansion at Berrington is set within grounds that were the final project of celebrated garden designer and architect, Lancelot 'Capability' Brown, before his death in 1783.

The 250 acres (101ha) of varied parkland surrounding the mansion is perfect for walks, encompassing woods and Berrington's pool. The gardens are a delight throughout the year – you'll find bluebells and other blossom in spring, scented roses in summer and apples and berries in autumn. This walk follows the waymarked purple trail, exploring the woodland, parkland and pool.

THINGS TO SEE

Berrington Pool with its intriguing, wooded island was designed by 'Capability' Brown to suggest a meandering river. As well as the dragonflies and other invertebrates that make their home at Berrington, otters have been spotted here – there's even an 'otter cam' set up to capture their activity, usually at night.

The Pool is a Site of Special Scientific Interest due to the large heronry which occupies Heron Island each year. It is the largest Heronry in Herefordshire and one of only two large heronries found in the West Midlands.

Paws for thought
You'll find grazing animals and wildlife across the estate, so please keep your dog on a lead. Assistance dogs only in the mansion and main tea-room.

Other walkies nearby
Follow the red waymarkers around the Berrington estate for a shorter (1-mile/1.6-km) walk that crosses the parkland and loops the Pool before returning to the house. For a longer walk, explore a section of the Herefordshire Trail, a circular, 150-mile (241-km), long-distance walking route linking the five market towns of Ledbury, Ross-on-Wye, Kington, Leominster and Bromyard, along with some picturesque Herefordshire villages and hamlets.

Above: The Hall seen within the wider parkland.
Overleaf: Berrington Park trails.

HOW TO GET HERE

Public transport Regular trains from Hereford to Leominster is the closest train station (4 miles/6.4km). The bus from Leominster to Ludlow stops at Luston (2 miles/3.2km away, across fields).

Car Signed from the A49 between Leominster and Brimfield. Satnav: HR6 0DW

OS map Explorer 203

Start/finish Berrington Hall car park, HR6 0DW, grid ref: SO510637

(Map showing Moreton, Camp Wood, Dinham Plantation, George's Plantation, Berrington Hall and Park, Long Wood, Moreton Ride, with numbered waypoints 1–7, parking and amenity symbols, and a 200m scale bar, N pointing up.)

DOG-FRIENDLY AMENITIES

Dogs are welcome in all areas of the parkland, courtyard and the gardens. The Stables Café, set within a converted stable, offers a dog-friendly indoor space to sit and enjoy refreshments with your dog.

Nestled in beautiful Marches countryside, in the Teme Valley to the north of Berrington, Brook Farm is a 16th-century former farmhouse surrounded by 9 acres (3.6ha) of garden, woodland and meadows. Two beautiful, dog-friendly self-catering cottages – the Hen House and the Hop Pickers' House sleep two people each. brookfarmberrington.co.uk

DIRECTIONS

Start/finish: Berrington Hall car park

1. Walk out of the car park and follow the path around Berrington Hall and towards the natural play area. You'll reach a gate into the parkland on your left.

2. Walk through the gate and out into the park, following the purple waymarked Parkland Walk. This trends left around the edge of the parkland. Carry on to reach the edge of a field on the right.

3. Cross the field and turn left, following the path along the tree line and into the woods. Take the next left marked with purple waymarkers, walk through the woods and across the park to the southern edge of George's Plantation.

4. Turn right and follow the path to the corner of the lake. Walk through the gate and follow the path around the shore, with the lake on your left. Continue around three sides of the lake until you return to the parkland with the Hall in front of you.

5. Follow the path to your right across the parkland, through a wooden gate and across to the driveway near the entrance. Turn left and follow the driveway to the reception and Triumphal Arch.

6. You can finish the walk by heading straight on to the car park, or continue and add an extra loop around Windmill Hill. To carry on, turn right and follow the pathway to North Lodge.

7. Bear left and follow the path along the edge of Camp Wood and then left around Windmill Hill. Head back across the parkland to reach the driveway; turn left and follow this back to the start.

46. Carding Mill Valley and the Long Mynd

Church Stretton Shropshire SY6 6JG 01694 725000
cardingmill@nationaltrust.org.uk

ABOUT THIS WALK

Distance 5.6 miles (9km)
Difficulty Challenging
Terrain Sometimes rugged moorland trails. Can be wet underfoot and exposed to the weather
Stiles No
Interest Wildlife

Set deep within the Shropshire Hills Area of Outstanding Natural Beauty, Carding Mill Valley and the Long Mynd cover nearly 5,000 acres (2,000ha) of rolling, heather-covered hills scored through by steep river valleys.

This adventurous walk starts out along the main path through Carding Mill Valley before climbing up to reach the head of Carding Mill Valley and the highest point on the Long Mynd – Pole Bank at 1,693ft (516m). This inviting trail offers outstanding views throughout. From here you'll make the well-earned descent into Townbrook Valley, tracing the snaking course of the brook to return to Carding Mill.

THINGS TO SEE

Look out for birds such as ravens, skylarks, grouse, snipe, wheatear and rare ring ouzels, and butterflies including the green hairstreak, orange tip, copper and small heath.

DOG-FRIENDLY AMENITIES

Dogs are welcome throughout Carding Mill Valley and the Long Mynd and can also join you for refreshments in the tea-room at the start/finish.

Stay at the dog-friendly Small Batch campsite, set in a picturesque green valley in Little Stretton, within walking distance of Carding Mill Valley and the Long Mynd. www.smallbatch-camping.co.uk

Paws for thought

To avoid frightening or harming wildlife and grazing animals, please keep dogs on leads. Particular care should be taken during the spring and summer (1 March–31 July) when new lambs and ground-nesting birds are highly vulnerable to dogs.

Other walkies nearby

You're spoilt for choice when it comes to walking in the Shropshire Hills, with a vast network of trails to explore. The Jack Mytton Way long-distance footpath traces nearly 100 miles (160km) of waymarked footpaths and bridleways around the Shropshire countryside.

Above: The Long Mynd at Carding Mill Valley.
Overleaf: View over Carding Mill Valley.

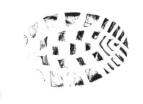

HOW TO GET HERE

Public transport Church Stretton train station is about 1 mile (1.6km) away.
Car Accessed through Church Stretton, off the A49. Satnav: SY6 6JG
OS map Explorer 217
Start/finish Carding Mill Valley car park, SY6 6JG, grid ref: SO440948

DIRECTIONS

Start/finish: Carding Mill Valley car park

1. Depending on where you park, follow the trail and the road up to the top car park. Then follow the stony track alongside the stream up Carding Mill Valley.

2. When the path forks, bear right, following the track known as Mott's Road. Walk steeply uphill and then level out as you reach the high plateau. Follow the path across the moorland to reach a wider track cutting across you.

3. Turn left and then left again onto the ancient Portway trail. Follow this along the edge of Wild Moor, staying right on a slightly smaller track when the Portway bears off left. Continue to the road.

4. Cross and follow the path opposite uphill over the heathery moor. Follow this path across a footpath and then the Medlicott track, continuing in the same direction up to the summit of Pole Bank. The trig point here is the highest point on the Long Mynd.

5. Retrace your steps about 270 yards to the path junction with the Medlicott track you crossed earlier. Turn right and follow this to the Burway Road.

6. Bear left onto the road and follow it for a short distance past Boiling Well spring. Continue to a path on the right, signed 'Townbrook'.

7. Follow this path, which walks roughly parallel to the road (on your left). Head downhill to reach a path junction at the head of the steep Townbrook Hollow.

8. Turn left, then bear right, following the narrow path down the valley to the Victorian reservoir.

9. Turn left, following the path along the edge of Old Rectory Wood and back to Burway Road. Cross the road and turn left, descending the Burway Track into Carding Mill Valley and back to the start.

47. Attingham Wildlife Walk

Atcham
Shrewsbury
Shropshire
SY4 4TP
01743 708170
attingham@nationaltrust.org.uk

ABOUT THIS WALK

Distance 2.5 miles (4km)
Difficulty Moderate
Terrain Grass, gravel and woodland paths, some sections are rough underfoot and can be muddy. Quite flat
Stiles No
Interest Wildlife, history

Attingham Park, set in the Shropshire countryside near to the market town of Shrewsbury, is an 18th-century estate with an imposing Regency Mansion at its heart. Surrounded by 200 acres (81ha) of gardens, pleasure grounds and parkland, the wider estate extends to 4,000 acres (over 1,600ha), encompassing woodland, tenanted farmland and a scattering of properties, some of which guests (and their dogs) can stay in.

Attingham was the home of the lords Berwick and was subject to the family's variable fortunes for more than 160 years before it was bequeathed to the National Trust in 1947 by the 8th Baron Berwick – who loved dogs. This circular walk starts in the Stables Courtyard and follows the Deer Park Walk, tracing centuries-old routes through scenic parkland, visiting the Repton Oak and the River Tern. There's an accessible option at the half-way point, making this walk suitable for PMVs with extra stability features.

Paws for thought

Dogs should be kept on leads at all times except in the signed off-lead area. 'Visiting Attingham with your dog' leaflets are available from Visitor Reception, containing helpful information, including walks and the locations of waste bins. Assistance dogs only in the café, shop, Mansion and second-hand bookshop, but there are tie-up points where you can leave your dog for a maximum of 10 minutes.

THINGS TO SEE

There are five species of bats at Attingham, including over 1,000 pipistrelle bats, which can be seen bug-hunting on dry evenings. If you're lucky you might also spot barn owls, ravens and buzzards here, as well as the herd of fallow deer, resident since the late 18th century.

The Mansion at Attingham Park Estate.

Public transport Shrewsbury is the closest train station (5 miles/8km). The 96 bus service from Shrewsbury stops at Atcham. Walk along the Severn Way to Attingham Park (2.5 miles/4km).

Car Off the B4380, between Shrewsbury and Cressage. Follow brown signs from Atcham. Satnav: SY4 4TP

OS map Explorer 241

Start/finish Attingham Park car park, SY4 4TP, grid ref: SJ547100

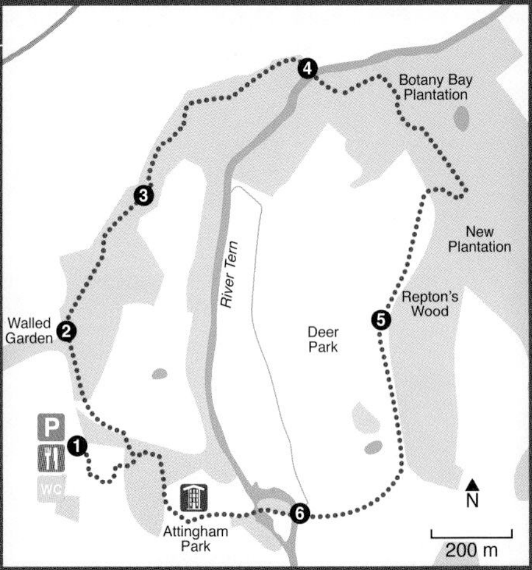

[Map showing: Botany Bay Plantation, New Plantation, Repton's Wood, Walled Garden, Deer Park, Attingham Park, River Tern, with numbered points 1–6, P parking, WC, scale 200 m, N compass]

Other walkies nearby

There's a wealth of wonderful walks exploring the wider estate at Attingham. The Mile Walk takes in a section of the Pleasure Grounds, visiting some fascinating trees along the way, and finally meets the Severn Way, which passes Attingham on its route along the entire Severn Valley from the source to the sea. Starting high on Plynlimon in mid-Wales's Cambrian Mountains, the Severn Way visits Hafren Forest, Llanidloes, Newtown, Welshpool, Shrewsbury and Ironbridge, then heads south through Worcester, Tewkesbury and Gloucester to Severn Beach, finally linking with the Avon into Bristol's city centre.

DIRECTIONS

Start/finish: Attingham Park car park

1. Walk through Reception and the Stables Courtyard and then left following the Mile Walk towards the Walled Garden.

2. Pass the left turn to the Walled Garden and continue on the Mile Walk to a path junction. This is where the Mile Walk bears right and loops back to the Mansion. Continue on, now following the Deer Park Walk.

3. Follow the path through woodland. You are now entering the area where dogs are permitted to be off-lead. Follow this path to the cable-stayed suspension bridge over the River Tern.

4. Cross and follow the Deer Park Walk through the Botany Bay Plantation. The path curves right and emerges onto the open deer park where dogs should be put back on the lead. Follow the path along the edge, with the woodland to your left and the park to the right. Pass the Berwick Memorial on your left.

5. Carry on following the path with Repton Wood on your left. Pass the Repton Oak and follow the path as it curves right and walks back towards the house. Continue to the Deer Park Bridge.

6. Walk up and past the Mansion, following the path around to the right and walking back to the Stables Courtyard. Return to the start.

Above: Attingham Park estate trails.

DOG-FRIENDLY AMENITIES

There's an off-lead area in the woodland to the north of the Mansion. In the Stables Courtyard you'll find 10-minute tie-up points where you can leave your dog while popping into the café, toilets or shop. You'll also find designated dog-friendly toilets near to the Mansion and Walled Garden, and water bowls in the Stables Courtyard.

Five newly converted, dog-friendly self-catering barns are available for guests on the Attingham Estate. As well as a cosy living area, the barns share an enclosed garden, with a lawn, a firepit ready for barbecues and a dining patio. You'll also find electric car charging points, a bicycle store and a dog shower (NT Holidays).

48. Shugborough Parkland and River Walk

Milford
Near Stafford
Staffordshire
ST17 0UP
01889 880160
shugborough@nationaltrust.org.uk

ABOUT THIS WALK

Distance 2.4 miles (3.9km)
Difficulty Easy
Terrain Gravel and grass paths, fairly flat
Stiles No
Interest Wildlife, history, gardens

Home to the Anson family from 1642 until the 1960s, when it passed to the National Trust, Shugborough's Georgian mansion is surrounded by 900 acres (364ha) of parkland. The grounds showcase work by many different designers and architects from over the centuries.

A walk here takes you past many unexpected sights, including the Chinese House (1747), the Shepherd's Monument (1750), Hadrian's Arch (c. 1762) and the Tower of the Winds (c. 1765). These follies were built to commemorate the family's various trips and influences and make for some intriguing points of interest as you walk through the estate.

THINGS TO SEE

In the early 1800s, architect Samuel Wyatt was tasked to design a model farm with a walled kitchen garden. The result – Park Farm – covered more than 2,000 acres (809ha), producing food for the estate, and included a functioning dairy. Today, you'll find the dog-friendly Park Farm café here.

Paws for thought

Woolly Southdown sheep and gentle longhorn cattle graze the parkland at Shugborough. Please keep dogs on leads at all times, including on the bridleway. Assistance dogs only in the tea-room, shops, house and Servants' Quarters.

Other walkies nearby

Just to the south of Shugborough, Cannock Chase covers over 16,800 acres (6,780ha) of mixed countryside, and is a great place to head for a walk, run or bike ride. Networked with footpaths and trails, there's almost endless scope for walks, as well as cafés, bike hire and toilets. The Chase welcomes dogs and offers information specifically for dog walkers on its website: cannockchase.org.uk/what-to-do/dog-walkers

Above: Shugborough Hall from the arboretum.
Opposite: Walking over the Garden bridge.

HOW TO GET HERE

Public transport Trains to Stafford. The 826 bus runs from Stafford station to Lichfield. Get off at the stop after the Barley Mow pub. Walk through the exit and along the bridleway to visitor reception.

Car Signposted from M6 J13, on the A513. Entry via Milford Gates only, to enable vehicle one-way system. Satnav: ST17 0XB

OS map Explorer 244

Start/finish Shugborough car park, ST17 0XB, grid ref: SJ990215

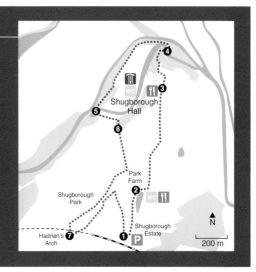

DIRECTIONS

Start/finish: Shugborough car park

1. Walk through reception and turn left, following the wide gravel track to Park Farm. There are toilets and a café here.

2. Go through the courtyard and turn left, following the path past the Tower of the Winds and onto a larger path. Follow this to the back of the Georgian house.

3. Walk past the house and turn left into the gardens, then turn right when you reach the river. Turn left just past the Chinese House, crossing the red footbridge.

4. Turn left after the bridge and follow the gravel path. The river Sow is on both sides of you, left and right, and the garden and glimpses of the house are to your left. Continue until you reach the blue footbridge on your left.

5. Cross and follow the path left along the river towards the trees. Turn right at the next junction and then right again; go through a gate to exit into the park.

6. Follow the grassy path across the park in the direction of Park Farm to reach a gravel track. Turn right and follow this track, then bear left, crossing the driveway and heading uphill to Hadrian's Arch.

7. Turn around and walk back down the parallel path, to the right (as you now look) of the ascent path. Continue until you reach the driveway. Turn right and follow this back to the start.

DOG-FRIENDLY AMENITIES

Dogs are welcome in Park Farm café and all outdoor areas of the estate, including the walled garden and pleasure grounds. You'll find several dog bins across the estate, and water bowls, taps and tie-up points in both Park Farm Yard and the Midden Yard.

49. Calke Abbey Estate Walk

Ticknall
Derby
Derbyshire
DE73 7JF
01332 863822
calkeabbey@nationaltrust.org.uk

ABOUT THIS WALK

Distance 2.9 miles (4.7km)
Difficulty Moderate
Terrain Grass, gravel and
woodland trails. Some
sections can be rough and
muddy. Undulating but no
big hills
Stiles No
Interest Wildlife, history,
gardens

Known as the 'un-stately' home, Calke Abbey is quite unlike anywhere else. Set within the open south Derbyshire landscape, on the banks of the Staunton Harold reservoir, this country estate of 600 acres (243ha) is a property where dereliction is part of the appeal.

With its aging paintwork and weedy courtyards, little restoration work has been undertaken here, leaving Calke frozen in time since the 20th century when so many grand country houses fell into neglect and disrepair. This walk loops the estate to the north of the abbey, passing the peaceful Mere Pond and Calke Park National Nature Reserve, ambling through Serpentine Wood and visiting Calke Explore, before crossing open parkland to finish.

THINGS TO SEE

There's lots to see on the Calke estate, including the Old Man of Calke – a 1,200-year-old oak tree; red and fallow deer in their restored enclosure; the Tramway Trail – an enjoyable exploration by bike or on foot; and the pleasure grounds and flower garden, with its unique auricula theatre.

Paws for thought
Assistance dogs only in the house and church. Please keep dogs on leads in the main visitor areas, nature reserve and around grazing animals.

Other walkies nearby
Calke is something of a meeting point for several long-distance walking trails, including the Cross Britain Way, the National Forest Way and the Ivanhoe Way. Along with other footpaths, these can be linked up to create enjoyable circular walking routes – or follow the Cross Britain Way as it skirts Staunton Harold reservoir for a scenic waterside walk.

Opposite: Buttercup meadow at Calke Abbey.

HOW TO GET HERE

Public transport Derby is the closest train station (9.5 miles/15.3km). From Derby take the No. 2 bus and alight at the Calke Abbey entrance. It's about 0.5 miles (0.8km) to join the walk from Ticknall.

Car Entrance is on the A514 at Ticknall, between Swadlincote and Melbourne. Satnav: DE73 7JF

OS map Explorer 245

Start/finish Calke Abbey car park, DE73 7LE grid ref: SK366228

DIRECTIONS

Start/finish: Calke Abbey car park

1. Follow the blue trail down the stepped path to the Mere Pond. Turn right and follow the edge of the pond until you can turn left and cross. Go through a pedestrian gate.

2. Under-control dogs are welcome to run off lead in the next section, providing they can come back upon first recall and remain in their owner's sight at all times. Follow the clear trail in front of you up the hill, with the deer park on your right, to a path junction at the northern edge of the woodland.

3. Turn left and follow the path along the edge of Serpentine Wood, passing through a pedestrian gate about half-way along. Continue to follow the path as it curves to the left until you reach a clearing. Leave the blue trail here, turning right down a stone track walking downhill until you reach a path junction with the National Forest Way and the red trail.

135

4. Turn right, following the red trail to a pedestrian gate and go through. Turn left and cross the main vehicular driveway here, watching out for oncoming cars. Head uphill with the driveway on your right, heading for a pedestrian gate in the trees on your left and on to the Tramway Trail.

5. Turn left and follow the Tramway Trail with the woods to your left and fields on the right. Make sure your dog is on a lead as you walk past Calke Explore on the left and continue to a path junction. It's fine to be off-lead again now.

6. Follow the red trail left, walking through Poker's Leys and out into the parkland. Follow the well-made winding trail to a crossroads with the driveway on your left. Go through a pedestrian gate and turn immediately right, following the track for a short distance to a fork in the trail.

7. Bear left onto the grass red trail and follow it across the parkland. Follow the red trail uphill continuing straight ahead with the woodland and old deer shelter on your left until you reach the driveway with St Giles Church in front of you.

8. Please put your dog back on its lead to finish off the walk. Turn left and follow the red trail and driveway back to the start.

DOG-FRIENDLY AMENITIES

Dogs are welcome across the parkland at Calke Abbey, where you'll find miles of woodland walks, open countryside and lots of ponds. You can also bring dogs to the stableyard, gardens, restaurant, shop and second-hand bookshop, provided they're on a short lead.

Dogs can be off-lead in many areas of the estate, as long as they're under close control. There is a handy dog-walking guide with specific details on where your dog can run free at www.nationaltrust.org.uk/visit/peak-district-derbyshire/calke-abbey/visiting-calke-abbey-with-your-dog

Calke Park meadow.

50. Clumber Park Estate and Lakeside Walk

Worksop
Nottinghamshire
S80 3BE
01909 476592
clumberpark@nationaltrust.org.uk

ABOUT THIS WALK

Distance 5.5 miles (8.8km)
Difficulty Moderate
Terrain Grass, gravel and
surfaced paths and trails.
Some sections can be
muddy. One small hill which
isn't very steep
Stiles No
Interest History, wildlife,
urban escape

Once the country estate of the dukes of Newcastle, and now a popular escape from the urban East Midlands, Clumber Park encompasses a landscape of open grass and farmland, heaths, woods and a majestic lake, in total covering more than 3,800 acres (1,536ha).

One of just a few Grade I-listed parks in the country, Clumber is networked by well-maintained trails, paths and roads, making exploring the wider estate enjoyable and accessible for all. This walk explores the park north of the lake, following winding woodland paths and bridleways, and finishing with a long stretch next to the lake.

THINGS TO SEE

Clumber Lake, at the heart of the estate, covers 87 acres (35.2ha) to the south of the site of Clumber House. It was built in 1772 by damming the River Poulter and excavating the river bed to form a wide expanse of water, a project that took 15 years to complete and cost £6,612 – around £800,000 in today's money.

Paws for thought
You'll often find animals grazing at Clumber. Please put dogs on leads around these and other wildlife, as well as in the main visitor areas including the Pleasure Grounds, the walled kitchen garden and Lake Brew at Hardwick village, as well as wherever signage requests you to do so.

Other walkies nearby
Clumber Park offers vast scope for dog walking, with a range of routes of different distances. Try the 2-mile (3.2-km) Walk for all Seasons; the 5-mile (8-km) Clumber Park waymarked walk, or the 7.5-mile (12-km) Clumber Park Curiosities walk.

The lime tree avenue.

Public transport From the train station at Worksop, take the Stagecoach Sherwood Arrow towards Ollerton, alight at Lake View Cottages, Carburton, 0.8 miles (1.3km) away.
Car Clumber Park is between Worksop and New Ollerton. Entry is via the A614 or B6034 to Lime Tree Avenue and the main crossroads. Satnav: S80 3BE
OS map Explorer 270
Start/finish Clumber Park car park, S80 3BE, grid ref: SK626747

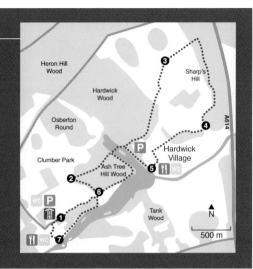

DIRECTIONS

Start/finish: Clumber Park Clock Tower

1. From the Clock Tower, follow the cobbled path under the archways and through Lincoln Stables. Follow the path to the end and turn right. Continue past Cycle Hub then straight on reaching red shale path with additional parking (Cow Pastures) on your left, following cycle no. 8 arrow signs.

2. At end of the path (stone arch on right), turn left, continue to follow cycle no. 8 arrow signs. Continue through the two stone pillars into Ash Tree Hill Woods. Take immediate left-hand path heading into the woods, passing a gate on left and then Bird Hide on right. Cow Pastures remains on your left. Upon reaching the road turn right towards the lake. Beware of traffic.

3. Follow the road which becomes a path, over the lake causeway and straight ahead. On reaching road, turn right and then fork left up onto Engine Hill (tarmac road), following cycle route no. 7. Road veers to right on hill. After red metal barrier, cross the road with care and go straight across onto path though wooden barrier into woods, signed Public Footpath. Go through gate and onto field path passing The Old School House on your left. Follow yellow marked posts. Path veers to right after School House, across field towards another gate. Go through gate and turn right on path.

4. Continue until you reach main red shale path and turn slightly right up the hill continuing on path turning right towards Hardwick village, following cycle no. 11 signs. At crossroads of paths turn right with a clear view of the Old School House on your right across field.

5. Go through 1st wooden gate onto path and then through 2nd wooden gate onto road. Turn left (beware of traffic) and head towards Hardwick village car park. With farm on the left head past the toilets with lake in front of you. Turn right at Lake Brew, keeping lake on your left and continue on path.

6. As path becomes a tarmac road, keep left. Cross the Causeway and immediately turn left signposted Lakeside Walk. Walk through the woods passing stone pillars on your right. Keep left, head through the stone arch, signposted The Pleasure Grounds and take path straight on towards the lake.

7. At the lake take right hand path with lake on your left and continue on Lincoln Terrace until you see Chapel on your right when you can walk across grass back to the starting point at the main visitor facilities.

DOG-FRIENDLY AMENITIES

Among the most dog-friendly of all National Trust places, Clumber Park has its own annual dog show, a weekly social dog walk and a monthly family dog walk. It also boasts its very own dog-friendly café, Central Bark, located between the walled kitchen garden and the cricket ground. Here, you'll find a welcoming space for you and your dog to shelter from bad weather, or sit out in the garden if it's sunny, and enjoy refreshments before or after your walk. There are dog bowls and toys on offer, as well as doggy products available to purchase. There's also a warm water dog wash for muddy paws. Open every day 9am–3pm.

You can also stay on the estate, with all the walks right on your doorstep. The dog-friendly Kitchen Garden Cottage is a restored gardener's cottage set in a peaceful spot on the estate with no passing traffic. Sleeping up to four people and a dog, the cottage has its own garden. Staying here, you'll have out-of-hours access to the estate, so you can explore to your heart's content once the crowds have gone home.

Opposite: The spire of the Gothic chapel, seen in the distance, over the serpentine lake.

51. Belton Park Walk

Grantham
Lincolnshire
NG32 2LS
01476 566116
belton@nationaltrust.org.uk

ABOUT THIS WALK

Distance 3.6 miles (5.8km)
Difficulty Easy
Terrain Surfaced and
unsurfaced tracks around
the estate. Flat but can get
muddy along the riverside
Stiles No
Interest Wildlife, history

Belton Park estate covers 1,300 acres (526ha) of wildlife-rich countryside, including formal gardens, pleasure grounds and 750 acres (304ha) of deer park, home to a herd of fallow deer.

This walk follows the Park Walk around the estate, starting at the impressive 17th-century decorative Carolean mansion and winding through leafy woodland, across open grassland and alongside a golf course. The return trip traces the gentle meanders of the River Witham – keep an eye out for kingfishers and green woodpeckers as you go – finishing through the Wilderness and back to the house.

THINGS TO SEE

As you walk alongside the River Witham, you'll pass the deserted medieval village of Towthorpe. Mentioned in the Doomsday Book of 1086, there's evidence of much earlier settlement, including Saxon and prehistoric findings.

Paws for thought
You'll almost always find grazing animals on the wider estate at Belton, so dogs should be kept on leads at all times. Only assistance dogs are allowed in the outdoor adventure playground, mansion, and the indoor adventure play area. There is a dog and owner waiting area just over the bridge leading into the adventure playground.

Other walkies nearby
For a shorter route, head for the Riverside Walk, an enjoyable 1.4-mile (2.3-km) loop that takes in a stretch of the River Witham and returns through the Wilderness.

Frost in the garden at Belton House.

HOW TO GET HERE

Public transport Grantham is the closest train station (3 miles/4.8km). Regular bus service 1 Grantham– Lincoln; 27 Grantham–Sleaford. The bus stop is just outside Belton Estate.
Car Located just off the A607, Grantham to Lincoln road. Belton Estate is signposted from the A1.
Satnav: input Belton Village
OS map Explorer 247
Start/finish Belton House car park, NG32 2LS, grid ref: SK928391

Map: 200 m scale. N. Belton House, Boathouse Pond, Bellmount Avenue, Belton Park, Alford Memorial, Old Wood, Villa Pond, Towthorpe Ponds, Manthorpe Mill, River Witham, A607, Belton Park Golf Club, Lion Gates. Points marked 1–6.

DIRECTIONS

Start/finish: Belton Estate car park

1. Walk out of the car park and turn right towards the house.

2. Facing the house, turn right and follow the small gravel path into the park. Keep the estate railing fence to your left and walk with Bellmount Avenue to your left and the parkland to your right. Continue through a gate and walk uphill to the next gate.

3. Don't go through; turn right and walk along the fence line, following a path through the back of Old Wood. At the edge of the wood follow the fence right, walking downhill with the golf course to your left. Walk past the Conduit House and through a gate to reach the Alford Memorial on your left.

4. Carry on along the path, then turn left at the end of the golf course. Follow the path through a gate at the head of Towthorpe Ponds. Continue to walk through the park – with the golf course to your left – to the Lion Gates at the far end of the park.

5. Turn right and walk up the avenue for a short distance, then turn left, following the waymarked path through some woodland and out onto open parkland with the River Witham to your left. Follow the river path to a wooden gate between the river and Towthorpe Ponds.

6. Walk through the gate and continue to follow the river path through woodland to reach a fence. Follow the path right to emerge onto the parkland in the southern avenue. Turn left and follow this back to the mansion and the start.

DOG-FRIENDLY AMENITIES

Dogs on short leads are welcome in the gardens, parkland and courtyard areas, including the gift shop, second-hand bookshop and Stables Café.

Just south of Grantham, in the conservation village of Folkingham, The Barn B&B offers a wonderful, peaceful escape. Dog-friendly, and with twin/double and single rooms available, breakfast is locally sourced, including eggs from the farm hens.

52. Gunby Estate Walk

Gunby
Spilsby
Lincolnshire
PE23 5SS
01754 890102
gunbyhall@nationaltrust.org.uk

ABOUT THIS WALK

Distance 4.6 miles (7.4km)
Difficulty Moderate
Terrain Field paths, tracks
and minor roads. Fairly flat
Stiles Yes
Interest Wildlife, history

Nestled at the edge of the rolling Lincolnshire Wolds, the 18th-century, red-brick Gunby Hall has an unimposing and homely character compared with many of its grand contemporaries. Surrounded by 8 acres (3.2ha) of picturesque gardens and 1,500 acres (607ha) of wider estate, there's huge scope for on-foot exploration here.

This walk explores the parkland and grounds, heading for the nearby hamlet of Bratoft. Along the way, you'll pass the church of St Peter and the church at Candlesby, the intriguing chapel at Monksthorpe (optional out-and-back) and the atmospheric remains of the house and garden of Bratoft Manor, a moated medieval site that was once home to the Massingberd family, prior to building Gunby. The homeward stretch follows a section of path that was formerly the East Lincoln Railway and operated between 1848 and 1971.

THINGS TO SEE

'Bratoft' is the name of the local hamlet and former manor, with Bratoft coming from the old Scandinavian *breithr* meaning 'homestead'. The moat would have surrounded a medieval manor and gardens, most likely to have been built during the mid- to late 13th century.

Paws for thought

You'll often find cattle grazing on the estate, as well as other animals and wildlife that makes its home here, so please keep dogs on leads. Assistance dogs only are welcome inside the house and tea-room serving area.

Other walkies nearby

The Lincolnshire Wolds Area of Outstanding Natural Beauty extends over 220 sq. miles (570 sq. km) of low hills formed from chalk, limestone and sandstone rock, laid down in the Cretaceous period. The characteristic open valleys were created through the actions of glaciation and meltwater during the last glacial period. The peaceful, rolling countryside, dotted with market towns and small settlements and networked with long-distance footpaths, makes it a great place to explore on foot.

Above: Exterior view of the house at Gunby Estate.

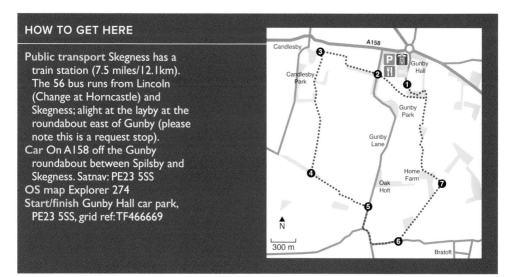

HOW TO GET HERE

Public transport Skegness has a train station (7.5 miles/12.1km). The 56 bus runs from Lincoln (Change at Horncastle) and Skegness; alight at the layby at the roundabout east of Gunby (please note this is a request stop).
Car On A158 off the Gunby roundabout between Spilsby and Skegness. Satnav: PE23 5SS
OS map Explorer 274
Start/finish Gunby Hall car park, PE23 5SS, grid ref: TF466669

DIRECTIONS

Start/finish: Gunby Hall car park

1. Walk through the courtyard and gardens or around to the right of the house towards the church. Leave the gardens by a gate, and go through another gate. Turn right after the church, go through another gate and turn right, following the path across Gunby Park and trending right to reach Gunby Lane.

2. Cross the lane and follow the path along the edges of fields with some woodland to your left. Continue across three fields towards Candlesby. Go over a stile to a path junction near Candlesby church.

3. Turn left and walk downhill through a gate into Candlesby Park. Follow the footpath, marked with yellow arrows to reach a concrete bridleway. You can turn right here to visit Monksthorpe Chapel. Follow the single track road, keeping left.

4. This walk turns left, following the bridleway track between fields to reach Gunby Lane.

5. Turn right and follow Gunby Lane, taking the next two lefts towards Bratoft. Pass a couple of cottages to reach a left turn onto the old railway line.

6. Follow the track of the old railway for about half a mile (1km) until it's crossed by a footpath.

7. Turn left onto the footpath and follow this, marked by yellow arrows, back to the church and Gunby Hall.

DOG-FRIENDLY AMENITIES

Dogs on short leads are welcome throughout the gardens and grounds, as well as in Orchard Gallery and the second-hand bookshop.

Stay on the Gunby estate and have the walks on your doorstep – the picture-perfect Whitegates Cottage is a thatched cottage with traditional mud and stud walls. It's super cosy inside, with many of the original features lovingly restored. Sleeps two people and one dog (NT Holidays).

53. Ilam and Dovedale

**Ilam
Ashbourne
Derbyshire
DE6 2AZ
01335 350503
peakdistrict@nationaltrust.org.uk**

ABOUT THIS WALK

**Distance 5.7 miles (9.2km)
Difficulty Challenging
Terrain Fields, gravelly paths
and woodland trails. Some
sections can be muddy and
wet. Steep hill out of
Dovedale
Stiles Yes
Interest History, geology,
wildlife**

The Peak District National Park lies mainly in Derbyshire, as
well as the surrounding counties of Staffordshire, Yorkshire
and Cheshire. In 1951, it became Britain's first National Park,
following decades of campaigning for access to open spaces for all.

The walking here is wonderfully varied, with stretches of level
riverside trail, edged by invitingly craggy fells where, should you
choose to take them on, tough ascents and rocky descents are
interspersed with glorious views. This walk begins at Ilam, where
you'll also find a second-hand bookshop, café and car park, and heads
across to explore Dovedale, following the river up past the famous
stepping stones to Ilam Rock. From here there's a good climb
through Dovedale Wood before a final wander through limestone
countryside returns you to Ilam Park.

THINGS TO SEE

Dovedale is a National Nature
Reserve, boasting ancient ravine
woodland, wild flowers,
limestone crags and a variety of
wildlife. Popular during the
summer holidays and on good
weather weekends, brooding
skies bring an extra level of
drama to the area.

Paws for thought
Ilam Park, Dovedale and the
White Peak are all set in beautiful
Peak District countryside, where
you'll find grazing farm animals.
The whole area is important for
wildlife such as birds and
invertebrates, as well as for
nature conservation generally, so
take care. Please keep dogs on
short leads.

Other walkies nearby
The 1.5-mile (2.4-km) Ilam Park
to Dovedale Stepping Stones
Trail takes in the famous
stepping stones at Dovedale –
always popular with younger
walkers – and takes in many of
the landmarks and scenic
highlights of the White Peak
area, including Thorpe Cloud,
1,000-year-old Saxon crosses
and a range of fascinating
wildlife. For a longer route, try
the 10-mile (16-km) Manifold
Valley Walk, which explores the
White Peak's Manifold Valley,
including views of Thor's Cave,
the River Manifold, Dovedale
and Ilam Park.

**Above: Looking towards Thorpe
Cloud at Ilam Park.
Opposite: Ilam Park Estate.**

HOW TO GET HERE

Public transport Use Buxton station which is connected by a daily bus service to Ashbourne; this runs along the A515. Alight at Fenny Bentley and walk approx 1.8 miles (3km) along footpaths to join the route at the stepping stones.
Car Ilam Park is off the A515 Ashbourne to Buxton road. Satnav: DE6 2AZ
OS map Explorer OL24
Start/finish Ilam Park car park, DE6 2AZ, grid ref: SK132507

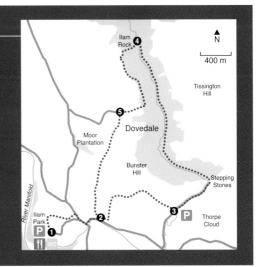

DIRECTIONS

Start/finish: Ilam Park car park

1. Walk out of the car park, turning right into Ilam Park and taking the path across the park to reach a footpath. Turn right and follow this to the road in Ilam village. Turn right and follow the road, bearing left at the Mary Watts-Russell Monument. After the last house turn left through a gate onto the moor.

2. Turn right and follow the footpath to a gate – signed Alternative Route – in the wall. You can continue across the next few fields to reach the Dovedale car park, but there are often animals in these fields. Our route turns left before the gate and follows the path alongside the wall, traversing under Bunster Hill and then right, to reach the road by the River Dove.

3. Turn left and follow this track into the valley. Cross the wooden footbridge on the right, then turn left and follow the riverside path upstream to the stepping stones. Continue on the riverside path, following the river to the left and walking through a gate. Walk up Dovedale, signed to Milldale, until you reach the next footbridge near Ilam Rock.

4. Cross and follow the footpath up the steep side of Dovedale Wood to a field at the top. Turn left and follow the edge of the woodland with fields to your right. Follow the path downhill, trending left and back into the woodland. The path then turns sharp right and walks back uphill past Air Cottage to Ilamtops Farm.

5. Turn left and follow the track up to the top of the hill. Bear right onto a footpath here and walk downhill, across a field and then down the steep side of Bunster Hill. Continue downhill to reach the road and your outbound path on the edge of Ilam village. Turn right and retrace your steps to the start.

DOG-FRIENDLY AMENITIES

Dogs on leads are welcome in all outdoor spaces and in the outdoor seating areas of the café and takeaway kiosk. There are water bowls around the welcome hub, in the Stableyard and outside the Manifold tea-rooms at Ilam Park, and in the car park at Dovedale. You'll also find dog friendly treats including ice cream available from the tea-room. There are bins for dog waste around the main welcome hub at Ilam Park and the car park at Dovedale.

145

54. Longshaw Explorer Walk

Longshaw
Near Sheffield
Derbyshire
S11 7TZ
01433 631757
peakdistrict@nationaltrust.org.uk

ABOUT THIS WALK

Distance 3.8 miles (6.1km)
Difficulty Moderate
Terrain Well-made but sometimes rocky paths, some steep steps
Stiles No
Interest Wildlife, history

The Longshaw estate covers 1,600 acres (650ha) of wild moorland, rugged gritstone edges and peaceful woodland in the heart of the Peak District National Park. Networked with paths and trails, many of which are accessible for buggy and wheelchair users, this is a wonderful place to explore with your dog.

Longshaw's fascinating and diverse landscape creates a species-rich environment, with native wildlife flourishing across the estate. As you go, keep an eye and an ear out for birds such as curlews, skylarks and pied flycatchers.

THINGS TO SEE

There's some fascinating human history to discover at Longshaw, from the Bronze Age ring cairns and hut circles high on the moors and the funerary cairn in the Sheffield Plantation, to the remnants of millstones that you'll find dotted about the estate. These massive wheels, made from local gritstone, date back to the 15th century, when millstones were made at nearby Yarncliffe Quarry.

Paws for thought
Please keep dogs on short leads to protect livestock, wildlife and the dogs themselves. Ground-nesting birds are often hard to see, but the birds and their nests are easily damaged by dogs. Farm animals and deer can also be found grazing in some areas in and around Longshaw.

Other walkies nearby
You're spoilt for choice when it comes to outstanding walks in the Dark Peak area of the Peak District. Head for popular Mam Tor to take in the views from the trig point; climb Jacob's Ladder to the Kinder Scout plateau; take in the views from the iconic gritstone edges, or head down to the Derwent valley to explore some less hilly riverside trails on the Derwent Valley Heritage Way.

DOG-FRIENDLY AMENITIES

You'll find water bowls around the welcome hub and café at Longshaw, alongside a range of dog friendly treats to purchase, including doggy ice cream. There's an indoor dog-friendly area inside the café and dogs on leads are welcome at the outdoor seating too.

You can stay on the Longshaw Estate at the gorgeous and dog-friendly White Edge Lodge. Standing alone on a vast expanse of heather moorland, this former gamekeeper's cottage starred as the home of the Rivers family in the 2011 adaption of Jane Eyre. Relax after a long day walking the local moors with a soak in the luxurious roll-top bath, gazing out over 20 miles (32km) of stunning landscape (NT Holidays).

Above: Burbage Brook.
Opposite: Longshaw estate.

HOW TO GET HERE

Public transport Grindleford train station is a 1.5 mile (2.4km) walk following the footpath up Padley Gorge and joining this walk between points 5 and 6.

Car Brown signs will direct you to Longshaw's main Woodcroft car park from the A625 and A6187 Sheffield to Hathersage road.

Satnav: S11 7TZ
OS map Explorer OL24
Start/finish Woodcroft car park, S11 7TZ, grid ref: SK266800

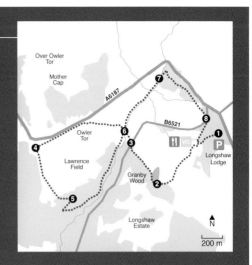

DIRECTIONS

Start/finish: Woodcroft car park

1. Follow the path down from the bottom of the car park to the Longshaw visitor centre and café. Cross the road in front of the café and turn left, walking between the wall and fence to a gate. Go through the gate and turn right, heading slightly downhill, then continue through another gate to the pond.

2. Turn right, following the pond and the path along the edge of Granby Wood to Granby Barn. Continue on the path down to the B6521. Cross carefully and walk through the gate.

3. Follow the path right, downhill to the bridge and cross Burbage Brook. Walk slightly right, joining Hollowgate and following it uphill towards the A6187. Don't go through the gate at the top of Hollowgate; turn left and walk up a sharp incline. Follow the path, walking past the weathered outcrop of Owler Tor to your left. Walk across Lawrence Field with the A6187 to your right.

4. At the edge of Lawrence Field you will reach a stile and gate, turn left just before these and follow the path downhill with the fence on your right. Walk down to a gate, go through and continue on the path, take the left fork and follow the path to the boundary wall and a gate.

5. Go through the gate and turn right, walking down a wide path for a short distance to a left turn. Take this and follow the path downhill to the main Padley Gorge footpath. Turn left and follow this gritstone path up the valley and back to the Burbage Brook bridge you crossed earlier.

6. Don't cross; continue to walk upstream on the path beside the brook. Carry on until you come to another bridge over the brook on your right.

7. Cross and follow the path uphill, turn right at the path junction and walk through the woodland, trending right until you reach a white gate and the B6521.

8. Carefully cross and follow the old driveway to the café in the Longshaw estate. Turn left just before the café to return to the car park.

55. Kinder Reservoir Walk

Near Hope Valley
Derbyshire
S33 8WA
01433 670368
peakdistrict@nationaltrust.org.uk

ABOUT THIS WALK

Distance 5.2 miles (8.4km)
Difficulty Challenging
Terrain Road, surfaced gravel/rocky trails and moorland paths. Can be muddy and exposed to bad weather. Hilly but not too steep
Stiles Yes
Interest Wildlife

The River Kinder rises on Kinder Scout, the highest point in the Peak District National Park. It then flows 98ft (30m) over the craggy cliffs at Kinder Downfall, and through Kinder Reservoir before joining the River Sett just 3 miles (4.8km) later.

Surrounded by dramatic Dark Peak scenery, shaped by the underlying gritstone bedrock, this walk circumnavigates the reservoir, starting through the quiet avenues of Hayfield before following the famous Snake Path up to reach the heather-clad moors surrounding Kinder. Surprise viewpoints and beautiful, peaceful moments make this varied, engaging walk a very special one.

THINGS TO SEE

As well as its place in history as a symbol of the right to roam, the area around Kinder is important for climate and nature.

Restoration work here has turned once bare peat into a landscape covered in moorland vegetation, rewetting the moorland and creating healthy peat bogs. This restoration work will help to sequester carbon, improve water quality and prevent flooding of the land below.

DOG-FRIENDLY AMENITIES

The Camping and Caravanning Club's Hayfield Campsite is perfectly placed for exploring the area around Kinder and beyond. Set out on a flat stretch of neatly kept grass, it's friendly, welcoming and great for dogs and families.

Paws for thought

Dogs should be kept on leads near to grazing animals, wildlife habitat and during bird nesting season (1 March–31 July).

Other walkies nearby

The 3.4-mile (5.5-km) Edale Circular Walk follows a low level route through open fields and along parts of the Pennine Way, following streams and stone-flagged paths through the Vale of Edale. Pop into the dog-friendly Penny Pot Café in Edale for refreshments at the end of your walk.

Above: The moorland above Kinder Reservoir.
Opposite: Kinder Reservoir.

Public transport New Mills Central is the closest train station (4.3 miles/6.9km). To get the bus, walk along Station Road, then Hague Bar Road, then turn right. Take the 61 or 358 bus service to Hayfield and join the route at point 2.
Car Hayfield is on the A6015 from New Mills and the A6, and on the A624 between Glossop and Chapel-en-le-Frith. The start is on the Kinder Road. Satnav: SK22 2LH
OS map Explorer OL1
Start/finish Bowden Bridge car park, SK22 2LH, grid ref: SK048869

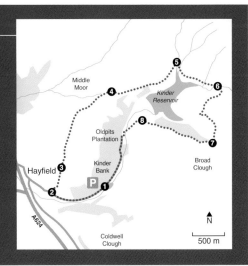

DIRECTIONS

Start/finish: Bowden Bridge car park

1. Turn right and follow Kinder Road back to the edge of Hayfield. Turn right onto the Snake Path, signed as a footpath. If you arrive by public transport you'll be walking from Hayfield to this point and the path will be on your left.

2. Follow Snake Path uphill through a couple of gates and over a stile. You're walking up through the fields and will soon reach the boundary of the Peak District National Park; this is also the edge of National Trust-owned land.

3. Continue to follow the path across a few more fields to the edge of the moorland. Stay right when another trail joins from the left and walk across Middle Moor to a path junction at a National Trust sign. There is a white shooting cabin to the left.

4. Take the path to the right, signed to the Snake Inn and Edale. Follow this path along White Brow, traversing the moorland above Kinder Reservoir (to your left). Trend right to descend to the footbridge over William Clough at the head of the reservoir.

5. Cross the bridge and follow the path right, traversing along the slopes above Kinder Reservoir. Walk through a couple of gates and then cross a small stream. Continue on the path, crossing a couple of stiles to reach a footbridge over the small River Kinder.

6. Follow the track ahead, walking uphill and curving to the right towards the pine tree plantations. Turn left at the National Trust sign, following the path up onto Upper Moor and then curving to the right and walking down to a gate. Walk downhill across the fields, cross a stile to reach the stream.

7. Cross carefully as it's often slippery here. Go over the next stile and follow the path right along the edge of the woods. Follow the path as it heads downhill and through a gate.

8. Turn left and follow the road down the valley. Cross the river and continue on the road back to the start. If you started in Hayfield, continue down Kinder Road to Hayfield.

North West

56. Park Moor and Knightslow Wood Walk at Lyme Park

Disley
Stockport
Cheshire
SK12 2NR
01663 762023
lyme@nationaltrust.org.uk

ABOUT THIS WALK

Distance 2.9 miles (4.7km)
Difficulty Moderate
Terrain Footpaths through parkland, moorland and woodland. Can be muddy in the wet
Stiles Yes
Interest History, wildlife

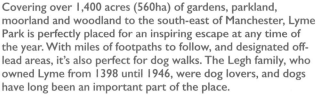

Covering over 1,400 acres (560ha) of gardens, parkland, moorland and woodland to the south-east of Manchester, Lyme Park is perfectly placed for an inspiring escape at any time of the year. With miles of footpaths to follow, and designated off-lead areas, it's also perfect for dog walks. The Legh family, who owned Lyme from 1398 until 1946, were dog lovers, and dogs have long been an important part of the place.

This enjoyable loop explores the wilds of Park Moor and the peaceful reaches of Knightslow Wood, returning along a wooded river valley on a stretch of the Gritstone Way long-distance trail. You'll also pass through areas where dogs can run free, which will be signposted. Keep an eye out for historic buildings and the resident herd of red deer as you go.

THINGS TO SEE

Lyme Hall dates back to the 16th century and is renowned for its Tudor architecture and elegant interiors. The formal gardens feature terraces, a reflection pool, and herbaceous borders. The estate is open 8.30am–5pm in winter and 8:30am–8pm in summer.

Paws for thought
You may encounter deer and other grazing animals on the estate – keep your dog on the lead in these areas. Dogs must also, by law, be on leads on open access areas between 1 March and 31 July. Dogs are not allowed in the house.

Other walkies nearby
Head up onto the windswept uplands of Park Moor to explore the trig point-topped summit of Sponds Hill at 1,355ft (413m), taking in the stunning views across the Peak District. To the east of Lyme rises the lonely Kinder Plateau, just above the village of Edale. The Pennine Way National Trail runs all the way from here to Kirk Yethlom in the Scottish borders, 268 miles (431km) north.

Above: Dog walk in the parkland at sunset.
Opposite: The Lantern at Lyme Park.

HOW TO GET HERE

Public transport The closest train station is Disley (half a mile/0.8km) from the entrance and a further 1 mile (1.6km) to the house and gardens.
Car Lyme can be accessed from the A6 in Disley. Satnav: SK12 2NR
OS map Explorer 268
Start/finish Lyme Park car park, SK12 2NR, grid ref: SJ962823

DIRECTIONS

Start/finish: Lyme Park car park

1. Leaving the car park, walk uphill to the left of the house and then to the left of the stable block to reach a road junction with a sign reading 'staff and volunteer vehicles only'.

2. Turn right, then walk past the staff car park and through the gate onto the off-lead trail. Follow this path straight ahead, ignoring the path on your right, and continue until you reach a gate and stile at the corner of Hampers Wood. Go over the stile (using the hole in the gate for your dog) and turn right.

3. Follow the trail to the right, along the edge of Park Moor with the woods on your right. You'll pass Hampers Wood and Knightslow Wood, then go through another gate before you reach a path junction with the Gritstone Trail.

4. Turn right through the gate into Knightslow Wood and then immediately turn left to follow a path at the edge of the woodland. Follow this path until you reach the corner of the wood with a stile on your left. Go over this stile, using the hole in the wall for your dog, and follow the path first down and then up a few steps. Follow the path here until you reach a small kissing gate below Paddock Cottage.

5. Go through the gate and head uphill to the cottage, from here go downhill with a fence on your right until you reach a gate on your right. Go through the gate and follow the track downhill until you reach a path junction. Turn right and follow this slightly uphill through Hase Bank Wood. Continue through a gate into the car park at the edge of the wood.

6. Follow the road across the parkland back to the main car park and the start.

DOG-FRIENDLY AMENITIES

Dogs are welcome in the Servants' Hall café and at the outside seating at the Timber Yard café. You can also take your dog into the Timber Yard shop and Crow Wood Playscape (please be extra vigilant here as it's a children's play area). You can also join a monthly social dog walking group at Lyme, taking in a different route each time.

Lyme East Lodge, set conveniently within the estate, is an attractive Edwardian lodge with a rear garden perfect for dogs. Offering great views to the Peak District, it sleeps four people and up to two dogs.

153

57. Rivers and Woods Walk at Quarry Bank

Styal
Wilmslow
Cheshire
SK9 4HP
01625 527468
quarrybank@nationaltrust.org.uk

ABOUT THIS WALK

Distance 2.7 miles (4.3km)
Difficulty Moderate
Terrain Some slopes; the riverside path can be muddy
Stiles No
Interest Wildlife, history

Fascinating to visit, but with a dark side, Quarry Bank is a complex window into a world gone by. Discover the elegant Georgian villa at Quarry Bank House – home to wealthy mill owners, the Greg family – adjacent to the mills where hundreds of workers, including children, spent their days weaving cloth.

The northern route wanders through mixed pleasure grounds and woodland, home to redwoods and folly bridges, once used by former owner Robert Hyde Greg to connect his home to the mill. On the southern route, pass the mill pond and weir as you trace the meandering course of the river through the woods, then following the old Apprentice Path back to the main site.

THINGS TO SEE

The village in Styal was built by mill owner Samuel Greg so his workers could live on-site, meaning efficient and cost-effective labour. You can still see the rows of terraced houses, each of which housed around seven people. As well as mill workers, the gardeners, labourers, farmers, butchers, engineers and managers lived in the village.

Paws for thought

Dogs should be kept on leads throughout the estate. Only assistance dogs are permitted inside the Weaving Shed Restaurant, mill, Quarry Bank House, the Apprentice House, Village Hub and Worker's Cottage.

Other walkies nearby

You'll find three great dog-friendly walks at Quarry Bank. The above walk combines two of these – the Southern Woods Walk and the Kingfisher Walk. Maps are available at the visitor welcome building detailing all of the walks, along with further information to make visiting with your dog as enjoyable as possible.

Above: Autumn walk at Quarry Bank Mill.
Opposite: The orchard during the Festival of Blossom.

HOW TO GET HERE

Public transport Styal train station is a half-mile (0.8-km) walk from Quarry Bank. Wilmslow train station is 2 miles (3.2km) away, approximately a 40-minute walk.
Car Quarry Bank is located off the B5166. Follow the A555 and exit at the Hollin Lane/Styal Road junction. Follow the brown oak leaf heritage signs. Satnav: SK9 4HP
OS map Explorer 268
Start/finish Quarry Bank Mill Yard, SK9 4HP, Grid ref: SJ835830ST778339

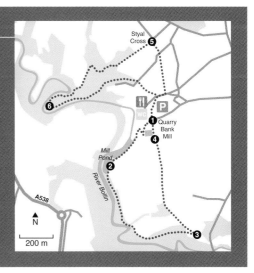

DIRECTIONS

Start/finish: Quarry Bank Mill Yard

1. Starting your walk in the Mill Yard near the second-hand bookshop make your way through the estate railing gate. The path passes to the left of the mill and follows the bank of the River Bollin.

2. Follow the path towards the mill pond, which used to control the flow rates for the mill. Continue on the riverside path, passing an old stone quarry and crossing the Heron's Pool Bridge over an area of wetland. Just before the next footbridge, turn left and follow the path uphill to a path junction.

3. Here you will find an Erratic Glacial stone; take the path to the left, and continue uphill, leading across fields, through a couple of gates and back to the main estate.

4. This is the end of the Southern Woods walk, our route continues and also completes what is known as the Kingfisher Walk in the woodland north of Quarry Bank. To continue, walk to Visitor Reception and follow the fingerpost to Styal Village. Cross a track with two gates through fields to reach Styal Cross.

5. Turn left and follow the path towards Norcliffe Chapel. Walk past the chapel and follow the path alongside a field, cross a large path and enter Chapel Woods. After a short distance, take the right-hand fork in the path and follow it downhill, with a gully on your left. Pass a steel bridge on your left and continue on the same path. Descend some stone steps and bear right to reach and cross Chapel Bridge. Then follow the path uphill and turn left, following this path down until you can see the river on your right. Continue to Oxbow Bridge.

6. Don't cross; stay on this side of the river and follow the path around the river bend to Kingfisher Bridge. Cross this and walk up the steep path, staying right at the next path junctions to return via a tarmacked drive to the start point.

Easter trail at Quarry Bank.

DOG-FRIENDLY AMENITIES

Dogs on leads are welcome around the wider estate and on a short lead in the Mill Yard, garden, Styal village, and footpaths through the main visitor areas of Quarry Bank. Dogs are welcome in the Upper Garden Café, visitor welcome building, the upper garden shop and the Mill Yard shop. You'll also find dog waste bins and water bowls on the estate.

58. Dunham Massey

Woodhouse Lane
Altrincham
WA14 4SJ
0161 941 1025
dunhammassey@nationaltrust.org.uk

ABOUT THIS WALK

Distance 2.4 miles (3.9km)
Difficulty Easy
Terrain Well maintained
estate paths
Stiles No
Interest History, wildlife

Dogs can expect a warm welcome at Dunham Massey, with 300 acres (121ha) of space to explore, including an off-lead area in the North Park next to the main car park and a dog-friendly café. With its grand Georgian house, formal gardens and extensive parkland networked by trails, including many that are accessible for buggy and wheelchair users, there's plenty for everyone to see and do here.

Records first mention the park at Dunham Massey in the 12th century, when deer parks were an important symbol of power and privilege. The estate has been home to a succession of remarkable women, including Lady Mary Booth, who inherited it from her father – a highly unusual occurrence in the 18th century – and oversaw extensive remodelling of the grounds. This enjoyable ramble takes in a varied loop of the deer park, passing the Hall, lake, obelisk and ice cream parlour.

THINGS TO SEE

As well as being dog-friendly, Dunham Massey is great for children. All through the year you'll find organised events that tie in with nature, being active and creative outdoors. From fungi trails and forest holiday clubs, to storytelling and guided walks, it's a perfect place to escape to for learning and fun.

Paws for thought
A large herd of fallow deer grazes in the deer park, while ground-nesting birds and other wildlife also make their homes here. Please keep dogs on leads in all areas other than North Park (see map for details of off-lead area) to avoid frightening or harming these animals.

Assistance Dogs only in the historic buildings, larger Stables Restaurant space, and in the gardens before 12pm.

Other walkies nearby
The Bridgewater Canal runs through the estate, connecting Runcorn, Manchester and Leigh over a distance of 41 miles (66km). With easy access to the towpath, it's perfect for peaceful, waterside walks. If you fancy taking on a bigger challenge, the Cheshire Ring is a 97-mile (156-km) route following the towpaths of six historic canals through Lancashire, Cheshire and Staffordshire. Doable in sections, or as a walking holiday stopping off at the various towns along the way, it's a fascinating journey through the history, heritage and nature of the area.

Dunham Park.

HOW TO GET HERE

Public transport The closest train stations are Altrincham (3 miles/4.8km) and Hale (3 miles/4.8km). From Altrincham, you can catch the hourly 280 bus which stops at the Dunham Massey entrance gate.

Car Dunham Massey is located on Woodhouse Lane in Altrincham, off the A56. Exit at J19 off the M6; and J7 off the M56. Satnav: WA14 4SJ

OS map Explorer 268 and 276

Start/finish Dunham Massey car park, WA14 4SJ, grid ref: SJ732874

DIRECTIONS

Start/finish: Dunham Massey car park

1. From the car park, walk to the left of the Visitor Centre and up to the pond via a gate. Turn right and follow the path alongside the water, through the double deer gate and into the deer park. Continue past the ponds and turn left around the stable buildings, walking towards the front of the big house.

2. Turn right and follow the Langham track to the obelisk. Turn left and follow smaller paths across the deer park, crossing Farm Walk and passing Island Pool to reach the wide Main Drive.

Watch out for the deer in Dunham Park.

3. Follow this track right, away from the house and between the deer sanctuaries to reach a T-junction with the boundary track.

4. Turn left and follow this track, with the boundary of the deer park through the trees to your right and the deer sanctuary on the left. Continue until you reach Charcoal Drive, which crosses in front of you. Turn left and follow this back to the path junction in front of the main house.

5. Walk up the driveway towards the house, but turn left before reaching it to enter the old stable courtyard near the café. Walk between the two buildings to reach the path by the pond used on the outbound walk. Turn right and retrace your steps back to the start.

The Stables buildings.

DOG-FRIENDLY AMENITIES

Dogs are welcome on leads across the deer park, North Park, and in the gardens from 12pm. North Park also has an off-lead area – you'll find further information and directions at the Visitor Centre.

For a frozen treat or warm drink, you can order and sit with your dog in the Ice Cream Parlour. The Stables Restaurant has a dog-friendly area as you enter (to the right) and also on the café terrace. You'll find dog waste bins and water bowls around these areas.

You can also stay on the estate with your dog in one of the National Trust's dog-friendly cottages. The gorgeous, newly renovated Hempfield Stables sleeps up to four people and their dogs. It has enclosed front and rear gardens and easy access to the estate and local walks.

59. The Standedge Circuit on Marsden Moor

Marsden Moor Office and
Information Room
The Old Goods Yard
Station Road
Marsden
West Yorkshire
HD7 6DH
01484 847016
marsdenmoor@nationaltrust.org.uk

ABOUT THIS WALK

Distance 10.4 miles
(16.7km)
Difficulty Challenging
Terrain Footpaths on
moorland, stone flagstones
and surfaced trails. A big
climb onto Marsden Moor
Stiles No
Interest Wildlife, history,
geology

Set among the rolling south Pennines, overlooking the town of Marsden, Marsden Moor covers more than 5,500 acres (2,226ha) of open moor and common land. Set partly within the Peak District National Park, the landscape is a patchwork of moorland, valleys, peaks and crags, marked extensively by human activities over the centuries.

This circular walk offers challenge and reward in equal measure, exploring the ancient Standedge crossing of the moors. As you walk, you'll discover valleys and reservoirs, take in far-reaching views from open moorland summits, and trace an old packhorse route and Huddersfield narrow canal back to Marsden.

THINGS TO SEE

Several different species of moorland bird can be seen, or more often heard, on Marsden Moor, including golden plover, red grouse, Eurasian curlew and twite.

Paws for thought

Dogs should be kept under close control at all times on Marsden Moor and, by law, must be on a lead during the bird breeding season (1 March–31 July).

Other walkies nearby

There's almost endless scope for walking on and around Marsden Moor. Try the 8-mile (12.9-km) Heritage Trail, the 4.5-mile (7.2-km) Deer Hill Walk, or, if you're visiting on a clear day, climb Pule Hill to take in the glorious 360-degree views from the top.

DOG-FRIENDLY AMENITIES

The Riverhead Brewery Tap in Marsden is a well-liked, dog-friendly pub where you can enjoy a selection of real ales and food with your dog.

DIRECTIONS

Start/finish: Marsden train station car park

1. Starting at the car park, walk back to the station then turn left, following Station Road across the canal and left towards town. Cross the river Colne and turn right, passing the church and following the road across a junction and then under the busy A62. Follow this road to a roundabout and

HOW TO GET HERE

Public transport The route starts at Marsden train station.
Car The train station car park, on A62 Manchester Road between Huddersfield and Oldham.
Satnav: HD7 6DH
OS map Explorer OL1 and OL21
Start/finish Marsden train station car park, HD7 6DH, grid ref: SE049118

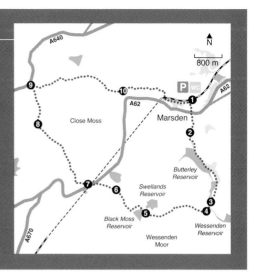

continue onto Binn Road. Take the track to the right that walks between the mill buildings, follow this towards the spillway.

2. Continue to follow this track as it forks left back to Binn Road. Take the next right onto a track marked as a bridleway. Follow this track up Wessenden Valley, passing Butterley and Blakeley reservoirs on your right.

3. At the next path junction, turn right following the Pennine Way down into the valley, across a footbridge and up to a path junction on the other side.

4. Turn right and follow the Pennine Way up Blakley Clough and across the moorland until you reach the corner of Black Moss reservoir.

5. Cross the footbridge and follow the path along the edge of the reservoir. Follow the flagged path around to the left, through a gate and right, downhill to a path junction with the Standedge Trail.

6. Turn left and follow the path until you get to Brun Clough car park.

7. From the car park, cross the A62 and follow the Pennine Way path ahead. Turn left at the top and continue on the Pennine Way to the next junction with a fingerpost. Turn right through the gate and head uphill, crossing a field with gates at both sides. Continue to follow the Pennine Way along Millstone Edge, passing the trig point and heading slightly downhill to reach a stone waymarker.

8. The waymarker is signed Oldham Way or the Pennine Way. Follow the Pennine Way right along a fence line and down to Haigh Gutter and the A640.

9. Just before you reach the A640 cross a ford and take a sharp right to reach a bridleway. Follow this down Willykay Clough to reach the bridge at Eastergate, also known as Close Gate Bridge.

10. Cross and follow the path alongside the River Colne to Waters Road. Turn right and follow the road signed 'Easter Gate return' back towards Marsden. At the road junction, turn right, leaving the road through a gate into Tunnel End Nature Reserve. Follow the path along the canal on the edge of the reserve up to the road and back to Marsden train station or the car park.

Marsden Moor footpaths.

60. Woods, Wetlands and Wildlife at Sizergh Castle

Sizergh
Near Kendal
Cumbria
LA8 8DZ
01539 560951
sizergh@nationaltrust.org.uk

ABOUT THIS WALK

Distance 3.6 miles (5.8km)
Difficulty Moderate
Terrain Estate and woodland paths, which can be slippery in the wet. Two hills on the route
Stiles No
Interest History, wildlife

Imposing, with its towering grey keep and battlements, medieval Sizergh Castle stands proudly at the gateway to the Lake District, and has been home to the Strickland family for more than 800 years. Surrounded by 1,600 acres (647ha) of estate, including wetland, woodland and orchards, it is a wonderful place to explore with dogs.

This varied walk takes you through the fields and farmland, historic parkland and ancient woodlands of the Sizergh Estate. From the high points you'll have fine views of the Lake District and across to Morecambe Bay. Look out for bright orange, fast-flying fritillary butterflies, deer and rare hawfinches as you go.

THINGS TO SEE

The medieval manor at Sizergh is filled with items collected by 26 generations of the Strickland family, including the internationally-recognised Inlaid Chamber, and fascinating to visit – although dogs (other than assistance dogs) aren't allowed into the house itself.

Paws for thought
Deer and other animals graze on the estate, which is also home to many wild birds and wildlife. Please keep dogs under control in all areas, and on the lead around animals and during the nesting season (1 March–31 July).

Other walkies nearby
From Sizergh, an intricate network of footpaths explores the area to the west of Kendal. Follow trails north for a glorious walk along the edge of the limestone scarp at Scout Scar, exploring the intriguing Helsington Barrows and taking in the awe-inspiring views from the top. Despite only rising to a height of 764ft (233m), choose a clear day and you'll be able to see Blackpool Tower, the Old Man of Coniston, the Langdales, the Howgill Fells and the Yorkshire Dales.

Above: View of the surrounding landscape from Park Moss wetland.
Opposite: Sizergh estate.

HOW TO GET HERE

Public transport From Kendal train station, take the hourly X6 bus or the 555, 755, 551 and 530 bus services to the Heave/Brettagh stop (ask the bus driver for Sizergh).
Car From the M6, exit at J36, take the A590 towards Kendal, then come off at the Barrow-in-Furness turning. Follow the brown signs, one of which comes quickly after the Brettargh Holt roundabout, so please be aware you should be in the right-hand lane.
Satnav: LA8 8DZ
OS map Explorer OL7
Start/finish Sizergh Castle car park, LA8 8DZ, grid ref: SD498878

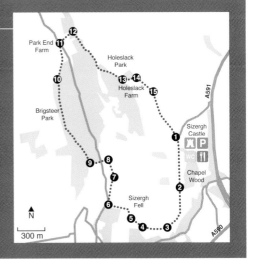

DIRECTIONS

Start/finish: Sizergh Castle car park

1. Leave the car park and follow the orange waymarkers signed to Sizergh Fell. Walk through a gate and into a field. Follow the wall to reach the far edge of the field and the corner of Chapel Wood.

2. Go through the gate into the next field, ignore the path to your right and continue walking in the same direction slightly uphill alongside the fence line. At the fence corner, follow the path right and uphill to the clump of trees.

3. Walk past the trees and follow the path across Sizergh Fell, staying left of the next clump of trees and starting to walk downhill.

4. Walk downhill and slightly right to reach a gate in the wall.

5. Go through the gate and turn right, following a track through a field to the next gate. Go through the gate and turn left. Follow this path downhill to a gate onto the road. Lane End Farm is opposite.

6. Turn right and use the pedestrian gate to follow a path through the field next to the road. At the end of the field, turn right and follow the path to another gate.

7. Go through the gate and left of the large ash tree. A small gate takes you into the next field, keep the wall to your left and follow the path across this field and through the gate on the other side to reach a footpath called Ashbank Lane.

8. Turn left and follow Ashbank Lane through a gate and across Brigsteer Road into a small car park. Follow the track out of the back of the car park into Brigsteer Park Wood.

9. Follow the track around to the right. When the track forks, take the left route, downhill to reach a path junction near the edge of the wood. Turn right and follow this path to a gate at the edge of the wood.

10. Go through the gate into Park End Meadow. Turn right and follow the path along the edge of the woods, then left across the meadow to a gate onto the road opposite Park End Farm's house.

11. Cross the road and follow the footpath through the farmyard and up the hill towards a couple of houses. Follow this path through a gate to a track junction.

12. Turn right and follow the track along the edge of woodland to reach a stony track. Follow this track right and downhill, past a cattle grid to Holeslack Farm.

13. Walk through the farmyard and past the barns to join the accessible trail.

14. Take the right fork and head downhill through a small gate into Rash Springs Wood. Stay on this path as it passes a small barn and continues back through fields, returning you to Sizergh Castle.

15. At the bottom of the hill, go through a gate onto a smaller shared footpath which takes you back to the car park and the start.

DOG-FRIENDLY AMENITIES

Dogs are welcome on a lead in the shop, café and wild play area, as well as on the wider estate. Dogs must be kept on a lead wherever there's livestock or nesting birds, including around the wetland at Park End Moss.

Get to know the estate more intimately with a stay at Holeslack. The cottage sleeps up to four people and two dogs, while the farmhouse sleeps up to eight people and two dogs – the two properties can be booked separately or together. Both have enclosed, dog-friendly gardens and access from the door to the estate's walking and cycling trails.

61.   Fell Foot

Newby Bridge
Windermere
Cumbria
LA12 8NN
01539 531273
fellfoot@nationaltrust.org.uk

ABOUT THIS WALK

Distance 1.7 miles (2.7km)
Difficulty Easy
Terrain Easy surfaced or
grassy trails
Stiles No
Interest Wildlife, history

In a picturesque setting at the very southern tip of Windermere, Fell Foot is a place to play, explore and relax. There's plenty of space here for all, whether it's a day out with kids; games or picnics on the sweeping lawns; paddling, swimming and boating in the lake, or an enjoyable dog walk.

In 1969, the National Trust took over running Fell Foot as a country park under the Countryside Act of 1968. Initially run as a holiday park with caravans and chalets, it's now a place for all, and one of the very few lakeside venues accessible to the public south of Bowness. This walk takes you out around the estate to explore some of Fell Foot's heritage, including the historic boathouses, a modern Active Base, and an 18th-century pleasure ground and pinetum.

THINGS TO SEE

The most enduring element of additions to Fell Foot is the Grade II-listed harbour complex comprising three piers and five Gothic boathouses, complete with crenellated turrets, arrow loops, doorways and rustic limestone decoration.

Paws for thought
Blue-green algae can sometimes be present in the lake, and can be fatal to dogs. Keep your dog on a lead and out of the water when it is present. Dogs should also be kept on leads in the parkland, along the lakeshore paths, around grazing or wild animals, and in the café.

Other walkies nearby
There's a fantastic variety of walks within easy reach of Fell Foot, as well as further afield in the Lake District. Windermere's western shore (see page 167) has lots to explore, including lakeside and woodland trails. Further to the north is Wray, with its mock-Gothic architecture and surrounding lakeside landscape. While dogs aren't allowed into the main building, the lakeshore path between Wray and Claife Viewing Station is a safe, car-free walk with plenty of shade and places for dogs to paddle and swim – perfect for warm days.

Sunrise at Fell Foot.

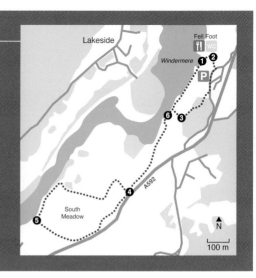

DOG-FRIENDLY AMENITIES

Dogs are welcome in all areas, including the
Boathouse Café, apart from the children's play
area. Water-loving dogs can swim in the lake, as
long as blue-green algae isn't present. For off-lead
walks, head to South Meadow where your dog can
run free provided cattle are not grazing there.

The lawns at Fell Foot,
heading for the harbour.

DIRECTIONS

Start/finish: Boathouse Café at Fell Foot Park

1. Follow the path towards the Active Base, then
    turn right following the path uphill, past a slate
    cottage to a gateway on the right.

2. Walk right, through the gateway and follow the
    path with the car park on your left and the
    open lawn area to the right. Continue in this
    direction until you reach a larger track cutting
    across in front of you.

3. Turn right and follow this track down to the
    lakeside path. Turn left onto this and follow the
    lake towards South Meadow.

4. Go through the gate and turn right, following
    the path towards the river and anti-clockwise
    around South Meadow.

5. Turn away from the lake and continue around
    the meadow and back to the gate. Go through
    and follow the same path back along the lake
    to the path junction. You can turn right and
    retrace your outbound route or continue
    along the lake.

6. Continue along the lake path, with the lawn on
    your right. This path will return you to the
    start.

62. Claife Heights and Windermere's Western Shore

Beside the Ferry on Windermere's west shore
Near Far Sawrey
Hawkshead
Cumbria
LA22 0LJ
01539 441456
claife@nationaltrust.org.uk

ABOUT THIS WALK

Distance 8 miles (12.9km)
Difficulty Challenging
Terrain The first half is challenging, with some steep slopes and potentially slippery ground. The return along the lake is easier, on flat, surfaced trails
Stiles Yes
Interest Wildlife, history

At around 11 miles (18km) long with a maximum depth of 219 ft (66.7m) deep, Windermere is the largest natural body of water in England. Dotted with islands – 19 in total – and alive with boats, this is a special place and a focal point for people and wildlife.

This walk explores the less-developed western shore of Windermere. Starting with a good climb, you'll ascend to Claife Heights and traverse the long, wooded ridge high above the water. The return trip winds through low-level woodland and parkland, offering great views of the islands and passing sites of interesting archaeology and the Victorian neo-Gothic Wray.

THINGS TO SEE

Wildlife abounds in this part of the Lake District. Claife Woods is one of the best places in the National Park to see wild deer, with both red and roe deer living here. If you're lucky, you might also spot the shy red squirrels, which are part of a monitoring and conservation project in this area.

Paws for thought
Dogs must be kept on leads in wildlife areas, at Claife Viewing Station, Wray (only assistance dogs are allowed inside the building) and at all times during the bird nesting season (1 March–31 July). Blue-green algae, which is highly toxic to dogs, may be present on the water in Windermere.

Other walkies nearby
Rising to the north of Claife Heights, Latterbarrow is a lovely hill to climb, with a wild feel. The path to the summit leads through ancient woodland and over streams, and reaching the stone cairn at the top is rewarded with stunning views. A thoroughly delightful walk starts at Wray and ascends Latterbarrow via High Wray. On your return you'll pass peaceful Blelham Tarn and St Margaret's Church, Low Wray, where Hardwicke Rawnsley was once vicar.

Claife Viewing Station.

HOW TO GET HERE

Public transport Train to Windermere, then take bus 599 to Bowness Pier. The Windermere ferry to the western shore is about 0.6 miles (1km) further down the lake.
Car J36 off M6, then the A684, which becomes the A591 to Windermere. B5285 from Windermere via Windermere ferry; B5286 and B5285 from Ambleside; B5285 from Coniston. Parking at Ash Landing. Satnav: LA22 0LJ
OS map Explorer OL7
Start/finish Ash Landing car park, LA22 0LJ, grid ref: SD388954

DIRECTIONS

Start/finish: Ash Landing car park

1. Leaving the Ash Landing car park, follow the track with a low wooden barrier uphill and up some steps to the ruin of Claife Viewing Station.

2. Turn left and continue uphill to a path junction with a walled bridleway and a sign pointing to Sawrey.

3. Turn left and follow the bridleway to a cross road in the path. Turn right and follow this uphill, curving right at the top of the ridge. Pass to the right of a pond (or marsh area in drier periods) and continue through a gate. Walk along this path beside a conifer plantation to a fork in the trail. Take the right fork and follow the footpath to reach a gate. Go through the gate and continue on the path.

4. Pass to the right of High Blind How and take the next left, walking uphill through woodland to a path junction beside the small lake. Turn right and follow the path along the lake shore to the next path junction.

5. Take the right fork and follow the path through woodland and across Belle Grange Beck to a path junction with a bridleway signed left to Hawkshead.

6. Cross and follow the bridleway opposite towards the National Trust Base Camp and High Wray. Follow this bridleway, staying right at the next fork and ignoring the paths going right. Continue downhill through a gate in a wall and past the National Trust Base Camp buildings to your right. Continue straight ahead to join the larger forest track and follow this downhill to the cattle grid and road at High Wray.

7. Turn right and follow the road to the left through the small village. Pass the village hall and then turn right onto a footpath just before the road bends left. Follow this footpath through a squeeze stile and gate and downhill to another stile and the Windermere lakeside path.

8. You can turn left here to walk to Wray and the café if you wish. Otherwise, turn right onto the lakeside path and follow it along the lake's edge all the way back to Claife Viewing Station and the start.

DOG-FRIENDLY AMENITIES

Dogs are welcome at Claife Viewing Station, outside on the Wray estate, and in Joey's Café in the courtyard. Dog-friendly Low Wray Campsite is perfectly placed for exploring Windermere's western shores, and offers a range of accommodation options, from spacious fields to pitch your own tent or park a camper van to pods (accessible pods on request), safari tents and tree tents available to let.

The shore of Windermere at
Low Wray Campsite.

63. Around Tarn Hows

Near Coniston
Cumbria
what3words- driven.
interlude.attending
07919 111620
tarnhows@nationaltrust.org.uk

ABOUT THIS WALK

Distance 2 miles (3.2km)
Difficulty Easy
Terrain Well-surfaced
lakeside trail
Stiles No
Interest Wildlife, history

Set in a low-level valley between Coniston and Hawkshead, surrounded by stunning mountain views, Tarn Hows offers gentler walking than many Lakeland destinations, along with easy route-finding and plenty of interest for all.

This walk takes in a full circumnavigation of the tarn, following the well-made trail that's great for keeping out of the mud during wet weather and also ideal for buggies and wheelchairs, although cycling is not permitted. An off-road Tramper mobility vehicle is also available to hire.

THINGS TO SEE

The tarn is a registered Site of Special Scientific Interest (SSSI), supporting a particularly diverse range of aquatic flora and rare, nationally important, plant habitats. Small herds of Belted Galloway cattle are contributing to conservation through their grazing, which significantly improves the diversity of wildlife in the landscape. You'll also spot the Lake District's famous Herdwick sheep here.

Paws for thought
Animals graze around the tarn throughout the year, so dogs need to be kept on leads at all times.

Other walkies nearby
You can extend this walk to Monk Coniston, at the northern end of Coniston Water, creating an enjoyable loop of about 5 miles (8km). Or, to explore further afield, part of the footpath around Tarn Hows follows the Cumbria Way, a 70-mile (112-km) long-distance track created in the 1970s by a local Ramblers group. Linking Ulverston in the south to Carlisle in the north, the route passes through the heart of the Lake District and offers vast scope for creating loops using surrounding footpaths and bridleways.

**Above: The surfaced lakeside loop.
Opposite: Tarn Hows.**

HOW TO GET HERE

Public transport Take the 505 bus
 service from Hawkshead to Coniston.
 Alight at Hawkshead Hill Chapel and
 follow road signs to Tarn Hows (about 1
 mile/1.6km).
Car 2 miles (3.2km) north-east of
 Coniston and north-west of Hawkshead.
 Signposted from B5285. Please don't
 follow satnav, follow the brown signs.
 what3words- driven.interlude.attending
OS map Explorer OL7
Start/finish Tarn Hows car park,
 what3words- driven.interlude.attending
 grid ref: SD326995

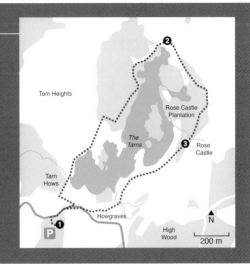

DIRECTIONS

Start/finish: Tarn Hows car park

1. Leave the car park and cross the road, take the
    left fork in the footpath down towards Tarn
    Hows. Go through the gate and follow the
    lakeside path clockwise around the tarn.
    Shortly before you reach the far end you'll
    pass a footpath heading off to the left, if you
    fancy a longer walk, take this up to the
    Cumbria Way where you can loop back
    around Tom Heights or via Yew Tree Tarn.

2. At the far end of the tarn cross a footbridge
    over one of the streams and continue on the
    tarn-side path. Follow this through Rose Castle
    Plantation to the next path junction.

3. Stay on the lakeside path for a level walk back
    to the start point. An alternative is to turn left
    here through the gate and up a hill to the
    viewing point above the tarn. From here follow
    the track back to the road and the short-stay
    car park and walk across the grass parallel to
    the road to return to the start.

DOG-FRIENDLY AMENITIES

The friendly and popular Green Housekeeper Café
(greenhousekeepercafe.co.uk) in nearby Coniston
has lovely outdoor seating where your dog can join
you to enjoy simple, home-cooked fare.

To the north of Tarn Hows, 1 mile (1.6km) from
the beautiful village of Grasmere, The Yan (www.
theyan.co.uk) is a family-run bistro housed in a
converted farmhouse and its outbuildings. You'll
find rooms, self-catering cottages and glamping
here, as well as delicious food, and it's all brilliantly
dog-(and family-)friendly.

64. Elterwater and Loughrigg Tarn

Above: Skelwith Force.

Great Langdale
Near Ambleside
Cumbria
LA22 9JU
01593 437623
langdale@nationaltrust.org.uk

ABOUT THIS WALK

Distance 4.4 miles (7km)
Difficulty Moderate
Terrain Well-maintained trails and country roads. The section between Loughrigg Tarn and Silverdale is rougher
Stiles No
Interest Wildlife, history

Nestled in the valley of Great Langdale, to the south of Grasmere and west of Windermere, the village of Elterwater is a great starting point for exploring this part of the Lake District.

This walk starts in Elterwater and follows the Cumbria Way alongside Great Langdale Beck to the peaceful, small tarn at Elter Water, which derives its name for the Old Norse for 'Lake of the Swans'. You'll often see swans visiting the lake today.

THINGS TO SEE

The pretty Lakeland village of Elterwater lies at the eastern end of Great Langdale, offering easy access to lovely riverside walks. Elterwater was once an important part of the area's gunpowder industry, and the old gunpowder mill lies just to the west of the village.

Paws for thought
You'll find grazing animals out on the fells all year round, as well as wildlife including birds, deer and red squirrels. Dogs should be under close control at all times and on leads near to other animals, as well as during nesting season (1 March–31 July).

Other walkies nearby
A delightful, if challenging, extension to this walk can be made by heading up Loughrigg Fell to the trig point at 1,100ft (335m). Despite being a relatively modest fell by Lake District standards, the views from here are some of the best around.

DIRECTIONS

Start/finish: National Trust Elterwater car park

1. Leave the car park by turning left onto the gravel river path and walking towards Elter Water and Skelwith Force. Follow the path across a meadow and through some woodland to a gate.

2. Walk through the gate and continue on the path as it follows the River Brathay downstream. Continue until you reach Skelwith Force, with a deviation down to the viewing area to your right.

3. Continue along the riverside path, heading downhill to the A593 at Skelwith Bridge.

Above: Skelwith Force.
Opposite: Silverthwaite House.

Public transport Windermere train station is 8 miles (12.9km) from Great Langdale. Catch 555 or 556 Keswick to Ambleside bus, then change to the 516 and alight at Britannia Inn in Elterwater.
Car J36 M6, then A591 from Kendal to Ambleside, A593 from Ambleside to Skelwith Bridge, then take the B5343 towards Great Langdale.
Satnav: LA22 9HP
OS map Explorer OL7
Start/finish National Trust Elterwater car park, LA22 9HP, grid ref: NY328047

4. Turn left and follow the road to the junction; cross and walk up steep Foulstep to the junction.

5. Follow the road right and then turn left onto a road signed as a bridleway. Follow this, passing Tarn Foot Farm and campsite on your left. Take the next left fork, staying on the bridleway and walking across the field to a path junction at the corner of Loughrigg Tarn.

6. Bear left and follow the path around the tarn and through a couple of gates to reach the road.

7. Turn left onto the road and then right up the track past some houses. Please keep your dog on a lead here as there are often chickens running free. Continue past the houses uphill on a stony track. Take the smaller path right just before you reach the wall and follow it over the hill and down the other side. The path turns left and follows the wall and edge of this area of moorland down to the car park at Silverthwaite.

8. Carefully cross the B5343 and walk down the small footpath opposite, through a gate and into the meadow beside the River Brathay. Cross the meadow and turn right onto the riverside path. Follow this back along the outbound route to return to the start.

DOG-FRIENDLY AMENITIES

Silverthwaite House is a grand, five-bedroom house built by suffragist, Amy Sharp, in the early 1900s. Sleeping up to eight people and two dogs, and with extensive wooded grounds, as well as a garden and patio area, it's an inspiring place to stay for visitors of all ages.

The Britannia Inn at Elterwater welcomes dogs and walkers. There's plenty of outdoor seating, good food and rooms; dogs stay free.

For lots more information and inspiration on visiting the Lake District with your dog, visit www. dogfriendlylakedistrict.com

65. Alcock Tarn

Allan Bank
Grasmere
Ambleside
Cumbria
LA22 9QB
01539 435143
allanbank@nationaltrust.org.uk

ABOUT THIS WALK

Distance 3.5 miles (5.6km)
Difficulty Challenging
Terrain Steep and rough
fellside trails both up and
down from the tarn
Stiles No
Interest Wildlife, history

The Lakeland village of Grasmere maintains its picturesque charm despite its popularity, which draws tourists in their thousands over the summer months. Described by William Wordsworth as 'the loveliest spot that man hath ever found', it's easy to see why.

Though fairly short, this loop of the fells above Grasmere packs in plenty of ascent, rugged terrain and a wonderful sense of being on a remote, mountain adventure.

THINGS TO SEE

Thirlmere pipeline runs over the aqueduct that crosses Greenhead Ghyll. It has been carrying water from Thirlmere 95 miles (153km) south to Manchester since 1894. The whole system is gravity-fed with no pumps along its route.

DOG-FRIENDLY AMENITIES

The rambling, creeper-clad country house hotel at Lancrigg is nestled in 30 acres (12ha) of gardens and woodlands, offering a tranquil and relaxing place to stay and soak up the beautiful surroundings of the Easedale valley. Dogs are welcome in eight of the main rooms and the four barn rooms, as well as the Poet's Café Bar. (www.lancrigg.co.uk)

Paws for thought
The rocky sections of this walk can become slippery in wet weather, and the softer ground can be boggy. Dogs must be kept on leads around grazing animals and during bird nesting season (1 March–31 July).

Other walkies nearby
From Grasmere, follow the bridleway up Easedale, climbing up alongside Sour Milk Gill to reach Easedale Tarn, a wonderful spot for a picnic or a swim. Level paths also trace the lakes at Grasmere and Rydal Water for a less challenging but still thoroughly enjoyable walk.

Above: Alcock Tarn.
Opposite: On the woodland trail at Allan Bank and Grasmere

HOW TO GET HERE

Public transport Use the Stagecoach Lancaster–Kendal bus service 555, or the open-top 599 service that runs between Bowness and Grasmere. Windermere is the closest train station.

Car From the north, follow the A591 south from Keswick to Grasmere, follow the signs for Grasmere village.

OS map Explorer OL7

Start/finish Red Bank Road car park, LA22 9SW, grid ref: NY335073

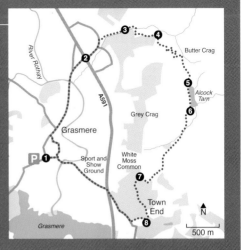

DIRECTIONS

Start/finish: Red Bank Road car park

1. Turn right out of the car park and follow the road past Tweedies Bar to Church Stile Road. Turn left and walk past the gingerbread shop and right onto College Street. At the far end, turn right onto Broadgate and follow this out of Grasmere to the busy A591.

2. Carefully cross and follow the road opposite to the right of the Swan Hotel. After about half a mile (0.8km) you'll see a sign pointing to Greenhead Gill and Alcock Tarn; turn right here and follow the smaller road uphill next to a stream.

3. At the top of the lane, turn right onto a path across a footbridge. Follow the path steeply uphill, turning right, then left and following the wall up to a path junction.

4. Turn right and follow this path as it zig-zags uphill and around to the left of a rocky outcrop. The path flattens out now as you walk through a (sometimes wet) area to the gate.

5. Go through the gate and follow the path to the right of Alcock Tarn. This is a wonderful place to let your dog have a swim while you paddle or picnic.

6. Follow the path through a gap in the wall and down the fairly steep and rocky path off the fell. Walk through another metal gate and down into the valley. After a zig-zagging section you come to a path junction in the trees.

7. Turn left and follow the path through woodland until you reach a small road.

8. Turn right and follow the road downhill; turn right again at the next junction and follow the slightly larger road down past Dove Cottage and the Wordsworth Trust Museum, to reach the A591. Cross the road and turn left at the roundabout following the B5287 into Grasmere. Turn left at the church to return to the start.

66. Aira Force and Ullswater

Near Watermillock
Penrith
Cumbria
CA11 0JS
01768 482067
ullswater@nationaltrust.org.uk

ABOUT THIS WALK

Distance 4.2 miles (6.7km)
Difficulty Challenging
Terrain Well-maintained but
steep and stepped trails
around the waterfall. The
Gowbarrow Fell section can
be muddy.
Stiles Yes
Interest Wildlife, water

At 9 miles (14.5km) long by half a mile (0.8km) wide, Ullswater is the second largest lake in the Lake District. This gleaming stretch of water snakes through the fells from Pooley Bridge in the north, through a peaceful patchwork of fields edged by dry-stone walls, to Glenridding in the south.

Here the ridges and summits of St Sunday Crag, Dollywaggon Pike and Helvellyn rise impressively on the skyline. While along Ullswater's northern shore, the mighty falls of Aira Force channel water from the fells to the lake. This walk begins with a tour of the falls before following the course of Aira Beck upstream to explore the peaceful open grasslands of Gowbarrow Fell, with its superb Lakeland views.

THINGS TO SEE

With their russet fur, bright eyes and fluffy ears, red squirrels are a delight to see, and the Lake District is one of its few remaining strongholds in England. Look for them amongst the branches as you wander through the pinewoods at Aira Force and also at Grasmere and Borrowdale further afield in the Lake District.

Above: The dramatic 65-foot waterfall at Aira Force.
Opposite: Over the bridge at Aira Force.

Paws for thought
You'll find animals grazing on the Lake District fells throughout the year. Please keep dogs on leads near other animals and during bird-nesting season (1 March–31 July).

Other walkies nearby
The Ullswater Way is a 20-mile (32-km) walking route that circumnavigates the entire lake at Ullswater. It can be undertaken as a full day walk in one go, or divided up into shorter sections combined with a boat trip or bus ride. You'll find villages and places to eat and drink dotted all along this enjoyable, low-level route.

HOW TO GET HERE

Public transport Penrith train station is closest (10 miles/16km). Use the Stagecoach bus service 508 that runs between Penrith and Windermere (runs from Easter to end of autumn half-term only).

Car Approach via Windermere and Bowness (A592) and Ambleside (The Struggle) for a scenic drive down the steep windy Kirkstone Pass. Or from J40 of the M6 and Keswick/Penrith on the A66.

Satnav: CA11 0JS
OS map Explorer OL5
Start/finish Aira Force car park, CA11 0JS, grid ref: NY400200

DIRECTIONS

Start/finish: Aira Force car park

1. Take the waterfall path out of the top of the car park and follow it through the picnic field. Where the path splits, stay left and follow the path through the arboretum to a gate in the wall with superb views towards Ullswater. Don't go through the gate; turn right and follow the path down some steps to the viewing area at the base of the waterfall.

2. Cross the small bridge and climb the steps to the left. At the top you can walk left to the upper bridge for another view of the waterfall, return to this point if you do. Follow the main path upstream, with the river to your left. Follow this path for about half a mile (0.8km) through a gate and across farmland to reach a path junction.

3. Turn right and follow the path with the wall to your left, through the fell gate and out onto Gowbarrow Park. Follow the well-maintained path uphill across the fell, with the wall to your left. Near the top, the path flattens out and bears right away from the wall to reach the summit and trig point of Gowbarrow Fell.

4. Leaving the summit, you follow the path back left towards the wall and downhill. The path curves to the right, passing the ruin of an old shooting lodge and leading around the edge of the fell. Follow this path towards Ullswater until you cross a stile and reach the stone memorial seat with amazing views over Ullswater.

5. Recross the stile and turn left, following the path downhill along the edge of the fell towards the woodland around Aira Force. At the edge of the fell you join another path near Lyulph's Tower; carry on walking towards the woodland. Just before you reach the woods, take the left fork, through a gate and through the glade back to the start.

Dog looking at the view from the Gowbarrow Fell trail.

DOG-FRIENDLY AMENITIES

Truly dog- and family-friendly, Another Place, set on the shores of Ullswater, offers a wonderful balance of relaxation and easy access to outdoor adventure. You'll find watersports, swimming (indoors in a pool or wild in the lake), great food and plenty of space here. Rooms at Another Place are split between a Georgian house and contemporary modern space, and there are also lakeside glamping options. (https://another.place)

67. Hadrian's Wall

Near Bardon Mill
Hexham
Northumberland
NE47 6NN
01434 344525
housesteads@nationaltrust.org.uk

ABOUT THIS WALK

Distance 8 miles (12.9km)
Difficulty Challenging
Terrain Well maintained
footpaths with steep and
rocky sections. Can be
muddy in the wet
Stiles Yes
Interest History, wildlife

Built on the orders of the Emperor Hadrian around AD 122, Hadrian's Wall took 15,000 men 16 years to build. Making strategic use of the natural igneous dolerite outcrop known as the Whin Sill escarpment, this is the Roman Empire's best-maintained outpost in northern Europe, and a UNESCO World Heritage Site.

This walk explores Hadrian's Wall country, starting at Housesteads Fort and looping one of the richest parts of the country for Roman archaeology. You'll also be able to get close to the vast wall affording a full appreciation of the scale of the undertaking.

THINGS TO SEE

Housesteads Roman Fort offers a fascinating insight into Roman military life. Here, you can discover the past behind the archaeological remains, explore the stone walls around the village south of the fort and imagine how the different chambers and rooms would have looked – you'll also get the chance to see some of the oldest toilets in Britain.

Paws for thought
Please keep dogs on a lead and under close control at all times. The route is on open grazing land for livestock, used all year round, and is an important habitat for ground-nesting birds.

Other walkies nearby
A vast network of trails explores the dramatic landscape to the north of Hadrian's Wall. Wander around the peaceful Greenlee Lough, or follow the Pennine Way as it covers the final miles of its 268-mile (431-km) journey from Edale in the Peak District to Kirk Yetholm, just across the Scottish border.

Above: The Romans held dogs in high esteem and our four-legged friends are welcomed at Hadrian's Wall.

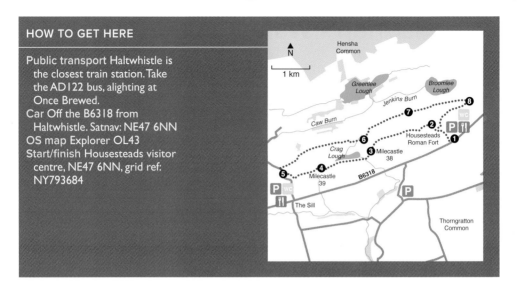

DIRECTIONS

Start/finish: Housesteads visitor centre

1. Leave the visitor centre and car park and follow the main path uphill towards
   Housesteads Fort. Walk to the left of the fort, following the path to join the
   Hadrian's Wall path in the woodland at the top of the hill.

2. Turn left and follow the wall path along the ridge, passing Milecastle 37 and dropping
   into the dip at Milecastle 38. Follow the farm track across the wall at this point.

3. Continue to follow the wall path, now on the north side of the wall. Walk through
   Crag Lough Woods, through the dip where the famous Sycamore Gap tree once
   stood and up to Milecastle 39.

4. Follow the wall path until you reach the road. Turn right and follow this to Steel Rigg car park.

5. Walk past the car park and down the road for another 100 yards to a stile with a footpath sign on the right.

6. Cross the stile and follow the track towards Hotbank Farm. Walk past the Peatrigg Plantation to reach the track junction near Hotbank Farm.

7. Stay on the track heading left and following footpath signs. Walk to the left of the plantation to reach a junction where the Pennine Way National Trail crosses your path.

8. Continue on the same path, walking parallel to Hadrian's Wall (on your right). Carry on through another small plantation and up through a gate to the Hadrian's Wall path. Cross the wall and turn right, following the path back to Housesteads Fort. Stay to the left of the fort to return to the outbound path. Turn left onto this and follow it back to the start.

Above: The footpath along the wall.
Opposite: Hadrian's Wall, Crag Lough can be seen in the distance.

DOG-FRIENDLY AMENITIES

Dogs are welcome throughout the site, and in the café at Housesteads visitor centre, which serves a range of hot and cold food and drinks and has both indoor and outdoor seating.

Situated right next to Hadrian's Wall, Peel Cottage is a sturdy single-storey cottage, perfect for a couple and up to two dogs. It was built in the 1850s and a plaque above the door records its opening by the late Queen Mother. A cosy hideaway at any time of the year, this is the perfect base from which to explore the wilds of Northumberland (NT Holidays).

Yorkshire & North East

68. Estate and Castle Walk, Wentworth

Wentworth Castle Gardens
Park Drive
Barnsley
South Yorkshire
S75 3EN
01226 323070
wentworthcastlegardens@
nationaltrust.org.uk

ABOUT THIS WALK

Distance 3.2 miles (5.1km)
Difficulty Easy
Terrain Mostly grassy or gravelled path, undulating but not steep
Stiles No
Interest History, wildlife

Wentworth was founded on the proceeds of the slave trade; a statement of wealth and power by its creator, the royal diplomat Thomas Wentworth. But today, 300 years later, this place that was once the privilege of the wealthy few has been reimagined as one that benefits many.

In a partnership between the National Trust, Barnsley Council and Northern College, Wentworth Castle Gardens is working to explore how it can be relevant to more people, valuing and celebrating the diversity of local communities. This walk heads out into the 500 acres (202ha) of parkland that surrounds Wentworth Castle, exploring the extravagant fantasy landscape and its collection of temples, water features, avenues and trees, including the Rotunda, Serpentine Bridge, the Sun Monument, the Gothic folly at Stainborough Castle and the formal garden.

THINGS TO SEE

There's always lots on for the community to get involved with at Wentworth. From workshops with local crafters, toy swaps and guided walks with a National Trust ranger, to a beginner-friendly running group, there's something to suit everyone.

Above: Originally built in the mid-1700s, the Rotunda is a copy of an ancient temple at Tivoli in Rome.
Opposite: The Sun Monument.

Paws for thought
Dogs are not allowed in the playground area and only assistance dogs are allowed inside the Conservatory.

Other walkies nearby
There's an extensive network of footpaths and bridleways to explore around Stainborough, to the south of Wentworth. Or, to the north of the park, the 9-mile (14.5-km) Dove Valley Trail runs on a former railway line from Silkstone Common towards Wombwell, passing through Dodworth and Worsbrough and forming part of the Trans Pennine Trail.

HOW TO GET HERE

Public transport Dodworth
train station is about 1.5 miles
(2.4km) from Wentworth
Castle Gardens.
Car Exit the M1 at J37, heading
towards Barnsley and follow
signs. Satnav: S75 3EN
OS map Explorer 278
Start/finish Lowe Lane car park,
S75 3EN, grid ref: SE320034

DIRECTIONS

Start/finish: Lowe Lane car park

1. Walk out of the car park and past the visitor reception, turning
    left and following the path to the parkland entry gate near the
    Long Barn Café. Turn left through the green gate and follow the
    grassy path, marked with pink arrows, across the parkland.

2. At the bottom of the hill you reach another green gate, turn
    right before the gate and continue to follow the pink arrows.
    Walk along the edge of the parkland, following a green fence on
    your left.

3. Pass the Serpentine Lake on your left and continue along the
    path to a wooden seat at the edge of some woodland. Turn right
    and follow the path around the edge of the woods until you
    reach a path junction.

4. Turn left, still following the pink arrows, and walk along the
    winding path to the Rotunda.

5. Leave the Rotunda and head back towards the parkland,
    following the path with the Shed Plantation to your left. Follow
    the path as it curves to the left, with the trees to your left and
    the parkland to your right. Continue to the far end of the
    plantation.

6. Continue on the path, curving to the left, walking through a metal gate and heading downhill towards Warren Wood. Go through the gate and turn right following the path to the Duke of Argyll monument.

7. Walk past the monument and go through the gate out of the woods and then head uphill across the parkland to the Great South Avenue. Turn left and follow the path up the avenue to reach the parkland gate back into the castle gardens.

8. Go through the gate to reach a T-junction in the path around the formal lawn. The next section of the walk loops the formal gardens; if you'd rather not, turn right and follow the path to point 12. To continue the walk around the gardens, turn left, following the path along the edge of the gardens and across the ha-ha bridge. Continue walking along the left edge of the gardens, past the Earl's Seat to reach the Sun Monument.

9. Carry on to Stainborough Castle on your right.

10. Follow the path around the castle and through the woods back to the formal gardens. Walk past the Victorian flower garden on your right to reach the Union Jack Garden.

11. Go through this and back over the ha-ha bridge to return to the park gate at point 8. Follow the path in front of you curving left past the castle and walking through the John Arnold Garden.

12. Finish off the walk by turning right and following the path past the Long Barn Café on your left to return to your outbound path, turn left and walk past the visitor reception to the car park.

DOG-FRIENDLY AMENITIES

There is dog-friendly indoor and outdoor seating in the Long Barn Café.

Wentworth Castle gardens.

69. Nostell Priory Obelisk Walk

Doncaster Road
Nostell
Near Wakefield
West Yorkshire
WF4 1QE
01924 863892
nostell@nationaltrust.org.uk

ABOUT THIS WALK

Distance 2.8 miles (4.5km)
Difficulty Moderate
Terrain Gravel and grassy paths, some sections of tarmac. Undulating but no steep hills
Stiles No
Interest History, wildlife

A masterpiece of 18th-century Palladian architecture, and built on the site of a 12th-century Augustinian priory, Nostell was a grand statement of wealth and importance by its creators, the Winn family. Approaching the magnificent frontage of the house, it's easy to imagine the elite of Georgian society sweeping up the long, curving drive in all their finery.

Outside the house, 300 acres (121ha) of landscaped gardens, stables and parkland await exploration, including meadows and grassland, leafy woodland and serene lakes. This walk loops the estate, sampling everything it has to offer. Starting at the car park, you'll follow paths and grassy trails to reach the eye-catching obelisk at the furthest point of the estate. From here you'll return through the park and woodland, skirting the lakes and passing by the house to finish.

THINGS TO SEE

The house at Nostell is a trove of fascinating treasures, including paintings by Brueghel, Hogarth and Kauffmann and a longcase clock by John Harrison, the man who solved the problem of calculating longitude at sea.

Paws for thought
Dogs aren't allowed in the house or garden (including the playground), the Treasure House or the front section of the Courtyard Café. Please be aware that there is a seasonal electric fence in use and that cattle may be grazing in the fields.

Other walkies nearby
The wellness trail at Nostell pinpoints ten new benches, each set in a tranquil position in the parkland such as under a tree canopy or by a lake. At each bench, you'll find words of advice and mindful activities to help you stop and appreciate the present moment. This trail was created in collaboration with Mindful Movers, a Wakefield-based mental health walking group. Pick up a trail sheet from the ticket office in the Stables Courtyard.

Above: Nostell Priory.
Overleaf: The Obelisk Lodge.

HOW TO GET HERE

Public transport Fitzwilliam train station is 1.5 miles (2.4km) away, but not easily accessed on foot. There is a regular bus service (496) from Wakefield to Upton via Fitzwilliam; the 485 also stops at Nostell.
Car On A638 towards Doncaster. Satnav: WF4 1QE
OS map Explorer 278
Start/finish Nostell car park, WF4 1QE, grid ref: SE409171

[Map showing the route at Nostell with labelled features: Obelisk Lodge, Obelisk Park, Priory Wood, Lower Lake, Weir, Middle Lake, Upper Lake, Nostell Park, Nostell Priory, Engine Wood, Wragby, A638, and numbered waypoints 1–4. Scale: 200 m. N indicates north.]

DOG-FRIENDLY AMENITIES

Nostell is very dog-friendly, and dogs are welcome almost everywhere. They can be off the lead but under close control across the parkland and in the dedicated 'dog run' but must be kept on a short lead in busy areas, including the courtyard and the Lower Lake, as well as any fields where animals are grazing. Dogs are also welcome in the rear section of the Courtyard Café.

DIRECTIONS

Start/finish: Nostell car park

1. Follow the path out of the far end of the car park, walking past the overflow car park and across a grassy area and then across an area of parkland planted with some trees. Reach a surfaced path and turn left, following it past a small lake on the left and through a gate to a path junction. Turn right and follow this around to the right to a band of trees.

2. Turn left and follow the grassy path uphill with trees to your right. Continue on this path until you reach the Obelisk Lodge.

3. Continue to follow the grassy path along the edge of the woodland. The path curves to the left and heads downhill until you reach a gate and the surfaced path on the shore of Lower Lake. Turn left and follow this path along the lake shore and then through the woods to a path junction.

4. Turn right and follow this through the woods, past the end of the lake and then over Boathouse Bridge. Follow the path as it curves right and walk past the front of the main house. Curve left passing the stables where you can leave the route to visit the café. Finish by walking down the main track, past the visitor reception and back to the start.

70. Seven Bridges Walk at Fountains Abbey

Fountains
Ripon
North Yorkshire
HG4 3DY
01765 608888
fountainsabbey@nationaltrust.org.uk

ABOUT THIS WALK

Distance 4 miles (6.4km)
Difficulty Moderate
Terrain Tracks, paths and
road on the estate.
Undulating but not very
hilly; can get wet and muddy
in winter
Stiles No
Interest History, wildlife

With its 900-year-old abbey and Georgian water gardens surrounded by 800 acres (324ha) of grounds, all set within wild North Yorkshire countryside, the World Heritage Site of Fountains Abbey is an extraordinary place.

This walk explores the wilder and more rustic side of the estate. Stride across the medieval deer park looking out for red, fallow and sika deer, explore a river valley and follow winding trails through ancient deciduous woodland, home to a wide variety of wildlife.

THINGS TO SEE

The majestic ruins of Fountains Abbey are the largest monastic ruins in the country. The abbey was founded in 1132 by 13 Benedictine monks from St Mary's in York, seeking a simpler and more peaceful existence.

Paws for thought

You'll encounter deer and cows grazing across the estate so dogs should be on leads. Dogs (other than assistance dogs) aren't allowed in Fountains Hall, the Porter's Lodge, Studley Royal tea-room or the children's play area.

Other walkies nearby

There's a wealth of wonderful dog-friendly walks at Fountains Abbey, including the 2.5-mile (4-km) Ancient Trees Walk, the 5-mile (8-km) Boundary Walk and, for those looking for a longer day out, the 8-mile (12.9-km) Ripon to Fountains Abbey Walk.

DOG-FRIENDLY AMENITIES

Dogs on leads are welcome in all outdoor spaces throughout the grounds. They can also join you in the restaurant at the visitor centre.

To the north of Fountains Abbey, near to the village of Masham, the delightful Hideaway Cottage is a perfectly-positioned cosy base from which to explore the Yorkshire Dales. Blending the original 18th-century farmworker's cottage with a contemporary living space, it sleeps two people and dogs are welcome.
www.hideawaymasham.co.uk

If you'd prefer to camp, and you're visiting over the summer months, Through the Kissing Gate is a dog-friendly, 28-day campsite nestled in a stunning location on the edge of the Fountains Abbey estate. More details at hipcamp.com

The Seven Bridges Valley.

HOW TO GET HERE

Public transport Regular buses from the nearest station at Harrogate to Ripon. Bus Service 139 runs from Ripon to Fountains Abbey on Mondays, Thursdays and Saturdays all year.
Car Follow the brown signs for Fountains Abbey from the A1. Fountains is a short distance off the B6265 between Pateley Bridge and Ripon. Satnav: HG4 3DY
OS map Explorer 298
Start/finish Fountains Abbey Visitor Centre, HG4 3DY, grid ref: SE272687

The bank of River Skell at Fountains Abbey.

DIRECTIONS

Start/finish: Fountains Abbey Visitor Centre

1. Leave the car park and follow the bridleway parallel to the main drive, signed to St Mary's Church. Go through the gates into the deer park and reach the church.

2. Pass to the right of the church and follow the path along the avenue to a cross-roads. Turn right and follow the path to the edge of the lake.

3. Follow the path past the lake and across a bridge flanked by sphinx statues. Continue to a left turn onto the Seven Bridges Valley Trail.

4. Walk up the valley, heading for the first stone arch bridge. Cross and carry on along this trail, crossing four more bridges and passing through a metal gate, reaching the Chinese Wood.

5. Carry straight on, then cross a green footbridge to your right. Once across, walk up the hill to a path junction in the woods.

6. Turn right and follow the bridleway along the edge of the Mackershaw Plantation, with a large field to your right. Keep the wall to your right and continue until you reach Mackershaw Lodge.

7. Walk through the lodge via the two gates on the left-hand side of the building. Follow the path ahead across Mackershaw Deer Park, heading downhill and through a gate. Continue until you return to the outbound path by the lake and the entrance to the Seven Bridges Valley Trail. Cross the bridge with the sphinxes and retrace your outbound route down the avenue and past the church back to the start.

71. Beningbrough Parkland and River Walk

Beningbrough
York
North Yorkshire
YO30 IDD
01904 472027
beningbrough@nationaltrust.org.uk

ABOUT THIS WALK

Distance 3.5 miles (5.6km)
Difficulty Easy
Terrain Fairly flat on riverside and estate footpaths
Stiles No
Interest History, wildlife

Beningbrough Hall's story took shape in the early 18th century when John Bourchier, a wealthy landowner, inherited the estate and commissioned the construction of the hall to replace a smaller, earlier house. Completed in 1716, it would have looked much as it does today.

In the 1800s, the hall passed from the Bourchiers to the Dawnay family, who undertook extensive remodelling, including installing electricity. In 1916, the estate was purchased by Lord and Lady Chesterfield. Barring a short period during the Second World War, when Beningbrough was requisitioned as a billet for RAF air crews, Lady Chesterfield – Enid Edith Scudamore-Stanhope – an heiress and racehorse breeder, lived at the hall until her death in 1957. This walk explores the wider estate, following clear paths through parkland and woodland and returning along a stretch of the River Ouse.

THINGS TO SEE

Often, dogs aren't permitted in formal gardens, but they're welcomed at Beningbrough. Wander around the 8 acres (3.2ha) of stunning gardens admiring many varieties of flowers, herbaceous borders, ancient trees, a walled garden filled with fruit trees and a new Mediterranean Garden.

Paws for thought

You'll often find cattle grazing on the estate, and at times there may be calves and a bull. Please keep to the paths in the parkland. Dogs must be kept under close control in the parkland, and on a short lead in all other areas.

Other walkies nearby

There's a range of wonderful waymarked walks at Beningbrough. Follow the blue waymarkers around the 1-mile (1.6-km) Woodland Larch Walk or the pink waymarkers around the 1.9-mile (3-km) Beningbrough Newton Walk.

Above: Dogs are welcome in the formal gardens.
Overleaf: The south front of Beningbrough Hall.

Public transport Nearest train station is York (8 miles/12.9km). Reliance bus service 29 stops at Newton-on-Ouse, 1.7 miles (2.7km) from Beningbrough Hall. Car Beningbrough is signposted off the A19 and A59; cars travel via Newton-on-Ouse. Satnav: Please follow signs rather than the satnav.
OS map Explorer 290
Start/finish Beningbrough Hall car park, YO30 1DD, grid ref: SE518585

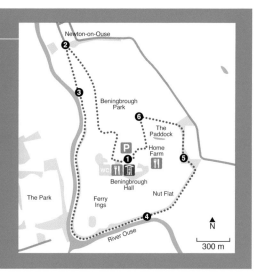

DOG-FRIENDLY AMENITIES

Dogs are welcome in the majority of the formal gardens, including the walled garden, pergola, south lawn, east and west formal gardens, double and south borders, as well as on paths in the parkland. You can also take your dog into the shop and sit at designated tables in the restaurant, or in the restaurant's outdoor seating area and the brew house.

DIRECTIONS

Start/finish: Beningbrough Hall car park

1. Start by walking along the path towards Beningbrough Hall. Turn right in front of the hall and follow the lime tree avenue to the junction with the driveway. Turn left and follow this to Newton Lodge at the edge of the estate.

2. Turn left just before the lodge and follow a smaller path through a gate to another path junction. Turn left and follow this path downhill to join the riverside path with some trees to your left.

3. Continue to follow the path along the River Ouse, with Beningbrough Park to your left. Walk past the Victorian water tower and follow the river around to the left. There is a river beach on the bend, and the River Nidd joins the Ouse opposite. Carry on walking along the river path to reach two sets of gates on the left, just before the river bends to the right.

4. Walk through these gates, bearing left away from the river and following the path through a linear wood towards Beningbrough Lodge on New Road. You turn left just before you reach the road and follow the path left through the woodland to reach the driveway.

5. Cross and follow the path opposite through Pike Ponds Plantation. The path curves to the left near the ponds and leads back towards the hall. Continue to a track junction near the picnic area.

6. Turn sharp left and follow this track through gates and across another track to reach Home Farm. Turn right and walk with the farm on your left along the path; it curves left and brings you back to the car park and the start.

72. Old Saltburn and Warsett Hill Walk

Near Ravenscar
North Yorkshire
TS12 1HH
01915 293161
yorkshirecoast@nationaltrust.org.uk

ABOUT THIS WALK

Distance 4.4 miles (7.1km)
Difficulty Moderate
Terrain Coast path and
inland farm tracks, often
muddy
Stiles Yes
Interest Coast, wildlife,
history

The stretch of coast at Old Saltburn in Cleveland is part of the Yorkshire Heritage Coast, a landscape sculpted by the sea and a long history of human use. Taking in a Roman defensive sight station on Warsett Hill, a series of locally-inspired sculptures, the remnants of an industrial and mining past, and a blaze of colourful coastal wild flowers in summer, this is a place of fascinating contrasts.

Starting on the seafront at pretty Saltburn-by-the-Sea, a popular seaside town in Victorian times that still boasts a pier and cliff lift, this walk heads out along the coast path. Near to where the route turns inland, you'll pass Guibal Fanhouse, which once extracted stale air from the mines below. The return trip explores the open fields and farmland across the headland, climbing to the top of Warsett Hill, where there are outstanding panoramic views of coast and countryside.

THINGS TO SEE

The grasslands and boulder-clay cliff along this stretch of the coast support a stunning variety of coastal flora, including wild flowers that bloom over the summer months. Look for hemp-agrimony, pyramidal orchid, fragrant orchid, bird's-foot trefoil and betony.

Above: Remains of the Guibal Fanhouse.
Overleaf: Circle by Richard Farrington.

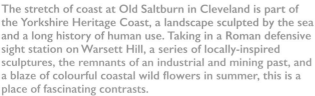

Paws for thought
Dogs should be kept on leads in areas where there are grazing animals, and during bird nesting times.

Other walkies nearby
A lovely, circular walk from the visitor centre at Ravenscar discovers the area's history and visits the old Peak Alum Works. You'll also pass an abandoned brickworks and disused Victorian railway bridge, as well as taking in the fine views across Robin Hood's Bay. The walk is 2.3 miles (3.7km) but has options to shorten or lengthen it.

HOW TO GET HERE

Public transport Saltburn station is
   less than a mile (1.6km) from the
   start of this walk.
Car The car park is just off A174 on
   the seafront. Satnav: TS12 1HF
OS map Explorer OL26
Start/finish Saltburn seafront car
   park, TS12 1HF, grid ref:
   NZ668215

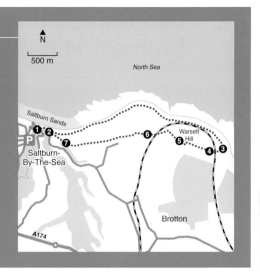

DOG-FRIENDLY AMENITIES

Taste in Saltburn is a well-liked,
dog-friendly café serving snacks,
meals and drinks. 01287 623777

DIRECTIONS

Start/finish: Saltburn seafront car park

1. Leave the car park and cross the road to the seafront. Turn right and follow the road with the sea to your left. The road curves right, away from the sea and you come to a National Trust and Cleveland Way sign to your left.

2. Turn left, joining the coast path and the Cleveland Way and follow this footpath along the coast for about 2 miles (3.2km). Cross the stile opposite the Fanhouse.

3. Follow this path inland over the stile and bearing left across a field to the railway crossing. Carefully cross using the stiles. Do not cross at the field gate.

4. Continue on the footpath across the fields and over stiles; climb up the steep hill to the trig point and summit of Warsett Hill.

5. Head down the hill in the direction of Saltburn. Follow the fence initially then bear left where the path forks; continue down to the railway crossing. Use the stiles to cross the railway.

6. Follow the path along the edge of the next few large fields, crossing an intersection near a cottage. Continue to a fork in the trail near a row of cottages.

7. Stay left, walking with the row of cottages on your right, and continue until you get back to the road at point 2. Turn right onto the road and return to the start.

73. Ormesby Hall and Lower Estate Walk

Ladgate Lane
Middlesbrough
North Yorkshire
TS3 0SR
01642 328904
ormesbyhall@nationaltrust.org.uk

ABOUT THIS WALK

Distance 3.2 miles (5.1km)
Difficulty Moderate
Terrain Woodland and parkland trails; can be muddy in wet weather. Fairly flat
Stiles No
Interest Wildlife, urban escape, history

The grand Georgian mansion at Ormesby Hall stands surrounded by 240 acres (97ha) of parkland and farmland – an oasis of green and calm set within Middlesborough's industrial cityscape.

This walk draws a figure-of-eight either side of the busy A174, which is safely crossed via a bridge and sits lower than the surrounding land so that it cannot be seen from the house. The first half of the walk takes you around the upper estate, through Crow Wood and across open fields and farmland. The higher ground here boasts impressive views of Ormesby Hall and Middlesbrough. The second loop heads north from the hall, around the former Pennyman estate, exploring woodland that's a haven for wildlife and passing St Cuthbert's Church.

THINGS TO SEE

The parkland at Ormesby Hall.

The gardens offer a peaceful and engaging place for ambling with your dog – and they're great for getting children interested in plants, too. Year-round colours and textures from a range of native and ornamental plants means there's always something to catch the eye.

Paws for thought

Only assistance dogs are allowed inside the house, the inside seating at the café and the second-hand bookshop. You'll find lots of farm animals grazing on the wider estate, so dogs should be kept on leads throughout.

Other walkies nearby

As well as the two routes that the above walk combines, the short estate walk takes in an enjoyable 1.2-mile (2-km) loop of the grounds nearest to the house.

HOW TO GET HERE

Public transport Marton train
station is 1.5 miles (2.4km) away.
Car From A19 take A174 to A172.
From Guisborough, the hall is
west of the A171. Please follow
the brown signs. Satnav: TS3 0SR
OS map Explorer OL26
Start/finish Ormesby Hall car park,
TS3 OSR, grid ref: NZ527167

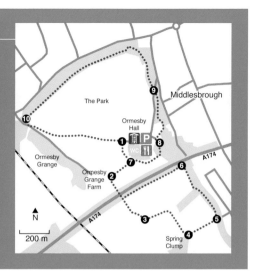

Ormesby Hall.

DIRECTIONS

Start/finish: Ormesby Hall car park

1. Start by walking out of the end of the car park
   towards the A174. Walk to the edge of the
   trees where you reach a farm track. Turn right
   and follow the track to a fork at the edge of
   Ormesby Grange Farm.

2. Bear left and follow the track across the
   footbridge over the A174 and into the large
   field opposite. Continue straight ahead and
   round to the left of a small clump of trees.

3. Follow the path to the left. Walk with the
   hedge to your left and the field to your right.
   Carry on around a bend to the right until you
   reach the edge of the woods known as
   Spring Clump.

4. The path splits here, turn left and follow the
   path along the edge of the field with the
   hedge to your left. Continue across the field to
   the edge of Crow Wood.

5. Turn left and follow the path through the
   edge of Crow Wood, with the beck on your
   right and the fields out to the left. Continue
   until you reach the corner of the field below
   the A174.

6. Follow the path left along the edge of the field, with the A174 to your right. Continue onto the track until you reach your outbound path. Turn right, re-crossing the bridge and following the track back towards the end of the car park. This is the end of the upper estate walk.

7. Don't turn left into the car park; carry on walking along the track as it curves to the right. You pass the back of the house on your left and walk into the woodland; the church is off to your right.

8. At the fork of the track turn right, walking past the stables (on your left) and along the drive towards a bridge. Just before you reach the bridge, turn left through a gate, and follow a path through woodland until you reach a tarmac road.

9. Cross and follow the path opposite through a gate into woodland, with the park to your left. Stay left at the fork in the path and follow the trail around the edge of the park until you pass through a gate to get to the driveway.

10. Turn left and follow the driveway through the clump of trees and back to the start.

DOG-FRIENDLY AMENITIES

Dogs are very welcome in the garden, woodland walks, parkland, the café's outdoor seating terrace and the courtyards. You'll find water bowls outside the café and dog waste bins across the estate.

74. Durham Riverside and Crook Hall Gardens

Frankland Lane
Sidegate
Durham
DH1 5SZ
01913 831832
crookhallgardens@nationaltrust.org.uk

ABOUT THIS WALK

Distance 4.8 miles (7.7km)
Difficulty Moderate
Terrain Mostly pavement
or the riverside path, some
steps and a couple of
short hills
Stiles No
Interest Urban escape,
history, gardens

Caught within a meander of the River Wear, central Durham is surrounded by water on three sides. Founded in 995 by Anglo-Saxon monks fleeing the Vikings, the church built by the monks to house the relics of St Cuthbert lasted only a century. Following the Norman Conquest, it was replaced by Durham Cathedral, which, alongside Durham Castle, is now a UNESCO World Heritage Site.

This walk can be started from Crook Hall Gardens, or nearby if you're not visiting the gardens and medieval hall itself, and takes in a beautiful stretch of the river. Enjoy the peace of the riverside path and avoid the busy city streets, while taking in some of Durham's most famous landmarks.

THINGS TO SEE

Bill Bryson described Durham as 'wonderful – a perfect little city' in his book, *Notes from a Small Island*. It's a great place to spend a weekend exploring, with lots of dog-friendly establishments. The city boasts a wealth of architectural treasures, from its Romanesque cathedral and fascinating Norman castle to Crook Hall itself.

Paws for thought

Only assistance dogs are allowed in the medieval hall. The car park is for those visiting Crook Hall Gardens and café only. If you're only planning on following the riverside walk, please use nearby Sidegate pay-and-display car park or travel by train. The gardens are closed over the winter months.

Intriguing paths lead you through acres of interlinked gardens, each with its own character and style.

Other walkies nearby
The Weardale Way runs for around 45 miles (72km) between Cowshill and Sunderland Bridge in County Durham (near Croxdale), offering waymarked walking through the heart of Durham city and out into the countryside to the north and south.

DIRECTIONS

Start/finish: Crook Hall Gardens car park

1. This walk starts at the National Trust Crook Hall Gardens, we suggest that you walk a loop of the gardens before or after this longer riverside walk. To follow the riverside walk, head out of the car park to Frankland Lane. Turn right and follow this with the River Wear to the left. Bear left onto Framwelgate Waterside. Follow the

Public transport Crook Hall Gardens is a 10–12 minute walk from Durham train station. Follow signs to the city centre to join the riverside trail.
Car Crook Hall Gardens is signposted from the A690. Turn left off Milburngate into Framwelgate Waterside and drive through the multi-storey car park. Pass the Durham Sidegate pay-and-display car park before reaching the entrance to Crook Hall Gardens car park. Satnav: DH1 5SZ
OS map Explorer 308
Start/finish Crook Hall Gardens car park, DH1 5SZ, grid ref: NZ274430

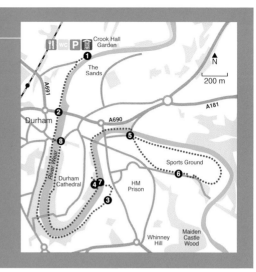

riverside path past a footbridge and under the A690 road bridge where the footpath splits away from the road.

2. Follow the riverside path along the bank of the River Wear. Walk under Framwelgate Bridge and continue along the river path to Prebends Bridge. Don't cross but continue walking on the river path past the footbridge and left as the river curves. The path starts to move right, away from the river and uphill, through St Oswald's Church graveyard to reach Church Street.

3. Turn left and follow Church Street downhill to the traffic lights, turn left here following the path across Kingsgate Footbridge. Walk up the steps at the far end of the bridge and turn left onto a cobbled path. Follow this down steep steps to the river path and turn left.

4. Follow the river path with the river on your right. Walk under Elvet Bridge into a small square. Go through the walkway with the car park on your left and a boathouse to the right. Carry on along the river path, walking under the new Elvet Bridge. Turn right and cross Baths Bridge to Elvet Waterside.

5. Turn left and follow the riverside path to the end of the road. Continue with the river to your left. Follow the path around the playing fields, curving right, away from the river and past the boathouse; continue to Federation House.

6. Walk with the sports fields to your right until you get back to the river on Elvet Waterside. Follow the outbound route back across Baths Bridge and left onto the riverside path. Walk along the river under the two Elvet bridges and back under Kingsgate Footbridge.

7. Don't cross but instead follow the river path around the bend, with Durham Cathedral above and to your right. Continue along the path past the Prebends Bridge and along the river until you reach Silver Street, which leads to Framwelgate Bridge.

8. Turn left, crossing Framwelgate Bridge. At the far side of the bridge, turn left and go down the steps to reach the riverside path under the bridge. Turn left again and follow the path back along your outbound route to Crook Hall Gardens.

DOG-FRIENDLY AMENITIES

The Garden Gate Café at Crook Hall Gardens (free entry for non-members) has indoor and outdoor dog-friendly seating. Dogs on a short lead are welcome in the gardens and café.

75. Durham Coastal Walk

Nose's Point Car Park
East Cliff Road
Seaham
County Durham
SR7 7PS
0191 529 3161
durhamcoast@nationaltrust.org.uk

ABOUT THIS WALK

Distance 5.2 miles (8.4km)
Difficulty Moderate
Terrain Coast path and
inland woodland trails; short
but steep hills; muddy
sections
Stiles No
Interest Wildlife, coast,
history

Durham Coast offers a wonderful sense of escape, boasting enjoyable walking and spectacular clifftop views. Once an area scarred by extensive coal mining, nature has reclaimed the land and, with some help from National Trust rangers and volunteers, as well as carefully managed conservation grazing, made it its own.

This walk sets out from Nose's Point, which is a nature reserve and Site of Special Scientific Interest for its fascinating geology and ecology. You'll explore the headland at Chourdon Point and the beautiful riverside woodland at Hawthorn Dene before returning along the England Coast Path.

THINGS TO SEE

The rare magnesian limestone that underlies this area has created a landscape of cream-coloured cliffs intersected by steep-sided, wooded gills. Above the cliffs, if you're visiting over the warmer months, you'll find the coastal grasslands colourful with wild flowers, attracting pollinators including the very special Durham brown argus butterfly.

Paws for thought
You'll find fragile wildlife, grazing animals and unfenced cliff edges along the Durham Coast, so please keep dogs under close control or on a lead.

Other walkies nearby
There's a wealth of incredible walking to the south of the route described above, following the undulating coast path to Horden, where you'll find the Durham Coast National Nature Reserve and Blackhall Rocks and Horden Grasslands nature reserves, all testament to the power of nature to restore and regenerate, even after extensive mining and industrial use.

Above: The Durham Coastal trails.
Opposite: Blast Beach.

HOW TO GET HERE

Public transport Seaham has a
  train station, walk to the sea
  and turn right to join this
  route (1.7 miles/2.7km).
Car Follow signs for Seaham
  from the A19. Satnav: SR7 7PS
OS map Explorer 308
Start/finish Nose's Point car
  park, SR7 7PS, grid ref:
  NZ435481

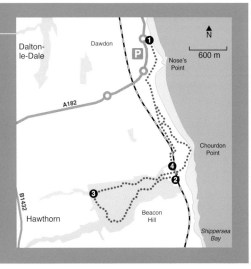

DIRECTIONS

Start/finish: Nose's Point car park

1. Follow the coast path south, walking away
   from Seaham with the sea to your left. Walk
   the winding and undulating path around
   Chourdon Point to reach a path junction
   under the Hawthorn Dene viaduct.

2. Turn right and follow the path under the
   viaduct, trending left uphill into Hawthorn
   Dene Nature Reserve. Walk up the wooded
   valley, staying to the right of the burn and
   curving to the right near the top. Continue to
   the path junction at the top of the hill.

3. The path to the left takes you towards
   Hawthorn village. Our walk turns right and
   heads back down towards the sea, through
   the Old Plantation, to reach the coast path
   and railway.

4. Turn left and follow the coast path with the
   railway on your right. Cross the footbridge and
   turn left, following the path with the railway to
   your left. Carry on along this path as it bears
   away from the railway and joins the coast path.
   Continue, reversing the outbound route back
   to the start.

DOG-FRIENDLY AMENITIES

The Durham Coast is a great place for dogs, who
are welcome to run, play and explore the beaches,
grassy meadows and wooded denes.

Along the coast to the north of this walk, you'll find
the iconic red-and-white striped Souter Lighthouse.
Stay in the dog-friendly Lighthouse Keeper's
Cottages, sleeping up to four people and two dogs,
with the spectacular coastline on your doorstep.

76. The Souter Saunter at Souter Lighthouse

Coast Road
Whitburn
Tyne & Wear
SR6 7NH
0191 529 3161
souter@nationaltrust.org.uk

ABOUT THIS WALK

Distance 2.3 miles (3.7km)
Difficulty Easy
Terrain Quite flat, well-maintained and mostly surfaced paths
Stiles No
Interest History, wildlife, coastal

Standing proud on a grassy coastal headland mid-way between the rivers Tyne and Wear, its red and white stripes vibrant against a backdrop of sky and sea, Souter Lighthouse is an impressive sight from many miles around. Opened in 1871 it was the first lighthouse in the UK designed and built to be powered by electricity.

The Souter Saunter is an enjoyable 2-mile (3.2-km) circular walking trail from Souter Lighthouse. You'll follow footpaths along the limestone cliffs and coastal grasslands to discover the location of a lost village; explore Whitburn Nature Reserve on the site of a former colliery; see vast numbers of seabirds, including kittiwakes, fulmars, cormorants, shags and guillemots, and admire the interesting rock formations and beautiful beaches and bays.

THINGS TO SEE

Just north of Souter Lighthouse you'll discover a large, flat field, popular with dog walkers and families. Looking across the grassy expanse today, it's hard to imagine that less than 70 years ago there was a bustling village on the site, housing the miners from nearby Whitburn Colliery. A combination of the closure of the colliery in 1968 and coastal erosion threatening many of the buildings, forced residents to move away and the village was demolished leaving no trace of its existence today. The site is now looked after by the National Trust, forming part of the Whitburn Coastal Park.

Paws for thought
Unfenced coastal cliffs and fragile wildlife, including nesting seabirds over the spring and summer months. Please keep dogs on leads.

Other walkies nearby
The beaches that dot this stretch of the coastline are fantastic places for dogs to run, explore and even swim. They're especially good out of season when you can often have acres of space to yourself. Dogs are allowed on Littlehaven Beach (next to Sandhaven) and Marsden Beach throughout the year. On Sandhaven Beach dogs are not permitted from 1 May–30 September between the hours of 8am and 6pm.

Above: Souter Lighthouse overlooks nature-rich clifftop grasslands.
Opposite: Rock stacks near Souter Lighthouse and The Leas.

HOW TO GET HERE

Public transport South Shields and Sunderland both have train stations. Stagecoach bus service E1 runs between these two locations; alight at the end of lighthouse drive.
Car Off the A183 coast road between South Shields and Sunderland. Satnav: SR6 7NH
OS map Explorer 316
Start/finish Souter Lighthouse car park, SR6 7NH, grid ref: NZ407640

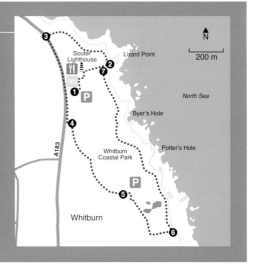

DIRECTIONS

Start/finish: Souter Lighthouse car park

1. Walk towards the lighthouse and through Foghorn Field to reach the King Charles III England Coast Path at Lizard Point, on the seaward side of the lighthouse enclosure.

2. Turn left and follow the coast path around the meadow, curving left to a path junction next to the A183.

3. Follow the path to the left, passing the lighthouse's white-walled entrance on your left. Turn left into the car park entrance, then right following signs to Whitburn Coastal Park.

4. Follow this road around the coastal park to reach Souter's lower car park.

5. Turn right and follow the path around the edge of the nature reserve. The path curves left at the end of the reserve and joins the coast path.

6. Follow the coast path left, back towards the lighthouse. Continue with the sea to your right until you reach Lizard Point and the outbound route.

7. Turn left and follow your outbound route back past the foghorn and lighthouse to the start.

DOG-FRIENDLY AMENITIES

Dogs are welcome across The Leas and Whitburn Coastal Park, but please keep them under close control and on a lead near cliff edges and other animals. Dogs are welcome on a short lead within the lighthouse grounds (Foghorn Field and all areas within the white walls) and in the Lighthouse Café, which serves drinks, snacks and light meals and has indoor and outdoor seating. Assistance dogs only in the lighthouse. Dog waste bins are dotted across the site.

Stay in the dog-friendly Lighthouse Keeper's Cottages, sleeping up to four people and two dogs, with the iconic red-and-white-striped lighthouse and spectacular coastline on your doorstep.

77. The Wonders of Nature at Gibside

Near Rowlands Gill
Gateshead
Tyne & Wear
NE16 6BG
01207 541820
gibside@nationaltrust.org.uk

ABOUT THIS WALK

Distance 5.2 miles (8.4km)
Difficulty Challenging
Terrain Gravel, dirt and
grassy paths. Some steep
sections and steps
Stiles No
Interest History, wildlife

Set within the spectacular Derwent Valley, Gibside is a rare example of a Georgian landscape garden. There's plenty to discover around the 600-acre (243-ha) estate, from wild deer and unexpected viewpoints to a Palladian Column to Liberty.

This walk follows the waymarked Wonders of Nature Trail, taking you on an adventure around the estate on well-maintained trails. Along the way you'll explore Gibside's Walled Garden, woodland and countryside, experiencing the area's natural beauty and peace.

THINGS TO SEE

Gibside's a great place to spot the local wildlife, including roe deer grazing in the woods and grasslands, red kites circling overhead, and even, if you're lucky, badgers, bats and otters.

Paws for thought
Dogs should be kept on a lead at all times, and on a short lead near to grazing animals.

Assistance dogs only in the chapel.

Other walkies nearby
Three further trails explore the estate, each marked with different coloured waymarkers. Take your pick from the purple Liberty Trail, the orange Explorer Trail and the pink Valley Views Trail – or try them all! The Derwent Walk is a popular 12-mile (19.3-km) linear route between Consett and Swalwell that also makes an enjoyable, level walk.

Above: The avenue at Gibside with views of the Column to Liberty.
Opposite: View from the Long Walk to the Palladian Chapel.

HOW TO GET HERE

Public transport Trains to the
Metrocentre or Newcastle.
The X45 bus runs from these
stations; alight at Station Road,
Rowlands Gill, half a mile
(0.8km) away.
Car The entrance is on the
B6314 between Burnopfield
and Rowlands Gill. Follow
brown signs from the A1.
Satnav: NE16 6BG
OS map Explorer 307
Start/finish Gibside car park,
NE16 6BG, grid ref: NZ169582

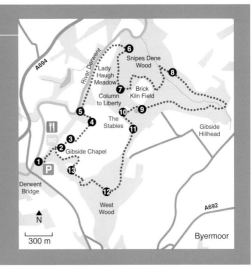

DIRECTIONS

Start/finish: Gibside car park

1. Walk up the wooden walkway that starts at
Visitor Reception. Follow the trail from the top
of the hill by the estate map.

2. Turn left through the doorway into the Walled
Garden and walk across to the wooden gates
at the far side.

3. Leaving the garden, turn right and follow the
path up to the avenue. Turn left and walk along
the avenue, passing the Orangery field and
then an area of woodland on your left. At the
far end of the woods turn left onto a footpath.

4. Follow this path down steps, along the edge of the wood and then through the
wood, down to the River Derwent.

5. Turn right, following the path and the river, with woodland to your right. Carry on
out of the woods and past the meadow known as Lady Haugh. After the meadow
the path trends right, away from the river and up into the woods.

6. At a junction with a forestry road, turn right and follow this uphill. Pass the Lily
Pond and continue to a cleared area of trees. To your right you can see down the
avenue while the Column to Liberty towers to the left.

7. Take the smaller path to your left, climbing up to the column. Walk past the column
and turn right at the next trail, follow this path through the wood with Brick Kiln
Field to your right. At the corner of the field you'll reach a path junction, turn left
and head downhill. Pass the old coalmine entrance on the right and take the right
turn when the path forks. Follow the trail as it starts to climb again.

8. Join a forestry road and turn right, following this track up Snipes Dene to the high point of the walk. At the top of the hill the track bends to the right, follow it around and walk back down the hill on the other side. Continue to the Octagonal Pond.

9. Walk around to the right of the pond and follow the path. Ignore the right-hand turns and continue to reach the Stables. There are toilets and a café here.

10. To continue, turn left and follow the path uphill. Pass the bothy to your right and the old saw mill on the left.

11. Continue up the hill, with Park Fields visible through the woods to your right. Ignore the right at the T-junction and carry on downhill to reach a crossroads in West Wood.

12. Turn right and follow the path signed to the Low Ropes Course; walk downhill through the woods to a larger track. Turn left and follow the path around the edge of the field to the children's play area.

13. Walk past the play area and follow the path around to the left which returns you to the end of the avenue. Continue behind the Chapel and back to the Market Place. Return to the start by your outbound route.

The Georgian landscape garden at Gibside.

DOG-FRIENDLY AMENITIES

Dogs are welcome on all 15 miles (24km) of paths at Gibside, but should be kept on leads in all areas other than the off-lead pen, which is next to the Stables. Your dog can join you at the indoor or outdoor seating at Market Place Café or Carriage House Coffee Shop. You'll also find a showering point to wash off muddy paws at Visitor Reception.

Burnhopeside Hall is a listed Georgian house on a 475-acre (192-ha) estate near Durham, offering bed and breakfast in the main house, as well as a self-catering cottage. Boasting elegant interiors, breakfasts made with locally sourced ingredients (often from the farm itself), walks from the door and a warm welcome from the hosts; resident springer spaniels Max and Barney welcome guests' dogs too. www. burnhopeside-hall.co.uk

78. River Walk at Wallington

Cambo
Near Morpeth
Northumberland
NE61 4AR
01670 773606

wallington@nationaltrust.org.uk

ABOUT THIS WALK

Distance 2.6 miles (4.2km)
Difficulty Easy
Terrain Fairly flat on
natural and surfaced
footpaths
Stiles No
Interest History, wildlife

Wallington is a landscape rich in culture and nature, shaped by its history as an agricultural estate. The intriguing history of Wallington Hall includes its transformation from country retreat to family home.

This walk explores the grounds, woodlands and ponds around the House at Wallington, at the southernmost end of the 13,500 acre (5431ha) estate. You'll follow a stretch of the River Wansbeck and finish with a loop of the West Wood. Keep your eyes peeled for the many different species of wildlife that make their homes here, including red squirrels, bats, birds of prey, dippers and white-clawed crayfish.

THINGS TO SEE

Wilder Wallington is an ongoing project to improve Wallington for nature and people. Work by staff, volunteers, tenants, partners and the local community aims to help nature recover across the whole estate and beyond. The project includes the reintroduction of beavers, planting tens of thousands of trees, work to slow river flows, encouraging pine martens onto the estate and surveying to track changes in biodiversity.

DOG-FRIENDLY AMENITIES

Dogs are welcome in almost all the outdoor areas including the woodland, along the River and Farm walks and in the Walled Garden. You can also take your dog inside the Clocktower Café and shops.

Stay at Wallington at Bolt Cottage, one of five dog-friendly holiday cottages on the estate. The cosy, stone-built cottage sleeps up to four people and a dog, and is surrounded by trees, with miles of walks on its doorstep.

Paws for thought

Dogs must be kept on leads at all times across the estate to avoid disturbing wildlife and livestock. Assistance dogs only are allowed in the House and play areas.

Other walkies nearby

The 6.3-mile (10-km) Wannie Line Walk explores both the Wannie and Rothbury railway lines as they cross Wallington estate, once carrying stone, lime, coal and livestock, as well as passengers. As you walk, you'll also discover other remnants of Wallington's industrial past, including an abandoned quarry and several old limestone kilns.

Above: Paine's Bridge.
Overleaf: The stepping stones over the River Wansbeck.

HOW TO GET HERE

Public transport Check for
  seasonal bus services from
  Newcastle.
Car Off the A696 from
  Newcastle. Satnav: NE61 4AR
OS map Explorer OL42
Start/finish Wallington car park,
  NE61 4AR, grid ref: NZ027843

DIRECTIONS

Start/finish: Wallington car park

1. Walk out of the car park, through the reception and right to the Clock Tower. Walk through to the Courtyard with the Clock Tower behind you.

2. Turn left and walk across the Courtyard and through the gate in the far left corner. Turn left, following the path away from the Courtyard to the B6342.

3. Cross and follow the footpath opposite along the serpentine walk through East Wood, continue to the corner of the Garden Pond.

4. Follow the path to the left of the pond and along its bank to the far end. Walk around to the right, continuing to the far end of the lake until you can turn left through Neptune Gate into the Walled Garden. Walk through the garden, past the conservatory (on your left) and exit at the far doorway.

5. Trend right, following Gooseberry Walk to a gateway and a minor road. You pass the seasonal Garden Kiosk to your right, before you reach the road.

6. Cross and use the gate to enter the woodland opposite. Follow the path to the River Wansbeck and cross the stepping stones. Turn right and follow the path along the river to Paine's Bridge. If the river is high, the stepping stones can become slippery or submerged, in which case keep on the road to miss out this section.

7. Walk under the bridge and follow the riverside path through the woodland of Wallington Dean until you reach Trout Bridge.

8. Cross and turn left, following the path uphill to a track junction. You can turn right here and follow the shorter path through West Wood, back to the start.

9. Our route turns left along Fenwick's Drive; curve to the right and then turn left at the path junction. The path then curves right through the woods, passing Top Pond on your left and Middle Pond on the right. Continue straight ahead on the path to return to the Courtyard. Retrace your steps under the Clock Tower and back to the start.

79. Cragside Crags, Quarries and Lakes Walk

Rothbury
Morpeth
Northumberland
NE65 7PX
01669 620333
cragside@nationaltrust.org.uk

ABOUT THIS WALK

Distance 4.2 miles (6.8km)
Difficulty Moderate
Terrain Rocky and gravel
sections, a couple of short
but steep ups and downs
Stiles No
Interest History, wildlife,
gardens

More than 40 miles (64km) of footpaths, including 7 waymarked routes, wind through the 1,000-acre (405-ha) estate at Cragside. It is an extraordinary place, from the grand Victorian house – the first in the world to be lit by hydroelectricity – to the maze of drives and paths that meander through forests of rhododendrons, around wildlife-rich lakes and past one of the largest rock gardens in Europe.

This walk initially follows the red waymarkers around the Gun Walk, taking in 3 miles (4.8km) through Cragside's craggy heart. You'll wind your way through impressive rock formations and Cragend Quarry, the largest of many quarries that once operated on the estate to extract sandstone to build the house. Look carefully and you can still see the blast marks on the sheer rock faces. After you reach Crozier's Kiosk – named after a former Cragside butler – where you can stop for drinks and snacks (seasonal opening times), you'll head out around the two artificial lakes at Nelly's Moss, taking in a loop of the lakes following the blue waymarkers. Rejoin the Gun Walk back at Crozier's for the final stretch back to the house.

Paws for thought
You'll find craggy, unfenced drops and resident wildlife including deer and red squirrels at Cragside, so please keep dogs on leads throughout your walk. Only assistance dogs are allowed in the house.

Other walkies nearby
Explore the vast network of footpaths extending around the Cragside estate, or head further afield to discover Northumberland's wealth of outdoor adventures, from the wild and windswept Cheviot Hills to the dramatic coast dotted with impressive castles.

Above: There are 40 miles (64km) of footpaths to explore across this 1,000-acre (405-ha) estate and all of these are open to dog-walkers. Overleaf: View of the north front at Cragside.

HOW TO GET HERE

Public transport The X14 Arriva service, which runs from Newcastle to Thropton, stops at Cragside.
Car From the A1 follow the signs for the A697, then the B6341. The entrance is off the B6341. Satnav: NE65 7PX; this may try to bring you in through the exit; follow brown signs for the entrance.
OS map Explorer OL42 and 332
Start/finish Cragside main car park, NE65 7PX, grid ref: NU072023

THINGS TO SEE

Described in 1880 as 'a palace of the modern magician', the Victorian mansion at Cragside was the home of Lord Armstrong and his wife, lady Armstrong. A prolific inventor, who made his fortune designing armaments including the Armstrong gun, Lord Armstrong filled the house and gardens with intriguing contraptions, including the first system in the world to light a house by hydroelectric power, an early design for a washing machine, fire alarm buttons, telephones, a passenger lift, a Turkish bath and the country's first flushing loo.

DIRECTIONS

Start/finish: Cragside main car park

1. Walk up from the car park to the house and through to the forecourt on the far side of the house. The Gun Walk is signed with red waymarkers from this point.

2. Follow the Gun Walk a few yards up the tarmac carriage drive to a path on the left, signed to Cragend. Follow this path and the red waymarkers through the woodland, slightly uphill. You will cross several path junctions; continue following the red waymarkers and signs to Cragend. Continue uphill to a sharper left curve in the path. At the next junction, turn right and head down to Cragend Quarry.

3. Continue on the path now signed to Viewpoint and Crozier. Follow this trail straight through the next junction, up a set of wooden steps and then uphill to the viewpoint. Carry on along this path, crossing the next junction, heading for the lake. Turn right following signs for the South Lake, cross a section of boardwalk and reach the estate drive by the lake.

4. The next section of our walk follows the blue waymarkers on the Nelly's Moss Lakes Walk. Cross the driveway and turn right, following the path signed 'Nelly's Moss South Lake/North Lake'. Walk along with the lake to your left and woods to the right. At the end of the South Lake, bear right on the path and walk around the North Lake until you get to the boathouse.

5. Continue on the stone path past the boathouse and walk with South Lake on your left and the carriage drive not far to the left. Near the end of the lake, follow the path right, across the drive and into the Crozier car park.

6. You are now following the red waymarkers of the Gun Walk again. Follow the path out of the car park, following signs to the Trim Trail. Continue until you reach a small, engraved stone and sign directing you left to the house. Follow this path down stone steps to Slipper Lake.

7. Turn right at the lake onto middle drive and follow this, bearing left at the next junction to return to the house and car park.

Everything you see at Cragside was sculpted, dynamited and planted to transform the bare moorside into a vast fantasy mountain landscape.

DOG-FRIENDLY AMENITIES

Dogs on leads are welcome in all outdoor spaces at Cragside, including the Rock Garden, Formal Garden, Pinetum and woodland, as well as the miles of paths. You can also bring your dogs into Cragside's shop and tea-rooms, where there is a dog-friendly seating area indoors.

The cottages on the Cragside estate aren't currently dog-friendly, but a stone's throw away, down the Coquet Valley, is the wonderful Brinkburn estate. Surrounded by 30 acres (12ha) of woodland, holiday cottages here sleep between two and nine, and can be booked together to accommodate larger groups. Dogs are given a warm welcome, with dog hampers containing treats and other items available to request on booking. www.brinkburnnorthumberland.com

Wales

Lakeside and Parkland Walk, Tredegar

Tredegar House
Pencarn Way
Newport
NP10 8YW
01633 811661
tredegar@nationaltrust.org.uk

ABOUT THIS WALK

Distance 1.7 miles (2.7km)
Difficulty Easy
Terrain Flat and mostly gravelled path; the grassy section can become muddy, particularly in winter
Stiles No
Interest Wildlife, history

Encircled by busy A-roads and the M4 motorway, Tredegar seems like an unlikely place for an escape. And yet, with its expanse of spacious parkland, mature trees and serene lake, the moment you set foot within the grounds, it feels a million miles away from the traffic.

This walk takes in a loop of the parkland, starting outside the 17th-century mansion and its stable block, and following the wooded lakeshore to reach the estate boundary. From here, you'll head back through the park.

THINGS TO SEE

The Grade I-listed mansion at Tredegar is a grand, red-brick house, built between 1664 and 1672. Along with its Grade II-listed park, Tredegar has been cared for by the National Trust since 2012.

Above: The lake and house in autumn.
Opposite: The parkland is a dog-walking haven.

Paws for thought
Dogs should be kept on leads across the Tredegar estate, and on short leads in the formal gardens, café, bookshop and visitor reception. Please don't let your dog chase the wildlife here. Tredegar is popular with families and picnickers – dogs should be kept well away from other people.

Other walkies nearby
Explore the former Tredegar estate to the west of the park, where a network of footpaths rambles through the peaceful hills and woodlands of the Rhymney Valley between Cardiff and Caerphilly. Here, you'll find the atmospheric ruins of Ruperra Castle, once the summer house of the Morgan family but gutted by fire in 1941, and Craig Ruperra, an Iron Age hill fort surrounded by wildlife-rich ancient woodland.

Public transport The nearest station is Newport (2 miles/2.3km). Local buses 30 and 36 stop within a 5-minute walk of Tredegar House.

Car Tredegar House is signposted from both the A48 and the M4. Satnav: When using satnav for directions please do not input the postcode, instead, use 'Pencarn Way', then follow signs for Tredegar House.

OS map Explorer 152

Start/finish Tredegar House car park, NP10 8YW, grid ref: ST288850

DIRECTIONS

Start/finish: Tredegar House car park

1. Walk to the right of the visitor reception and through the courtyard past the café. Continue through a gate into the courtyard area next to the house.

2. Go through the gates on the right and out onto the turning circle by the Victorian entrance to the mansion. Walk around the turning circle to the edge of the lawns.

3. Follow the path towards the lake, with the Italianate sunken garden on your right. When you reach the lake, turn right and follow the lakeside path to the lake's end.

4. Walk over a small bridge and follow the path through woodland with the lake to your left. Carry on until you reach a path junction.

5. Take the middle path and follow it through woodland, curving to the left and eventually reaching a small bridge on the left.

6. Cross the bridge and walk out onto the parkland, passing the old gatehouse on your right. Walk across the park, following the path across the grass to another bridge over the stream.

7. Head across the grassland to the small wood on the far side. Follow the path around the woods and left along the boundary of the estate. Continue past a pond on your right to reach a track. Turn left and follow the track around the buildings and in front of the large courtyard. Turn right and follow the track towards the main house.

8. Walk past the house and back to the turning circle and Victorian entrance. Turn right through the gate and walk back through the courtyard, past the café and back to the start.

DOG-FRIENDLY AMENITIES

Dogs are welcome across all of Tredegar's parkland. You're welcome to explore the formal gardens with your dog; the Cedar Garden lawns are a favourite spot for dogs who like to bask in the sun. You can also enjoy post-walk refreshments at the Brewhouse café, or a wander around the bookshop with your dog.

The lake and boathouse at Tredegar House.

81. Summit and Valley Walk, Skirrid Fawr

Abergavenny
Monmouthshire
NP7 8AP
01874 625515
brecon@nationaltrust.org.uk

ABOUT THIS WALK

Distance 3.5 miles (5.7km)
Difficulty Challenging
Terrain Steps, mountain
trails, some rocky sections
Stiles No
Interest History, wildlife,
mountains

The Black Mountains lie at the eastern edge of the Bannau Brycheiniog (Brecon Beacons) National Park, on the border between Wales and England. The ridges and steep slopes form an intriguing and inviting skyline, with more achievable summits than those in the higher ranges further east.

One such summit is at Skirrid Fawr, a hill shrouded in local myth and legend. Its distinctive shape, carved by its underlying geology, has drawn people to its slopes over the centuries. Walking here offers a real sense of being high up and away from it all, yet it's achievable for most people with a good general level of fitness. This is wonderful dog-walking country, with plenty of shade in the wooded areas for keeping cool over the summer months.

THINGS TO SEE

The medieval chapel of St Michael, the remnants of which can be seen near to the trig point, was used for services until the late 17th century.

Paws for thought

You'll often find sheep grazing on the grassland here, so dogs should be kept under close control, and on a lead during lambing/bird-nesting season (March to September).

Other walkies nearby

Skirrid Fawr's neighbouring mountain, Sugar Loaf, is another fantastic dog-friendly place to walk. It's recommended to park at Fairfield car park in Abergavenny Town Centre and walk up to the southern slopes where several obvious paths lead invitingly to the summit. Views from the trig point at the top reach across to the distinctive summit of Pen y Fan.

Skirrid Fawr summit ridge.

Public transport Abergavenny is the closest train station, but you'll have to take a taxi or walk from there, 4 miles (6.4km) on the Beacons Way.
Car The car park is a lay-by on the B4521 east of Abergavenny. Satnav: NP7 8AP
OS map Explorer OL13
Start/finish B4521 National Trust car park, NP7 8AP, grid ref: SO328164

DOG-FRIENDLY AMENITIES

A short hop across the Usk Valley from the Black Mountains, the National Trust's Kymin Stables is a peaceful retreat, perfect for enjoying with your dog. Set on one level and with its own private garden, walks from the door explore the surrounding woodland and countryside including Offa's Dyke, the Forest of Dean and the 9-acre (3.6-ha) grassy pleasure grounds surrounding the Round House. After your walk, head to the dog-friendly Cwtch Café in nearby Abergavenny for coffee and cake.

DIRECTIONS

Start/finish: Car park at grid ref SO328164

1. Follow the gravel track out of the back of the car park and around a sharp right-hand bend. Continue on the main path through the woodland and up the hill to reach a wooden gate at the dry stone wall.

2. Go through the gate and follow the uphill path to your right, emerging onto open hillside and ascending the main ridge to the trig point at the summit.

3. From the trig point, retrace your steps for a short distance until you can turn left onto a footpath, which is also the Beacons Way. Follow this down the hillside to the valley below, turning left when you reach the path at the bottom of the slope.

4. Follow the path around the base of Skirrid Fawr, passing through woodland and below the craggy western flanks of the hill. Continue until you reach your outward path, turning right here and following it back to the car park.

The Beacons Way long distance trail climbs to the summit of Skirrid.

82. Hills and History at Dolaucothi Estate Walk

Pumsaint
Llanwrda
Carmarthenshire
SA19 8US
01558 650177
dolaucothi@nationaltrust.org.uk

ABOUT THIS WALK

Distance 3.9 miles (6.2km)
Difficulty Challenging
Terrain Paths, tracks and
lanes, a steep climb and
descent. Some sections can
get muddy
Stiles No
Interest Wildlife, history,
geology

Mined for gold since Roman times, the Dolaucothi estate covers over 2,500 acres (1,012ha) of farmland, woodland and the site of the original Dolaucothi house and surrounding parkland. Nature has taken over the once busy industrial landscape here, but the wooded hillsides hold many intriguing secrets, waiting to be discovered.

This adventurous walk climbs to the highest point on the Dolaucothi estate to discover the trig point and beautiful views over the winding River Cothi, the former gold mines and the village of Pumsaint. You'll cross the bridge over the Cothi. If you're lucky you might spot otters, dippers, kingfishers or herons. You'll return along an old railway route, following the River Cothi, which was used in the past for transporting timber down the valley.

Other walkies nearby
You'll find over 15 miles (24km) of footpaths exploring the estate at Dolaucothi, from gentle riverside walks to scenic upland trails. Just a little further afield, you'll find the rolling expanse of the Bannau Brycheiniog National Park – a dark sky reserve with hundreds of miles of wonderful walks to explore, including the Beacons Way, which runs for 99 miles (159km) across the full length of the park.

THINGS TO SEE

Book onto a tour of the Roman mine (dogs welcome), exploring the SSSI, which is significant for its upland oak woodland – a segment of ancient temperate rainforest where plants such as the rare hay-scented buckler fern grow. The old mines are also home to many types of bat.

Paws for thought
All dogs taken on the tour of the Roman mine and the mine yard must be kept on short leads. The tour itself is up steps, over uneven ground and through woodlands, which may be slippery, especially during wet weather.

There are plenty of footpaths to explore throughout the estate.

HOW TO GET HERE

Public transport Llandovery is the closest station (10.5 miles/16.9km), but there is no bus from there.

Car Follow signs for Dolaucothi Gold Mines from the A482 near Pumsaint. Satnav: SA19 8US

OS map Explorer 186

Start/finish Dolaucothi Woodland car park, SA19 8US, grid ref: SN662403

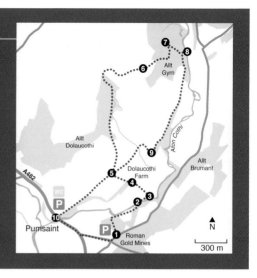

DIRECTIONS

Start/finish: Dolaucothi Woodland car park

1. The woodland car park is opposite the gold mines car park. Walk through the woodland car park and follow the path at the far end through the trees to reach the River Cothi. Turn right and follow the path to the footbridge.

2. Cross the bridge and turn right, following the riverside path into a small area of trees where you will find a path turning off to the left.

3. Turn left and follow this footpath through the woods and across a field, then walk through a gate onto the Dolaucothi Farm track.

4. Follow the track to a junction, cross and follow the track opposite between two fields to another track junction with a forestry road.

5. Cross and go through the gate opposite onto a footpath. This heads right and uphill across a field. Reach a path junction at the edge of some woodland, take the right-hand track and follow this through the woods. At the far end of the woods follow the path as it curves to the right and walk uphill along the edge of a field to the trig point at the summit.

6. Walk down the steep hill into the woods and turn left onto a track. Follow this to reach a path junction.

7. Turn a sharp right and follow the path downhill through woodland to return to the River Cothi.

8. Follow the river path downstream, with the river on your left and fields to the right. The path stays quite straight while the river meanders down the valley.

9. The path takes a sharp right and heads away from the river and uphill to the forestry road. Turn left and follow the forestry road past waypoint 5 and down the valley to the A482 in Pumsaint village.

10. Turn left and walk along the pavement and over the bridge. Follow the A482 and bear left on the smaller road signed to Dolaucothi Gold Mines. Follow this back to the start.

DOG-FRIENDLY AMENITIES

All areas at Dolaucothi are dog-friendly, from tours of the Roman mine to the miles of footpaths to explore across the estate. Just a short walk from the main gold mine area, Dolaucothi Caravan and Motorhome Park offers a dog-friendly place to stay, right in the middle of this area's beautiful natural surroundings. There are no toilet or shower facilities at the site, and it's not suitable for tents — all campers and caravaners must have their own facilities.

Opposite: Site of the Roman Pumsaint Fort.
Left: Dolaucothi Gold Mine.

83. To the Castle at Dinefwr

**Dinefwr Park
Newton House
Llandeilo
Carmarthenshire
SA19 6RT
01558 825910**
dinefwr@nationaltrust.org.uk

ABOUT THIS WALK

Distance 3.6 miles (5.8km)
Difficulty Moderate
Terrain Grassy trails and
gravel paths; can be muddy
and wet
Stiles No
Interest Wildlife, history

The historic Newton House, built in 1660 by Edward Rice and modified over the centuries, stands surrounded by an 800-acre (323-ha) estate with woodland, parkland and Dinefwr Castle to explore. This is a place with a fascinating history dating back to the Romans, whose forts can still be seen here.

This walk loops Dinefwr's historic parkland, visiting some of the best spots for wildlife-watching, admiring the magnificent veteran trees and appreciating the glorious views. You'll pass the medieval castle and 17th-century mansion. There's also a separate off-lead area in an expansive meadow with views of the house and valley.

THINGS TO SEE

You can also explore Dinefwr Castle, which is managed by Cadw and owned by the Wildlife Trust. Standing proud in an imposing, hilltop position overlooking the Tywi Valley, this ruined castle features strongly in Welsh history.

Paws for thought
Grazing animals can be found at Dinefwr all year round. Please keep dogs on leads at all times, other than in the off-lead meadow.

Other walkies nearby
Dinefwr lies right at the edge of the Bannau Brycheiniog National Park, a dark skies reserve and wonderful place for walking. The 99-mile (159-km) Beacons Way runs from Abergavenny in the east to Llandeilo in the west, finishing a stone's throw from Dinefwr. An enjoyable, but hilly, loop follows the Beacons Way from Llandeilo to Carreg Cennen Castle, returning along the Heart of Wales Line Trail.

Above: Newton House from the parkland at Dinefwr.
Opposite: The estate in September.

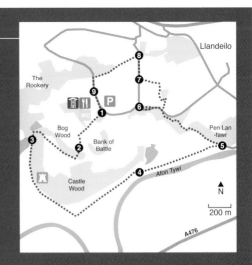

Public transport Llandeilo train
station is 1.7 miles (2.7km)
from Dinefwr.

Car If you're travelling from the
east or west, please use the
A40 to Llandeilo or use the
A483 from Swansea. Satnav:
Postcode misdirects; search
'National Trust Dinefwr' and
follow the brown oakleaf signs.

OS map Explorer 186

Start/finish Dinefwr car park,
SA19 6RT, grid ref: SN615224

DIRECTIONS

Start/finish: Dinefwr car park

1. Walk out of the bottom of the car park
    towards the castle. Cross the cattle grid and
    follow the stony track past the deer house.
    Continue to follow the track downhill past
    Mynachdy, an old, red-brick gamekeeper's
    cottage.

2. Walk past the right turn signed 'Bogwood' and
    follow the path through the wood to a
    T-junction. Turn right following the track along
    the edge of Bogwood with a field to your left.
    Continue into the woodland and through to
    the corner of the millpond. Follow the path
    left, past the millpond and the old pumphouse
    on your right. Carry on through woodland to
    reach the oxbow lake on your right.

3. Continue on the path that walks around the
    edge of the Dinefwr estate. The river is to your
    right and the castle remains tower up to the
    left. Carry on until you reach the edge of the
    meadow and a tree-lined drainage ditch.

4. Cross into the next meadow and follow the
    Tywi Valley until you reach a track cutting across
    your path at the edge of some woodland.

5. Turn left and follow the track past
    Llandyfeisant Church to the Dinefwr driveway. Turn left onto this and follow it for a
    short distance until you reach a sharp right turn through a gate onto the meadow.

6. Walk through into the meadow area; this is the designated off-lead area. Dogs can run free for the next section. Follow the path uphill and left, in front of the clump of trees. Continue to follow the path trending left until you reach the edge of the meadow area and a larger track.

7. Turn right and follow this track downhill to a path junction with a gate and path to your left. Animals are often grazing in the next field.

8. Go through the gate and follow the path slightly uphill, with a field on your left and an area of woodland on the right. Turn left at the path junction at the end of this path to reach the gates to Newton House.

9. You can take your dog into the café and explore the ground floor of the house. Or follow the path in front of you downhill back to the start.

DOG-FRIENDLY AMENITIES

Dogs are welcome on the ground floor inside Newton House, as well as in the outer park and café, which has indoor and outdoor seating. The town of Llandeilo, which adjoins Dinefwr, is an enjoyable place to visit, with lots of independent shops and cafés. Diod is a family- and dog-friendly café and wine bar, serving good coffee and food all day (diod.cymru).

Dogs are welcome all year round and there's plenty for them to enjoy.

84. Coast and Lily Ponds at Stackpole

**Stackpole
near Pembroke
Pembrokeshire
SA71 5LS
01646 623110**
stackpole@nationaltrust.org.uk

ABOUT THIS WALK

Distance 6 miles (9.7km)
Difficulty Moderate
Terrain Beach, coast path
and gravel trail, lots of steps
Stiles No
Interest Coast, wildlife,
history, geology

The Stackpole estate covers 2,000 acres (809ha) of stunning coastal and countryside landscapes in the far south-west of Wales. Part of the Pembrokeshire Coast National Park, it is both a listed designed landscape and an internationally important nature reserve.

This walk sets out from Stackpole Quay, crossing the beautiful stretch of sand at Barafundle Bay and across the dramatic cliffs and wildlife-rich grassland of Stackpole Head. Pause at Broad Haven South beach before exploring Bosherston Lakes and famous lily ponds. The home stretch takes you across the deer park and back to Stackpole Quay.

THINGS TO SEE

Bosherston Lakes were created in the 18th century by the Cawdor family, who dammed the river valley during the process of 'designing' the landscape. Initially intended as a scenic backdrop for the Cawdors' mansion, these shallow lakes have since evolved into a rich, wildlife habitat where otters, water birds and a staggering 24 species of dragonfly can be seen.

Paws for thought

To protect wildlife and grazing animals, dogs should be kept on leads around Stackpole Warren, the coastal grassland between Barafundle and Broad Haven South, and around Bosherston Lakes.

Other walkies nearby

The accessible Secrets of Stackpole Court walk is a shorter trail exploring the landscape and parkland designed by the Cawdor family to complement their grand mansion, Stackpole Court, which was demolished in 1963.

Barafundle Bay, near Stackpole Quay.

Public transport The nearest train
  station is Pembroke (4.5
  miles/7.2km). The 387/388 Coastal
  Cruiser from Pembroke stops at
  Stackpole Quay, with a limited
  service in the winter.
Car B4319 from Pembroke; follow
  Stackpole Village signs then brown
  tourist signs for Stackpole Quay.
  Satnav: SA71 5LS
OS map Explorer OL36
Start/finish Stackpole Quay car
  park, SA71 5LS, grid ref: SR990958

DIRECTIONS

Start/finish: Stackpole Quay car park

1. Leave the car park and follow the coast path
   towards Barafundle. Walk up some steps and
   across the headland before descending to
   Barafundle beach.

2. Cross the beach and climb the steps on the
   other side, following the coast path to
   Stackpole Head.

3. Continue on the coast path walking with the
   sea on your left and Stackpole Warren
   grassland to your right. Carry on to the
   narrow inlet of the Ramming Hole and the
   path junction just beyond this.

4. You can walk any of the three path options in
   front of you; all follow the coast along the
   southern edge of the nature reserve. Continue
   on the coast path around Saddle Point to the
   outlet at the back of Broad Haven Beach.

5. Follow the path inland to the small stone
   bridge over the spillway from the Bosherston
   Lily Ponds.

6. Cross and follow the western arm of the Bosherston Lily Ponds to Bosherston Causeway.

7. After walking across the causeway, follow the path right and along the edge of the lily ponds.

8. Don't cross this, carry on following the path with the lily ponds to your right. Follow the eastern arm footpath up to the Eight Arch Bridge.

9. Cross the Eight Arch Bridge and follow the deer park track in front of you across Stackpole Park and back to the start.

DOG-FRIENDLY AMENITIES

Dogs are welcome across the wider Stackpole Estate, along the coast path from Stackpole Quay, and on the beach at Barafundle Bay, Broad Haven South and Freshwater West all year round. You can also take your dog inside visitor reception areas, the exhibition room, indoor picnic areas and the Boathouse Tea-room. In Bosherston village, near to the lakes, you'll find dog-friendly refuelling spots at Ye Olde Worlde Café and St Govans Country Inn.

Rosemary and Thyme Cottages on the Stackpole Estate offer good value, dog-friendly accommodation with the beaches on your doorstep (NT Holidays).

The lily ponds on the Stackpole estate.

85. River and Woodland Walk, Llanerchaeron

Ciliau Aeron
Near Aberaeron
Ceredigion
SA48 8DG
01545 573010
llanerchaeron@nationaltrust.org.uk

ABOUT THIS WALK

Distance 2.3 miles (3.7km)
Difficulty Moderate
Terrain Grassy and
woodland footpaths and
tracks. The first section can
get muddy
Stiles No
Interest Wildlife, coast,
history

Llanerchaeron is a traditional Welsh country estate with an elegant Georgian villa, designed by celebrated architect, John Nash, at its heart. It was intended as a model self-sufficient farm. Surrounding the house is a red-brick walled garden, ornamental lake and rambling parkland. This peaceful place remains much as it would have been 200 years ago.

This walk explores the wider estate at Llanerchaeron. You'll head out on the Kingfisher Walk, which follows the meandering River Aeron. As the trail's name suggests, you'll often spot kingfishers here, along with many other birds such as diminutive brown and white dippers. You'll pick up the Red Kite Walk, which takes you out to the organic farm at Lanlas, and then head into ancient woodland, a protected Site of Special Scientific Interest for its ground flora. Staying in the woods, you'll join the Goldcrest Walk for a loop of the steeper ground at Penparc, finishing along the Nuthatch, which follows the river back to the main visitor area.

THINGS TO SEE

In Llancharaeron's farmyard, you can see local and rare breeds of horses, pigs and sheep. Dogs (other than assistance dogs) aren't allowed in this area, but if you're visiting with kids it's a great place to see some interesting and friendly animals up close.

Paws for thought
The first section of this walk on the Kingfisher can become flooded after heavy rain, if this is the case, join the walk via the Red Kite trail. Assistance dogs only allowed in the Villa and in the farmyard. You'll find grazing animals across the parkland, so please keep your dog on a lead at all times.

Other walkies nearby
A spectacular 3-mile (4.8-km) circular coastal walk takes you along the cliffs from the bay at Cwm Tydu to Cwm Soden. As well as being one of the few sites for the pearl-bordered fritillary butterfly in Wales, this walk offers opportunities to spot a variety of other invertebrates, including the forester moth, Welsh chafer and the giant lacewing.

Opposite: Waymarkers in the woods at Llanerchaeron.

HOW TO GET HERE

Public transport Train to Aberystwyth, regular buses to Aberaeron. Then walk the Allt y Graig Woodland Trail to Llanerchaeron (2.5 miles/4km).
Car Follow the A482 east from Aberaeron Satnav: SA48 8DG
OS map Explorer 198 and 199
Start/finish Llanerchaeron car park, SA48 8DG, grid ref: SN480602

DIRECTIONS

Start/finish: Llanerchaeron car park

1. Walk out of the car park following the Kingfisher Walk upstream along the River Aeron. Follow this trail through the woods, then along the road. Stay left on the dead end lane and follow this to the farm at Pandy. Walk through the gate and yard then turn left following the path through woodland and across a footbridge. Turn left and follow the path to a path junction and marker post at the edge of the woods.

2. Leave the Kingfisher Walk, turning right and following the footpath uphill across the field to join the Red Kite Walk at a track junction. Turn right, then left at the waymarker following the track to the south of Lan-las. Cross the stream and follow the path left, walking downstream back to the track. Turn right and follow the track downhill to a path junction and waymarker at the end of the Red Kite Walk.

3. Turn right following the Nuthatch Walk for a short distance to the next path junction and waymarker. Turn right at the next path junction and follow the Goldcrest Walk uphill through the woods. At the top the path turns sharp left and descends back through the woods to a path junction and waymarker.

4. Leave the Goldcrest Walk and bear right to rejoin the Nuthatch Walk. Follow this down to the river and left, walking upstream until you reach the bridge. Cross and return to Llanerchaeron and the start.

DOG-FRIENDLY AMENITIES

Dogs on leads are welcome in the walled gardens, lake, pleasure grounds and wider estate, car park, and visitor centre and café.

Conti's Café, located in a green-roofed building next to the visitor centre, is run by a local family business from Lampeter. As well as serving hot and cold drinks, including excellent coffee, you can buy Conti's multi-award-winning ice cream here. Using the same family recipe that Angelo Conti began making in the 1930s, today it's produced using organic milk and cream, along with organic raw cane sugar. You'll also find dairy-free options and even a Welsh whisky flavour! www.contisicecream.com

A short drive from Llanerchaeron, The Three Spaniels is a stunning Welsh smallholding with a microbrewery and dog-friendly shepherds' hut, which sleeps two. www.thethreespaniels.co.uk

The Kingfisher trail, which follows the River Aeron.

86. Cemlyn Shingle and Headland Walk

**Cemlyn Nature Reserve
Cemlyn
Cemaes Bay
Anglesey
LL67 0DY
01248 714795**
cemlyn@nationaltrust.org.uk

ABOUT THIS WALK

Distance 3.7 miles (5.9km)
Difficulty Moderate
Terrain Beach, coastal path and lane. Short but steep hills which can be muddy
Stiles No
Interest Coast, wildlife, geology

Set on the wild, north-western edge of Anglesey, Cemlyn's intricate coastline of rocks, small bays and headlands is fascinating to explore. This area is both a National Nature Reserve and a designated Area of Outstanding Natural Beauty. It's home to rare plants, such as the spotted rock rose, and breeding colonies of Sandwich, common and Arctic terns.

This stunning walk makes the most of the area's extraordinary geology, setting out with a crossing of the shingle ridge that separates the lagoon from the Irish Sea at Cemlyn Bay. Making it to the far side of the spit, you'll take in a loop of the remote headland, discovering its intriguing geology, vast array of coastal wildlife and the church of St Rhwydrus. Returning via a quiet country lane to the lagoon, you'll make a return crossing of the shingle to finish. Please note the Cemlyn Bay area, including the car parks and the bridge leading across to Esgair Gemlyn, is prone to flooding, so check tide times carefully before visiting.

THINGS TO SEE

The remarkable shingle ridge that separates the lagoon from the sea is known as Esgair Gemlyn, and was formed by the process of longshore (or littoral) drift – the movement of material along the shoreline by wave action. The ridge is home to some wonderful coastal plants, including sea kale, sea campion and yellow horned poppy, all of which thrive on its shifting stones.

Paws for thought
At high tide in stormy weather, the car park and beach sections can be flooded and dangerous. Access to the top of the shingle ridge is limited. When the terns are nesting, this area is patrolled by North Wales Wildlife Trust wardens and will be signed when out of bounds. As this is an area that's home to many seabirds, seals and other wildlife, dogs should be kept on leads at all times.

Other walkies nearby
Plas Newydd, on the eastern edge of Anglesey and overlooking the Menai Strait, is another great place to walk with your dog. Dogs are welcome in almost all areas of the gardens and grounds, including outside the mansion, the Rhododendron Garden and the Camellia Dell, as well as, further afield, the Coronation Meadow and the Arboretum through to Church Wood.

HOW TO GET HERE

Public transport Holyhead is the
closest station (12 miles/19.3km).
Take the Holyhead to Amlwch
bus, alighting at Tregele. Cemlyn
is 1.6 miles (2.6km) from Tregele.
Car Follow signs to Cemlyn
National Nature Reserve from
the A5025 in Tregele. Satnav:
LL67 0DU
OS map Explorer 262
Start/finish Cemlyn Bay car park,
LL67 0DU, grid ref: SH335931

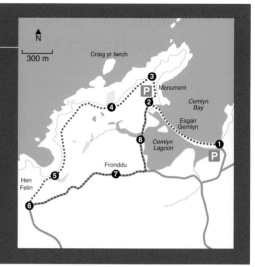

DOG-FRIENDLY AMENITIES

Just along the coast to the east
of Cemlyn, the beautiful house at
Bryn Llywelyn stands in its own
grounds, overlooking the bay at
Llanlleiana. Sleeping up to seven
people and two dogs, it's walking
distance to the sea and Wales
Coast Path (NT Holidays).

For post-walk refreshments, head
to The Bell, a small, independent
café on Cemaes Bay High Street,
a short walk from the beach. It's
dog-friendly and serves
homemade cakes, fresh coffee,
Red Boat gelato ice cream,
breakfast and light lunches.

DIRECTIONS

Start/finish: Cemlyn Bay car park

1. Walk onto the beach and turn left, following the shingle bank
   known as Esgair Gemlyn to the Bryn Aber car park at the far end.

2. Turn right and follow the coast path past the monument to the
   headland.

3. Go through the gate and continue on the coast path, walking
   with the sea to your right until you reach a small beach.

4. Follow the coast path, passing a turning on your left which would
   take you on a detour to St Rhwydrus's Church. Carry on walking
   to the small bay known as Henborth.

5. After passing Henborth leave the coast, bearing left through a
   gate and following the path inland towards Hen Felin (Old Mill).
   Turn left, cross a bridge and reach a small lane.

6. Follow the lane left towards Cemlyn Bay, passing Fronddu Farm.

7. Take the next left and follow this road towards the sea, with the
   Cemlyn lagoon on your right. Carry on to the causeway.

8. Follow the lane across the causeway and back to Bryn Aber car
   park. Turn right and follow the shingle beach back to the start.

Previous page: Aerial seascape of the
shingle ridge at Cemlyn.
Left: View from the beach at Cemlyn.

87. Forests and Waterfalls at Dolmelynllyn

Dolmelynllyn car park
Ganllwyd
Dolgellau
Gwynedd
LL40 2TF
01341 440238
eryri@nationaltrust.org.uk

ABOUT THIS WALK

Distance 4.2 miles (6.8km)
Difficulty Moderate
Terrain Woodland trails are rocky and rooty in places. Some tarmac. Steep and muddy sections
Stiles No
Interest History, wildlife

The Dolmelynllyn Estate covers around 1,200 acres (486ha) of farmland, woodland and parkland near the village of Ganllwyd in southern Eryri (Snowdonia). Once owned by William Madocks, the architect of Porthmadog, today it's free to explore, with trails winding through ancient woodland, including pockets of rare temperate rainforest where lichens, mosses and ferns thrive.

On this walk, you'll trace the River Gamlan, passing the spectacular cascades of the Rhaeadr Ddu – the Black Falls – which have inspired many generations of artists and writers.

THINGS TO SEE

During the 19th-century Welsh gold rush, Cefn Coch was one of the richest mines in the Merionnydd gold belt, which was then known as New California. As you explore, you'll see early and more recent stamping mills, as well as the barracks and a powder hut.

DOG-FRIENDLY AMENITIES

Mostyn Cottage, in the heart of nearby Coed y Brenin Forest Park, offers dog-friendly self-catering accommodation in two cosy log cabins. You're also just a short hop from the beach at Barmouth and the Rhinogydd and Cadair Idris mountain ranges.
www.mostyncottage.co.uk

Paws for thought
Dogs should be kept under close control in woodland and on leads on farmland. The rocky areas near to the river can become very slippery, especially after wet weather.

Other walkies nearby
The Ornamental Lake Walk (0.6 miles/1km) is an accessible, buggy- and wheelchair-friendly circuit around the lake at Dolmelynllyn, with viewing platforms extending out over the lake edge. It's a wonderful place to watch wildlife, and dog-friendly, too.

Above: The trail towards Rhaeadr Ddu falls.
Overleaf: Rhaeadr Ddu is a waterfall which cascades over 60ft.

Public transport The nearest
train station is Barmouth
(12 miles/19.3km). The
Dolgellau to Blaenau
Ffestiniog bus stops in
Ganllwyd.
Car On the A470 between
Dolgellau and Trawsfynydd.
Satnav: LL40 2TF
OS map Explorer OL18
Start/finish Ganllwyd car
park, LL40 2TF, grid ref:
SH727243

DIRECTIONS

Start/finish: Ganllwyd car park

1. Cross the A470 and follow the tarmacked road uphill with the River Gamlan to your left. Near the top of the hill, bear left onto a stony path and follow this to a wooden footbridge.

2. Walk across the bridge and turn right, following the path upstream to the Rhaeadr Ddu viewpoint.

3. Follow the path uphill and curving to the left, walking through woodland with the wall and boundary on your right. Follow this, staying right, past a path junction to reach a gate.

4. Continue along the path, following the waymarkers through the kissing gate. A little further on, take the path to your right and cross the wooden footbridge. Carry on along the path to your right, up a tarmac road and through a gate into recently clear-felled NRW forestry.

5. After about 110yds (100m) turn left up the forestry track. Follow the waymarkers over a rustic oak footbridge and onto the open mountain. From here the waymarkers will take you past the 19th-century gold workings. The path will lead you down to the ruined cottage of Berthlwyd, and returning to the track. Turn right and follow this downhill to the stone house on the left (Ty'n y Coed).

6. Take the path on the right, through a gate and follow the path up into the woods. Follow this path out of the woods.

7. Carry on along this path until you reach a junction. Take the turning to the left and follow the waymarkers down through the woods. This path will bring you to the Merionnydd National Trust work base. Turn right and follow the tarmac road downhill to the A470 near the Ty'n y Groes Inn.

8. Cross the A470 and follow the footpath opposite down to the River Mawddach and the road at the T'yn-y-Groes bridge. Turn left and follow the road back up to the A470. Turn right and follow this back to the start.

88. River Glaslyn and Cwm Bychan Walk

Near Beddgelert
Gwynedd
LL55 4NG
01766 510120
eryri@nationaltrust.org.uk

ABOUT THIS WALK

Distance 5.5 miles (8.9km)
Difficulty Challenging
Terrain Gravel path, rocky mountain trails and rocky river path. Steep and sometimes muddy sections
Stiles No
Interest History, wildlife

This challenging and adventurous walk takes you along the spectacular Aberglaslyn gorge, traversing the rocky Fisherman's Path, which winds its way above a spectacular stretch of the River Glaslyn.

As you go, you'll pass Bedd y Ci – the grave of Prince Llywelyn's faithful hound, Gelert, in the popular Welsh legend; the pretty village of Beddgelert – a perfect place to stop off for mid-walk refreshments; serene Llyn Dinas – said to be the resting place of the red dragon; and the atmospheric remnants of the copper mine workings of Sygun and Cwm Bychan.

THINGS TO SEE

The River Glaslyn is a real highlight of this walk, tumbling down its rocky gorge and widening out into shingly shallows, perfect for paddling. Its turquoise colour, which makes it look even more magical, comes from copper sulphate running from the surrounding hills.

Paws for thought

Dogs should be kept on leads near wildlife or grazing animals, and at all times during bird nesting season (1 March–31 July). There are sheer, unfenced drops along the Fisherman's Path, as well as uneven, rocky terrain which can be slippery after wet weather. Keep to paths as the area is dotted with tunnels, spoil heaps and pits.

Other walkies nearby

Gelert's Grave Walk is a 1-mile (1.6-km) flat, accessible trail that's suitable for buggies and wheelchairs. It takes in a loop of the surfaced trail that follows either side of the River Glaslyn, heading out through trees, crossing a bridge, and returning across a wide, grassy area, home to Gelert's Grave and a former Augustinian Priory.

DOG-FRIENDLY AMENITIES

Bistro Hebog in Beddgelert offers great food and drink, with dog-friendly outdoor seating in the pretty garden by the river. Ybistroynyrhebog.com Just a couple of miles outside Beddgelert, on the Craflwyn estate, Stabl Bach is a stunningly converted stable, offering accommodation for four people and a dog. Set out on one floor, the former loose boxes have been cleverly incorporated into the design. Walks from the door take you out into the wilds of the estate, and all the way to Yr Wyddfa (Snowdon) if you choose (NT Holidays).

Above: A tranquil day at Llyn Dinas lake near Bwthyn Mai.
Overleaf: The narrow path beside the Glaslyn river.

HOW TO GET HERE

Public transport Train station at Porthmadog (7.6 miles/12.9km), regular buses from there to Beddgelert on the S4 route. Alight at the Natmor Turn and follow the road to the start.

Car On the A4085 south of Beddgelert; drive from Beddgelert or Penrhyndeudraeth. Satnav: LL55 4YG

OS map Explorer OL17

Start/finish National Trust car park, Nantmor, LL55 4YG, grid ref: SH597462

DIRECTIONS

Start/finish: Nantmor National Trust car park

1. Leave the car park through a gate and follow the path – signposted Aberglaslyn – uphill into the woods, turning left and descending to the river path at Aberglaslyn.

2. Turn right onto the Fisherman's Path and follow this carefully upstream, with the River Glaslyn to your left. The path is rocky and twists up and down above the river, then hugs the edge as it follows the trail cut into the rocky cliffs. Carry on as the path gets easier until you reach a gate.

3. Go through the gate and cross the narrow-gauge Welsh Highland Railway. Stay on the right of the river and follow the gravel path upstream. Walk through a decorative gate and continue to the footbridge in Beddgelert. Cross here to visit the village and cafés.

4. This route doesn't cross to the village; instead turn right and follow the riverside path across the green and to the left of the houses. Carry on along this path through a gate to reach the road with a bridge to your left.

5. Follow the road right to the entrance to the Sygun Copper Mine.

6. Continue on the road downhill towards the river. Turn right through a gate and onto the riverside path, walking upstream with the river to your left. Follow this path until you go through a gate to reach Llyn Dinas and the small beach at its south-west end.

7. Turn right and follow the stony path steeply uphill; it zig-zags slightly but trends generally up and right onto the mountainside. As it flattens out continue to follow the path, ignore the first proper right turning and continue gently uphill to reach a path junction and wall at Bwlch y Sygun.

8. Follow the path down Cwm Bychan towards Aberglaslyn. As you descend, you'll pass the remains of the pylons and other mine equipment. Carry on down the valley, trending right at the bottom into the woodland. Turn left to reach Nantmor car park and the start.

89. Chirk Castle Woodland Walk

Chirk Castle
Chirk
Wrexham
LL14 5AF
01691 777701
chirkcastle@nationaltrust.org.uk

ABOUT THIS WALK

Distance 2.1 miles (3.4km)
Difficulty Easy
Terrain Mostly flat on gravel, grassy or tarmac surfaces
Stiles No
Interest History, wildlife

The imposing bulk of Chirk Castle dominates the surrounding landscape from its position on an outcrop high above the confluence of the rivers Dee and Ceiriog. Construction began in the late 13th century by the English during the reign of Edward I, and was intended as a Marcher castle – a fortress against the last princes of Wales.

Chirk boasts award-winning gardens, a wooded pleasure ground, and a terrace overlooking the 18th-century ha-ha – a means of keeping animals enclosed without the use of unsightly fences – and affording fine views out over the Cheshire and Shropshire countryside. This gentler walk follows mostly flat paths through woodland, finishing through open fields, popular in summer with wild flowers and pollinators. It's fully waymarked — follow the blue arrows throughout.

THINGS TO SEE

The veteran sweet chestnut tree you'll pass at around the half-way point of your walk is about 25ft (8m) in girth, and is over 500 years old – meaning it dates from around the time of King Henry VIII.

Paws for thought
No dogs other than assistance dogs are allowed in the formal gardens, kitchen garden, Pleasure Ground Wood or inside the castle rooms. You'll find animals grazing across the estate and fragile wildlife, so please keep dogs on leads and under close control at all times.

Above: A winter view of Chirk Castle from the north-west.
Overleaf: Chirk Castle estate.

Other walkies nearby
If you're visiting between April and September, as part of this route is permissive, head out on the fascinating, 3-mile (4.8-km) Battle of Crogen walk, which takes you to the Gates of the Dead with its ancient oak and the site of the 1165 Battle of Crogen.

DOG-FRIENDLY AMENITIES

Dogs are welcome on leads across the estate, and in the castle courtyard, where there's outdoor seating for the café. You'll find water bowls at Home Farm (where there's also a refreshment kiosk for owners on busier days) and by the castle, and waste bins across the estate.

You can stay in Chirk Castle's grounds in Chirk Home Farm Cottage. Inside is bright and airy, with room for four people and two dogs (NT Holidays).

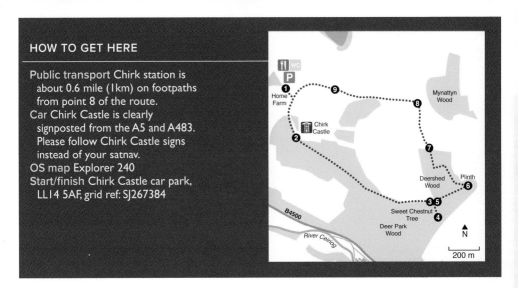

HOW TO GET HERE

Public transport Chirk station is about 0.6 mile (1km) on footpaths from point 8 of the route.
Car Chirk Castle is clearly signposted from the A5 and A483. Please follow Chirk Castle signs instead of your satnav.
OS map Explorer 240
Start/finish Chirk Castle car park, LL14 5AF, grid ref: SJ267384

DIRECTIONS

Start/finish: Chirk Castle car park

1. Leave the car park and follow the road to the left of the Home Farm visitor reception and café buildings, walking towards the castle. Carry on past the left turn up to the castle and follow the footpath signed Woodland Walk.

2. Continue on the path, passing the bird hide on your right and bearing left where the path forks. Continue on this path until you reach a gate into Deershed Wood.

3. The next section is an out and back to visit the old sweet chestnut tree. You can continue straight on towards point 5 if you wish. To visit the tree turn right and follow the path through the woodland.

4. The veteran tree is on your left. Retrace your steps back to the gate at point 3.

5. Turn right and walk through the gate into Deershed Wood. Follow the path ahead uphill through the woods to reach the plinth where a statue of Hercules used to stand.

6. From the plinth, take the right-hand path down the hill and turn right. Follow the path until it bends to the left and then slightly uphill to a larger path.

7. Walk through the gate and follow the blue waymarkers and the path across the field to a path junction at the field corner.

8. Turn left and go through the gate, following the blue waymarkers and the edge of the field until you reach the castle driveway.

9. Cross and follow the grass path opposite between the ha-ha ditch and the road, curving to the left back to the start.

90. Erddig Woods and Meadows Walk

Wrexham
LL13 0YT
01978 355314
erddig@nationaltrust.org.uk

ABOUT THIS WALK

Distance 3.4 miles (5.5km)
Difficulty Easy
Terrain Fairly flat with one steeper climb towards the end. Mainly grassy, gravel and woodland trails. Often muddy in the winter
Stiles No
Interest History, wildlife

Standing proudly on an escarpment above the Clywedog river, Erddig Hall (pronounced 'Erthig') is a grand, 17th-century country mansion surrounded by a fully restored 18th-century garden and 1,200-acre (486-ha) landscape pleasure park. A wonderful place to escape at any time of the year, this is a peaceful haven that's perfect for exploring and relaxing.

This varied and enjoyable walk follows the red waymarked route through a lush mixed landscape of riverside paths, woods, lakes and meadows. You'll walk through Big Wood, an ornamental woodland with a diverse range of broadleaved trees; the French meadow, with its extensive lake, and the Cup and Saucer cylindrical waterfall designed by William Emes in the 1770s.

THINGS TO SEE

There are more than 30 ponds across the estate, attracting a wide variety of water-loving wildlife. The lake in the French meadow, which you'll pass on this walk, was formed in the 1980s by subsidence caused by coal mining. Today it is home to many different birds, mammals and invertebrates.

Paws for thought

You'll find grazing animals across the wider estate, which continues to be worked by tenant farmers. Dogs should be kept on leads other than in the signed designated off-lead area.

Other walkies nearby

Erddig's riverside walk follows the green waymarkers on a 1.5-mile (2.4-km) loop, visiting some intriguing natural and archaeological features. You'll visit the famous 18th-century Cup and Saucer waterfall and follow the River Clywedog along the bottom of Wat's Dyke and Court Wood into the historic village of Felin Puleston, where you'll find the off-lead area.

Above: Erddig Country Park.
Overleaf: Erddig Hall.

Public transport Wrexham
   Central station is about 1.7 miles
   (2.7km) walk away. Follow the
   Wat's Dyke Way to join our route.
Car Follow the brown signs from
   the A525 Whitchurch Road or the
   A483 as satnav isn't always helpful.
Satnav: LL13 0YT
OS map Explorer 256
Start/finish Erddig car park,
   LI13 0YT, grid ref: SJ326481

DIRECTIONS

Start/finish: Erddig car park

1. Walk out of the car park onto the road by the dovecote, turn left and follow this
    around the edge of the car park and left. Follow the track with the formal gardens
    and ha-ha ditch on your left to reach the corner of the field at the edge of Big Wood.

2. Turn right and follow the waymarkers along Lime Walk. This path follows the edge
    of the French meadow and the River Clywedog, which runs parallel to the path
    through the trees to your left. Carry on until you reach a gate onto Sontley Road.

3. Follow the road to your left, walking steeply downhill and across Sontley Bridge.
    Carry on for a short distance, then turn left into Sontley Road car park.

4. Walk through the kissing gate into the French meadow. Follow the path across the meadow, going through a gate half-way across and continuing until you reach the stony footpath of Erddig Road. This section can get wet and muddy; to avoid it walk past the car park and take the next footpath on the left, walking through Coed-y-Glyn Wood to reach Erddig Road.

5. Turn left onto the path known as Erddig Road and follow it over the stone bridge. Follow this path across the parkland and over another stone bridge. Continue until you reach a path junction with a wooden bridge to the right.

6. Walk across the wooden bridge and up to the Cup and Saucer water feature. Stay to the left of the Cup and Saucer, walk through the wooden kissing gate and follow the red waymarker sign. This path traces the course of Black Brook. The path curves right and then left, away from the stream, and through a kissing gate up to the main drive.

7. Turn right and follow the drive for a short distance, then turn left through a gate onto Green Lane footpath. Follow this path towards the next path junction.

8. Take the next left and follow this to Sontley Lodge Farm.

9. Pass the farm on your right and follow the stony path towards Forest Wood. Turn right and continue until you reach a gate on your left.

10. Go through the gate and follow the central path through Forest Wood. Turn left onto Forest Drive and follow this over a cattle grid. Leave the drive, turning right and following the path along the edge of Erddig Park with Forest Wood to your right. Continue across the parkland to the road by the dovecote and return to the start.

DOG-FRIENDLY AMENITIES

Dogs on leads are welcome across the wider estate, and in the tea garden and Midden Yard. You'll find water bowls and waste bins dotted around, and a signed off-lead zone at Felin Puleston, where your dog can stretch its legs and play.

241

91. Rhosili Beach and Downs Walk

Rhosili,
Swansea,
SA3 1PR
01792390707
visit.rhosili@nationaltrust.org.uk

ABOUT THIS WALK

Distance 4.4 miles (7.1km)
Difficulty Challenging
Terrain Steep steps, uneven moorland paths and beach or coast path
Stiles No
Interest Coast, wildlife, history

Beautiful Rhosili bay (Rhossili), with its 3-mile (4.8-km) stretch of stunning sandy beach, is backed by the rolling grasslands of Rhosili Down. From the top of the down, the highest point on the Gower Peninsula, views stretch out over The Vile – a medieval open field strip system – along the undulating Welsh coast, and across the Bristol Channel to Lundy Island and the North Devon coast.

This walk sets out from Rhosili village, passing St Mary's Church, which was built in the 12th and 13th centuries – look out for the unknown sailor's grave in the corner of the churchyard. You'll climb steeply up to reach The Beacon at the top of Rhosili Down, but the views once you get there are well worth the effort. Descending takes you past a Second World War radar station and through an area of heathland, bright with pink and purple heather in late summer and early autumn.

THINGS TO SEE

The Vile, at Rhosili, is a well-preserved example of a medieval open field strip system. There are many other interesting archaeological features to discover along this stretch of the coast, including Neolithic burial chambers, Bronze Age cairns and Iron Age forts.

Paws for thought
Dogs are allowed on the beach all year, but must be kept on leads around grazing animals on the downs, and seals out on the rocks.

Other walkies nearby
From the National Trust shop in Rhosili village, a level walk takes you along the grassy clifftop to the Old Coastguard Lookout. If the tide is out, the sure-footed can cross the rocky causeway to the tidal island of Worms Head. This is an exhilarating place for watching the waves and seabirds, and you'll often spot grey seals lazing on the rocks below. Be sure to make it back across the causeway before the tide comes in and Worms Head becomes an island again.

Above: Rhossili beach.

Public transport Trains to Swansea. Regular bus services on route 118/119 from Swansea to Rhossili. Currently no Sunday service.
Car From Swansea, follow the A4118 then the B4247 to Rhossili. Satnav: SA3 1PR
OS map Explorer 164
Start/finish Rhosili National Trust car park, SA3 1PR, grid ref: SS414880

DIRECTIONS

Start/finish: Rhosili National Trust car park

1. Walk out of the car park and back onto the road, turn right and follow this to the churchyard. Follow the footpath to the left of the church and turn left at the next path junction. Follow the track up to a gate marked with a National Trust sign for Rhosili Down.

2. Go through the gate and follow the path uphill across the heathland to reach the trig point at the summit of The Beacon. You're at the highest point of the walk.

3. Follow the path along the Rhosili Down ridge, undulating slightly but generally losing height as you go. You'll pass the remains of Stone Age burial chambers and a Second World War radar station. Climb up slightly to the north summit and then descend quite steeply towards Hillend Campsite and the road.

4. Turn left and follow the road onto the site, past Eddie's Café and head down onto the beach.

5. Walk left along the beach, with Rhosili Down up to your left. Pass the wreck of *The Helvetia* out to your right and head for the path and steps on the left under Rhosili Cliffs.

6. Leave the beach and follow the path and steep steps back up to the top of Rhosili Cliffs by the National Trust shop. Turn right to return to the start.

DOG-FRIENDLY AMENITIES

The Ship Inn at Port Eynon (a 15-minute drive from Rhosili) and The Britannia Inn in Llanmadoc (a 30-minute drive from Rhosili) both welcome dogs inside.

Dogs are very welcome at the NT Rhosili shop, which sells a range of goodies for dogs, including doggie ice cream. Open between Easter and the end of October; check website for opening times.

Stay at South Pilton Green Farmhouse in Rhosili, which sleeps up to five people and one dog. The house has a footpath that leads straight onto the breathtaking clifftops of the Wales Coast Path with views to Lundy Island off Devon on a clear day (NT Holidays).

Northern
Ireland

92. Ancient Woodlands and Ruined Castles at Crom

**Upper Lough Erne
Newtownbutler
County Fermanagh
BT92 8AJ
02867 738118**
crom@nationaltrust.org.uk

ABOUT THIS WALK

Distance 3.5 miles (5.6km)
Difficulty Easy
Terrain Grassy and woodland paths, fairly flat but can be muddy
Stiles No
Interest History, wildlife

Set on the shores of Upper Lough Erne, the scenic, 2,000-acre (809-ha) estate at Crom is made up of tranquil islands, ancient woodlands and an atmospheric ruined castle. It is also one of Ireland's most important conservation areas.

This walk has water at its heart, setting out from the shores of Lough Erne and following the loughside trail towards the old castle and yews. You'll past the boathouse, with its glorious views out across the lough and its numerous waterbirds, before crossing the White Bridge onto Inisherk Island. A full loop of the island takes you past the walled garden before returning across the bridge to the deer park.

THINGS TO SEE

Close to the ruins, in the Old Castle Garden, are Crom's famous Yew Trees, named among the '50 greatest British trees'. Thought to be almost 400 years old, this conjoined pair of a male and female English yews has a combined circumference of 377 feet (115m) and a diameter of 115 feet (35m). In the 19th century, parties of 200 people are said to have dined beneath their branches.

Paws for thought
You'll often find sheep and cattle grazing on the Crom estate. You may also see some deer. The estate is a patchwork of sensitive and delicate habitats for a rich diversity of wildlife that can be easily disturbed. Dogs should be kept on a lead and under effective control throughout the estate.

Other walkies nearby
The Argory, an estate in Dungannon, County Armagh, is another great place to visit with dogs. For a scenic, peaceful riverside walk, follow the River Blackwater around the estate and across the intriguing, industrial-age Bond's Bridge. If you're lucky, you might spot the bright blue flashes of kingfishers, flying low along the water.

Public transport Take the Enniskillen to Clones bus (connections from Belfast), alight at Newtownbutler, 3 miles (4.8km) away.
Car On Newtownbutler to Crom road. Follow signs from Lisnaskea. Satnav: BT92 8AJ
OSNI map Lough Erne Activity Map
Start/finish Crom visitor centre, BT92 8AJ, grid ref: H370239

Upper Lough Erne

West Derrybeg

White Bridge

Crom Castle

Lough Nalughoge

Old Castle

The Boathouse

Deer Park

Walled Garden

Old Castle

Old Castle

Jetty

N

300 m

DIRECTIONS

Start/finish: Crom visitor centre

1. Turn left out of the visitor centre courtyard and follow the main avenue towards Crom Castle. Turn left onto the Old Causeway, signed 'to the Old Castle'.

2. Follow this path to the Old Castle, a fascinating ruined 17th-century castle.

3. From the Old Castle turn left, back onto the stone lane and follow the loughside path, past a boathouse to reach the White Bridge.

4. Cross to Inisherk Island and turn right, following the Inisherk Trail around the edge of the island. Walk past the walled garden and back to the White Bridge. Cross again and turn left following the path through the trees with the lough to your left.

5. Continue walking along this path, passing the Summer House, Ice House and Boat House, with the lough to your left. Carry on along the path as it curves to the right, joining the tarmacked avenue back towards the visitor centre.

DOG-FRIENDLY AMENITIES

Dogs are welcome along the trails and in the visitor centre. Water bowls are provided near the visitor centre, a dog wash station is located near the toilets in the main visitor car park, and you'll find dog waste bins around the estate.

There are several dog friendly holiday cottages available at Crom, and the campsite is also dog-friendly. Up to two dogs can stay in each tent or, if you'd prefer, you can book into a dog-friendly glamping pod.

Opposite: A group of kayakers by the ruins of the old castle at Crom.

93. Murlough Dunes and Woods Walk

Keel Point
Dundrum
County Down
BT33 0LW
02843 751467
murlough@nationaltrust.org.uk

ABOUT THIS WALK

Distance 4.8 miles (7.7km)
Difficulty Moderate
Terrain Paths and beach with some short but steep sections
Stiles No
Interest Wildlife, coast, history

Murlough National Nature Reserve encompasses a fragile, 6,000-year-old sand dune system, managed as Ireland's first nature reserve since 1967. Beyond the dunes stretches a wide expanse of sandy beach, with a pebble ridge marking the high watermark.

Rising above this spectacular coastal setting, the granite peaks of the Mourne Mountains dominate the horizon, including Northern Ireland's highest mountain, Slieve Donard, at 2,790ft (850m). This is a truly awe-inspiring yet utterly peaceful place to visit. This walk explores Murlough's wide range of habitats, including heathland, species-rich grassland, scrubland and woodland, as well as some points of historical interest along the way.

THINGS TO SEE

The eye-catching marsh fritillary butterfly overwinters as a caterpillar and can be seen in flight in late spring and early summer. Numbers of these brightly-patterned butterflies are declining all over Europe, although the UK is considered a stronghold and it's a priority species in Northern Ireland. The caterpillar feeds on the tall, purple devil's bit scabious flowers, which bloom across mountain and moorland in late summer and early autumn and are popular with many pollinators.

Above: Murlough National Nature Reserve.

Opposite: The beach and dune habitat at Murlough Nature Reserve.

Paws for thought

Dogs should be kept on leads at all times while in the reserve. When possible, please keep to the marked pathways and boardwalks in order to avoid disturbance to wildlife. Please be aware of animal grazing areas and ground-nesting bird sections of the reserve, where dogs are not allowed – these will be signed.

Other walkies nearby

The Murlough Woodland Walk is a lovely, shorter walk that explores the wooded area around Murlough House and the North Point. You'll discover a range of different trees, most of which were planted in the late 1800s, and a developing flora, which comes alive during springtime. Closer to the North Point, you'll walk through a more natural woodland of hazel, blackthorn and spindle.

HOW TO GET HERE

Public transport Belfast Great
Victoria and Belfast Central are
the closest train stations. Use
the Ulsterbus 20 from Belfast to
Newcastle, alight at Lazy BJ
Caravan Park after Dundrum.
Car Belfast is about 25 miles
(40km) north on the A24. Newry
is 25 miles (40km) west and
Downpatrick is 10 miles (16km)
to the east, both on the A25.
Satnav: BT33 0LW
OSNI map Mournes Activity Map
Start/finish Murlough Car Park,
BT33 0LW, grid ref: J394338

DIRECTIONS

Start/finish: Murlough car park

1. Walk out of the pedestrian gate in the centre of the car park, turn left and follow
the boardwalk into the nature reserve. Follow the boardwalk past a junction and
through the dunes to the beach.

2. Turn left and walk along Murlough beach. Pass a black marker and then a yellow
marker; both of these mark paths that can be followed back inland for a shorter loop.
Continue walking along the beach until you reach a green marker close to the channel.

3. Follow the green topped marker post left up a steep sandy path over the dune and
through an area of woodland. Turn right just before the gardens of Murlough House.
When you reach the end of the Murlough House garden you will see a miniature
chapel. Turn left up a short rise, continuing to follow the green topped posts.

4. Continue on the path on the seaward side of the house, walk through an area of
woodland and keep right, following the path down the slope to the beach next to
the boathouse.

5. Turn left and walk along the beach until you reach the next left, signed with a green post. Follow this up the bank on the Hazel Path to a junction with a larger track.

6. Follow this track right, staying close to the channel on the right. Walk down through the gorse scrub and stay right back to the beach.

7. Turn left and walk along the beach until you can see a set of stone steps on your left. Walk up the steps and follow the path back into the nature reserve. Continue in this direction until you reach the minor road that crosses in front of you.

8. Follow the road left for a short distance, then turn right through the gate onto a path. Follow this path along the edge of the nature reserve, with farmland to your right. Follow the edge of the fields around to the right, back towards the inner bay and Exmoor Kraal.

9. Go past the Kraal, over a stile, until you turn left onto the gravel road. Follow the yellow topped posts back to the car park and start.

View of the Mourne Mountains across the sand dunes.

94. Castle Ward and Strangford Lough

Strangford
Downpatrick
County Down
BT30 7BA
02844 881204
castleward@nationaltrust.org.uk

ABOUT THIS WALK

Distance 8 miles (12.9km)
Difficulty Challenging
Terrain Well-surfaced paths,
with lots of gates and some
steep sections
Stiles No
Interest History, wildlife

With its eccentric 18th-century mansion – a mixture of Gothic and classical architecture – and over 800 acres (324ha) of landscaped gardens and rolling parkland overlooking the peaceful expanse of Strangford Lough, Castle Ward is a must-visit for nature lovers and a wonderful place to explore with your dog.

This walk follows the popular and well-waymarked Boundary Trail, taking in everything this fascinating property has to offer. You'll wander along the windswept shoreline, through leafy woodland, across open grassland – spectacular with wild flowers in summer – and through magnificent parkland, with plenty of places to stop and take in the views. There are also several opportunities to shorten the route if required.

THINGS TO SEE

Strangford Lough is the largest sea lough in the British Isles, a unique and beautiful place that's internationally important for nature conservation. It stretches from Angus Rock, where it joins the Irish Sea, to the vast sand flats at its northern end, some 20 miles (32km) away, and is dotted with around 100 islands.

Paws for thought

As the trail is multi-use, be aware of cyclists, horse riders, runners and other walkers. Cattle and sheep may also be grazing in some areas. Only assistance dogs are permitted in the house and shop.

Other walkies nearby

There's a great choice of different waymarked trails around Castle Ward and Strangford Lough, including the 1.8-mile (2.9-km) Castle Trail, the 1.2-mile (1.9-km) Shore Trail and the 2.5-mile (4-km) Farm Trail. Pick up a leaflet detailing all these at the visitor centre.

Visitors walking towards
Temple Water.

Public transport Take the bus from Downpatrick to Strangford, alight at Castle Ward gates.

Car Castle Ward is 7 miles (11.3km) north-east of Downpatrick, and 1 mile (1.6km) from Strangford on A25. Satnav: BT30 7BA and follow signs for Castle Ward only.

OSNI map Strangford Lough Activity Map

Start/finish Shore car park, BT30 7BA, grid ref: NW677031

DIRECTIONS

Start/finish: Shore car park

1. This walk follows the red waymarked Boundary Trail throughout. Turn left out of the car park and follow the multi-user Shore Trail along the coast and past Audley's Castle. Continue around to the left and into Audleystown Wood.

2. Continue on the path heading inland and back past the castle (now on your left) to reach Audleystown Road. Cross and follow the farm trail opposite to the right of Temple Water. Follow the path right through mature woodland to West Park, behind the old walled garden. Turn sharp right at the back of the Walled Garden to stay on the Boundary Trail, which continues parallel to road.

3. Carry on walking along the Boundary Trail to the edge of Mallard Wood, where you turn left and follow the path through the mature coniferous woodland to Downpatrick Avenue. Turn right and follow this for a short distance, then follow the Boundary Trail left and left again at the next junction. Walk through Castle Ward Forest, crossing the Hoof Trail and reaching a path junction.

4. Turn sharp right and continue on the Boundary Trail to the viewpoint in Castle Ward Wood. Walk along the trail through the woodland to reach a junction with the Hoof Trail near the edge of the small lough.

5. Cross the Hoof Trail and walk across parkland and through some smaller areas of trees. The trail bends to the left and crosses Park Road. Walk through Windmill Plantation to reach Church Walk.

6. Cross Church Walk and continue on the Boundary Trail across parkland to Strangford Avenue on the coast. Turn left and follow this back to the start.

DOG-FRIENDLY AMENITIES

Dogs on leads are welcome across the estate, in the garden and in the Stableyard Tea-room. There's a designated dog exercise field located near the admission hut and main car park where you can let your dog have a stretch off the lead.

Opposite: The 18th-century mansion at Castle Ward. Left: The Lough trail.

95. Giant's Causeway Clifftop Walk

**44 Causeway Road
Bushmills
County Antrim
BT57 8SU
02820 731855**
giantscausewaytic@nationaltrust.org.uk

ABOUT THIS WALK

Distance 3.6 miles (5.8km)
Difficulty Challenging
Terrain Coastal paths,
gravel trail and grassland.
Sections of narrow and
steep path which can be
slippery in the wet
Stiles No
Interest History, geology,
coast, wildlife

Northern Ireland's only UNESCO World Heritage Site, the Giant's Causeway, captures the imagination of all who see it. Set in a dramatic landscape of coastal cliffs, and backed by the swelling Atlantic, this is a place where the magic of geology takes centre stage.

This walk follows the waymarked Yellow Trail, accessible from the seaside village of Portballintrae. Setting out from just beyond Runkerry House, you'll climb onto the clifftops, passing around the edge of Runkerry Head and taking in fantastic coastal views. You'll pass the dolphin and basking shark bench – a wonderful spot to stop and admire the views to the Giant's Causeway, the Skerries, Donegal and the distant hills of the Inishowen Peninsula. If you're lucky you might also see dolphins playing in the waves.

THINGS TO SEE

When the Giant's Causeway was formed, about 60 million years ago, the island of Ireland was still joined to North America. As Europe split away from North America, huge rifts were created in the Earth's surface. Magma (molten rock) bubbled up through the cracks, cooling and solidifying into basalt rock as it reached the surface.

Over the millennia that followed, erosion created a river valley through the basalt. Successive flows of lava along the river valley, inching toward the coast and cooling when they came into contact with the sea formed columns of layered basalt. The pressure between these columns sculpted them into the fascinating polygonal shapes we see today.

Paws for thought

This wild, coastal landscape is exposed to high winds, and you'll encounter sheer cliffs, uneven terrain and unstable rocks here. Keep dogs on leads and stay well away from cliff edges.

Other walkies nearby

The accessible Green Trail follows a 2-mile (3.2-km) clifftop trail towards Runkerry. You'll be treated to views of the Giant's Causeway as you go, and on clear days glorious views stretch to Scotland and the Inishowen Peninsula.

**Above: Waves crash against the Giant's Causeway.
Opposite: The Giant's Causeway Visitor Centre.**

Public transport Train services from Belfast and Londonderry (Derry) to Coleraine then Ulsterbus service 172 or seasonal buses.

Car The Giant's Causeway and Visitor Centre is located on the B147 Causeway road. It is 2 miles (3.2km) from Bushmills village. Satnav: BT57 8SU

OSNI map Causeway Coast and Rathlin Island Activity map

Start/finish Runkerry Head, BT57 8SU, grid ref: C940438

Map labels:
Port na Spaniagh · Hamilton's Seat ⑤ · The Amphitheatre · Benanouran Head · Grand Causeway · The Organ · Croyer Hill · Great Stookan · Giant's Chair ③ · ② · ① · Causeway Hotel · Runkerry Head P · Causeway Head · Hall · B146 · Carrowreagh Bridge · ④

N · 500 m

DIRECTIONS

Start/finish: Runkerry Head

1. Turn right and follow the Yellow Trail and clifftop path around Runkerry Head to the Causeway Hotel.

2. Continue on the coast path and onto the roof of the Giant's Causeway Visitor Centre. Walk past the top of the steps and take a slight left. Pass the viewfinder map and head uphill to Weir Snout.

3. Follow the clifftop path with the sea on your left, pass the Shepherd's Steps where the Blue and Red trails turn left. Carry on walking along the clifftop trail.

4. As you get further from the Giant's Causeway the path becomes a bit smaller and quieter. Continue on the path to reach Hamilton's Seat.

5. Hamilton's Seat is a wonderful viewpoint to look along the coast at the interesting rock formations. When you're ready, turn around and follow the same path back along the coast to the start.

DOG-FRIENDLY AMENITIES

Dogs on leads are welcome in all areas of the Visitor Centre, including in the café, and across the World Heritage Site. Dogs on leads are also welcome on guided tours.

Scotland

**St Abb's Head
National Trust for
Scotland
Northfield
Eyemouth
TD14 5QF
01890 771443**
st.abbs@nts.org.uk

ABOUT THIS WALK

Distance 3.3 miles (5.3km)
Difficulty Moderate
Terrain Coast path and track
Stiles No
Interest Coast, geology,
wildlife

Lying on the north-east coast of Berwickshire, in the southern Scottish Borders, the dramatic and windswept coastal headland of St Abb's Head is renowned for its vast seabird colonies. Looked after by the National Trust for Scotland, the area has been a designated National Nature Reserve since 1984.

This enjoyable walk explores the headland, starting out to the north and taking in a loop around Mire Loch, passing the remains of St Abb's Nunnery, Kirk Hill and St Abb's Head lighthouse. The return stretch follows the intricate coastline, passing numerous rocky pinnacles and arches rising from the sea, with spectacular views and plenty of birdlife to watch.

THINGS TO SEE

From the swans, damselflies, dragonflies, eels, perch and sticklebacks in and around the loch to thousands of nesting seabirds on the rocky outcrops, St Abb's is a special place for wildlife. Look for guillemots, razorbills, puffins, kittiwakes, fulmars, shags and herring gulls gathering on the rocks and soaring over the waves. Away from the water, a carpet of wild flowers spreads out across the grassland – including sea pinks, rock rose, wild thyme and purple milk vetch.

Paws for thought
St Abb's Head has lengthy sections of unfenced cliff edge, as well as populations of breeding birds and delicate flora, so keep dogs on leads.

Other walkies nearby
The coast path offers spectacular walking in either direction: north past Coldingham Loch to Fast Castle Head, or south past Coldingham Bay, with its stunning stretch of sandy beach, to the village of Eyemouth. The fort at Eyemouth was constructed first by the English, and then by the French, in the 1500s.

Above: Starney Bay.

Public transport Berwick-upon-Tweed
train station is 14 miles (22.5km) away.
Take the 235 Borders Bus service to
St Abb's Head.
Car From the A1 follow the B6438 via
Coldingham. Satnav: TD14 5QF
OS map Explorer 346
Start/finish St Abb's Head car park,
TD14 5QF, grid ref: NT913674

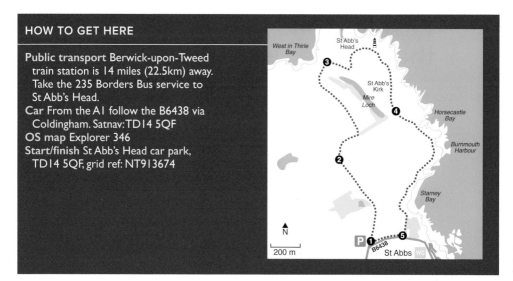

DIRECTIONS

Start/finish: St Abb's Head car park

1. Turn right out of the car park and walk past
   the visitor centre. Take the left fork after the
   cottages and follow this track across fields to a
   track junction.

2. Stay on the track as it curves right and walk
   towards the end of a linear wood. Turn left at
   the edge of the wood and follow the track
   parallel to Mire Loch, heading towards the
   coast. The track curves to the right and joins
   the coast path.

3. Turn right and follow the Berwickshire Coastal
   Path up and around St Abb's Head. Pass above
   the lighthouse and head downhill with the sea
   on your left to walk past the ruins of St Abb's
   Kirk. Continue to the corner of a field near the
   end of the loch.

4. Follow the coast path with the field boundary
   to your right and the sea to the left. Walk
   around the headland above Burnmouth
   Harbour and to the seaside of Bell Hill. Follow
   the path right at the edge of the woodland to
   reach a right turn just before the B6438.

5. Take this path to the right and walk across the
   field back to the car park and start.

DOG-FRIENDLY AMENITIES

In St Abb's village, just to the south of this walk,
you'll find two great cafés. Ebbcarrs, overlooking
the harbour, has dog-friendly outdoor seating,
which can be blustery, but the views are second
to none. The Old School Café, at the Ebba Centre,
allows dogs inside. Both are popular and serve
good, local food.

97. East Lomond and the Maspie Den

Back Wynd car park
Falkland
Cupar
KY15 7AN

ABOUT THIS WALK

Distance 4.6 miles (7.4km)
Difficulty Challenging
Terrain Mountain trails,
grass, gravel and sections of
road. Some sections are
steep and can be slippery
Stiles Yes
Interest History

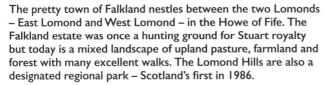

The pretty town of Falkland nestles between the two Lomonds – East Lomond and West Lomond – in the Howe of Fife. The Falkland estate was once a hunting ground for Stuart royalty but today is a mixed landscape of upland pasture, farmland and forest with many excellent walks. The Lomond Hills are also a designated regional park – Scotland's first in 1986.

This walk begins in the heart of Falkland, heading through woodland and up onto the open hillside of East Lomond, climbing steeply to the top for glorious views across the Fife countryside, to West Lomond and to the Forth Estuary. For a simple out-and-back walk, you can turn around and retrace your steps to Falkland, however, the second half of the walk is packed with fascinating features, including a rock-cut path that passes excitingly behind a waterfall and the Maspie Den – a network of paths laid out in the 19th century to showcase the Falkland estate.

THINGS TO SEE

Falkland is most famous for its fine Renaissance palace, inspired by the grand châteaux of France and once a favourite haunt of Mary, Queen of Scots. Looked after by the National Trust for Scotland, it boasts spectacular architecture, beautiful gardens and one of Britain's oldest tennis courts (paid entry/NTS membership).

Paws for thought
You'll often find grazing animals on the hills in this area, so keep dogs under close control at all times.

Other walkies nearby
You'll find 17 miles (27.3km) of trails to explore around the Falkland Estate, which is free to enter and has parking on-site. There's also a shop and café here.

Neighbouring West Lomond makes a great walk, starting in peaceful woodland and heading up onto open hillside to follow clear trails up to the trig point-topped summit for expansive views out across Loch Leven and the Ochil Hills.

Above: Descending from East Lomond, with West Lomond in the distance.
Opposite: East Lomond summit.

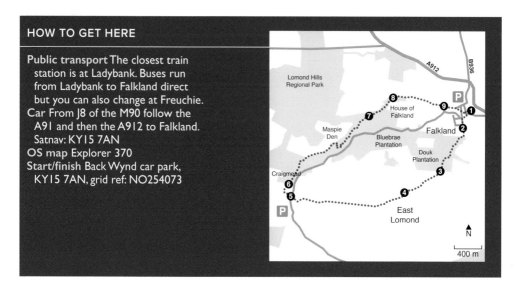

HOW TO GET HERE

Public transport The closest train station is at Ladybank. Buses run from Ladybank to Falkland direct but you can also change at Freuchie.
Car From J8 of the M90 follow the A91 and then the A912 to Falkland.
Satnav: KY15 7AN
OS map Explorer 370
Start/finish Back Wynd car park, KY15 7AN, grid ref: NO254073

DIRECTIONS

Start/finish: Back Wynd car park

1. Turn right out of the car park and walk along the road past the library; then turn right onto Back Wynd. Follow this and turn right where the road forks then left onto East Loan. Follow East Loan out of town.

2. Continue on the road marked 'Private road and footpath', it turns into a track and bends to the right. Take the left fork and follow the wooden steps uphill through the beech woods and then up some more steps to the edge of the moorland.

3. Follow the mountain path right and uphill; cross a stile and steeper ground to reach the trig point and topograph on the summit of East Lomond.

4. Continue on the path heading downhill. The path is initially steep and rough, but you soon merge with a larger track, which you follow downhill to the road at Craigmead.

5. Turn right onto the road then left into Craigmead car park. Walk through this to the far corner, where you join a footpath signed to West Lomond. Go through a gate and follow this briefly to the path junction at the edge of the trees. Turn right onto another footpath heading downhill, signed to Falkland. Follow this to a track and the edge of the Bluebrae Plantation.

6. Go through a gate and walk downhill through the plantation; take the left fork in the path then cross a footbridge and trend right through another gate. Take the second path on the right, which passes behind a waterfall. Continue along the far side of the burn to reach the Maspie Den. Cross several wooden footbridges and a stone bridge by a waterfall. Carry on down the path ignoring the bridges to the right and crossing another bridge to reach a track which crosses your path.

7. Cross the track and carry on down the path, ignoring the bridges to the right and walking through a stone tunnel. It can be dark, but there should be enough light to get through. Carry on down the Den, pass under a bridge and walk past the House of Falkland and across another bridge to reach West Port road.

8. Turn right and follow West Port back towards Falkland. Pass the Falkland Estate stables and the car park (both on your left) and reach the road junction with the High Street.

9. Bear left, following the High Street into Falkland. Stay right where the road forks, walking along Braunton Street and then Horse Market until you can turn left, rejoining the outbound walk along Back Wynd. Turn right to return to the start.

DOG-FRIENDLY AMENITIES

The Falkland Estate is an organic working farm and has lots to see and do, including walking and cycling trails, a shop selling local crafts and produce, a gallery, and a welcoming café – The Stables. With dog-friendly indoor and outdoor seating, and water bowls provided, it's a perfect post-walk stop. The Coachman's Cottage on the estate offers dog-friendly, self-catering accommodation set within the stunning Lomond Hills and sleeps up to four people. www.falklandestate.co.uk

West Lomond from the summit of East Lomond.

98. Along the Pass of Killiecrankie

Killiecrankie
Near Pitlochry
Perthshire
PH16 5LQ
01796 473233
killiecrankie@nts.org.uk

ABOUT THIS WALK

Distance 3.6 miles (5.8km)
Difficulty Moderate
Terrain Sometimes rough riverside trail and sections of lane
Stiles No
Interest History, wildlife

This adventurous walk follows in the footsteps of Jacobite troops and English redcoats, who travelled through the Pass of Killiecrankie on 27 July 1689. Set within an impressive, wooded gorge, this popular beauty spot is well known for the battle that took place nearby.

The gorge is a Site of Special Scientific Interest and lies within the Loch Tummel National Scenic Area. There's a wildlife feeding station near the visitor centre, which is well placed for spotting red squirrels, pine martens (if you're very lucky), woodpeckers and nuthatches.

THINGS TO SEE

The Garry Bridge is an iconic suspension bridge that spans the River Garry. Built in 1969, it offers stunning views of the river below, and is a fantastic spot for photographs.

Paws for thought

The gorge and surrounding woodland are an important habitat for wildlife, including rare flora and fauna that can be easily disturbed or damaged. Please keep dogs under close control at all times. You'll also encounter unfenced drops along the gorge.

Other walkies nearby

Adjacent to the Pass of Killiecrankie, Tay Forest Park is a wonderfully varied area, networked with paths to explore and rich in wildlife and history. Start your visit at the Queen's View, where you can admire the beautiful vistas over Loch Tummel. Then head for nearby Allean Forest, where you'll find an 18th-century farmstead and ruined Pictish ring fort.

HOW TO GET HERE

Public transport Pitlochry has
 a train station and there are
 regular buses from Pitlochry
 towards Blair Atholl; alight at
 Killiecrankie.
Car The visitor centre and car
 park are 3 miles (4.8km) north
 of Pitlochry off the B8079.
Satnav: PH16 5LQ
OS Map Explorer OL49
Start/finish Killiecrankie visitor
 centre car park, PH16 5LQ,
 grid ref: NN917626

DOG-FRIENDLY AMENITIES

Dogs are welcome across the
site and inside the visitor centre,
including in the Jacobite Café,
but must always be kept under
control (and on a lead when
indoors). The centre is open
every day except Christmas Day,
Boxing Day and New Year's Day:
10am–4pm (November–March
inclusive); 10am–5pm (April–
October inclusive).

DIRECTIONS

Start/finish: Killiecrankie visitor centre car park

1. Walk past the visitor centre, following signs to Riverside Walks
   and the Soldier's Leap. Follow the path down the steps towards
   the River Garry. At the bottom of the stairs you'll reach a path
   junction, turn right, following the path down more steps to the
   Soldier's Leap view point.

2. Return to the main path and continue following signs towards
   the Pass of Killiecrankie. Follow this trail down river to reach the
   green footbridge.

3. Cross and follow the path left downstream, taking the right fork
   and then climbing a flight of stairs to reach the B8019 road at
   Garry Bridge. To stay off the roads, turn around here and retrace
   your steps back to the start.

4. To continue the loop, turn right, walk through the car park and
   along the path adjacent to the B8019 for a short distance, then
   turn right onto a smaller road. Follow this road uphill through
   woodland and then back down hill to the River Garry. Cross the
   river and then the railway to reach a junction with the busier
   B8079 in Killiecrankie.

5. Turn right and follow the road on the right for a short distance
   and then cross to follow the path on the other side signed to
   Pitlochry. Cross the road again and follow the path back towards
   the Soldier's Leap. Rejoin the outbound path and turn left up the
   steps and back to the visitor centre and start.

The pass of Killiecrankie.

99. Balmacara Estate

Balmacara Estate
Lochalsh House
Balmacara
Kyle
IV40 8DN
01599 566325
balmacara@nts.org.uk

ABOUT THIS WALK

Distance 8.5 miles (13.7km)
Difficulty Challenging
Terrain Forest and
moorland trails and paths
Stiles No
Interest History, wildlife

Covering the rocky moors and wooded hills overlooking the Kyle of Lochalsh, Balmacara is a traditional Highland crofting estate, looked after by the National Trust for Scotland. Rich in wildlife and history, yet peaceful and relatively undiscovered; ease of access and a network of well-maintained trails make it ideal for on-foot exploration.

This walk sets out from pretty Balmacara Square at the heart of the estate, with its friendly café, art gallery and visitor information centre. From here there's a good climb following waymarked trails through slender birch trees, emerging high on open moorland with views across to the exhilarating skylines of Torridon and Applecross. A little farther on is remote Loch Achaidh na h-Inich, with its tiny, cairn-topped islet – the remains of an ancient, inhabited crannog. After looping the loch, the return trip explores the pine-forested foothills of Sgùrr Mòr and the ancient, lichen-clad oak woods at Reraig, just above Loch Alsh. A final climb gains grand views to Skye and the Cuillin Ridge, from where it's downhill to the finish at Balmacara Square.

Paws for thought
The estate is home to a diverse array of delicate flora and fauna. You'll often find deer and other grazing animals here, too. Keep dogs on leads and under close control.

Other walkies nearby
The Isle of Skye, just over the bridge from the Kyle of Lochalsh, boasts a vast range of beautiful walks. One of our favourites starts at Glenbrittle, where you'll find a campsite and café, and heads up towards the dramatic peaks of the Cuillin Ridge, returning via the waterfalls at Eas Mor.

THINGS TO SEE

In Balmacara Square, you'll find lots of information on the local area at the visitor centre. While you're here, visit the Steadings Gallery, a contemporary art space, which exhibits a range of work by local and national artists. There's also a café, shops and parking here.

Birch woodland.

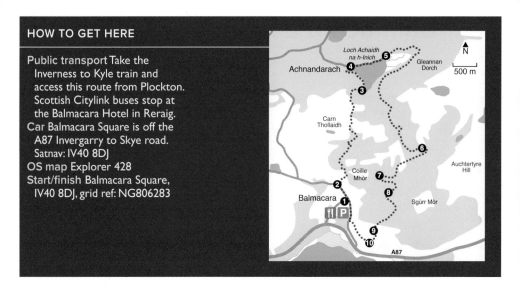

HOW TO GET HERE

Public transport Take the Inverness to Kyle train and access this route from Plockton. Scottish Citylink buses stop at the Balmacara Hotel in Reraig.

Car Balmacara Square is off the A87 Invergarry to Skye road. Satnav: IV40 8DJ

OS map Explorer 428

Start/finish Balmacara Square, IV40 8DJ, grid ref: NG806283

Balmacara Bay.

DIRECTIONS

Start/finish: Balmacara Square

1. Follow the road towards Plockton. When you get about 300 yards out of the village, turn right onto the track signed to Achnahinich.

2. Walk along this track, ignoring the smaller tracks which turn off. Cross a stream and after the track bends to the right, take the path on the left. Follow this through a gate signed to Achnahinich. The path is mostly downhill from here, it winds across moorland and through areas of birch woodland. There are good views from the open areas. Walk downhill through another area of birch to the edge of Loch Achaidh na h-Inich.

3. Turn left and follow the shore path around the loch, walk through a gate and then, a short distance later, cross the sluice gate to reach the road.

4. Follow the road right, along the edge of Loch Achaidh na h-Inich, to its end and a track junction. The right fork goes to the farm, so take the left fork uphill.

5. Walk up this track to a staggered crossroads, turn right here and follow the track. It curves to the right, crossing a stream and traversing the hill above the farm. Continue to follow this track with great views down to the loch and further afield. Follow it uphill, curving left and passing the Allt a' Ghlarsair. Carry on uphill to reach a viewpoint of Skye and the Cuillin hills next to a wooden bench.

6. Continue to follow the track downhill, then after a short distance, turn right onto a smaller grassy path signed 'Waterfall Route'. Follow this downhill, curving to the right and walking through woodland to reach a gate at the edge of the moorland. Go through the gate and follow the path across the moorland to a path junction.

7. Turn left, following the smaller path across the Balmacara Burn and up to a larger track junction.

8. Cross and follow the track opposite, take the right fork onto a smaller path and follow its wiggly course across an area of felled woodland, then moorland, to reach a larger track. Turn right and follow the track up to the summit and viewpoint.

9. Turn around and follow the track back downhill; pass the path you walked down on your left and continue on the track, curving to the right to a track junction.

10. Follow this track right, across moorland and then through a thin patch of woodland until you reach the road. Turn right and follow the road back to Balmacara Square and the start.

DOG-FRIENDLY AMENITIES

Ferry and Craggan cottages, located on the north shore of Loch Alsh, both welcome dogs, sleep up to four people, and are set along a small track, well away from the main road. You'll have woodland and coastal walks right on your doorstep, with the Isle of Skye and the Kintail mountains just a short drive away. www.nts.org.uk/stories/dog-friendly-holiday-accommodation-in-scotland

Footpath near Reraig.

Isle of Iona
SW of Mull
Argyll & Bute
PA76 6SP
01681 700659
iona@nts.org.uk

ABOUT THIS WALK

Distance 4.4 miles (7km)
Difficulty Moderate
Terrain Minor roads, beach and optional steeper and rougher climb up to Dùn Ì, which can be muddy
Stiles Yes
Interest History, wildlife, coast

Just off the coast of the Isle of Mull, in Scotland's Inner Hebrides, Iona holds a wealth of treasures to be discovered. The island makes an enjoyable day trip from Mull, or immerse yourself in its peace and beauty for longer by staying in the village.

This walk explores the northern end of the isle of Iona, passing the nunnery at Baile Mor, the Benedictine abbey, and the wild and remote north coast, with its intricate bays, rocky headlands and spectacular white sandy beaches edged by an impossibly blue sea. There's an optional out-and-back detour to the top of Dùn Ì to take in the beautiful views back to Mull and the Highlands, and out to the Inner and Outer Hebrides.

THINGS TO SEE

Since the arrival of Irish abbot and Christian missionary, St Columba, on Iona in AD 563, the site of the abbey has formed the focal point of the island. Despite intermittent raids by the Vikings from AD 795 onwards, the abbey remained in use until the 12th century. In June 2021, the abbey reopened following a £3.75M renovation, fund-raised by the community of Iona.

Paws for thought
The crofting land on Iona is used for grazing – please keep dogs on leads.

Other walkies nearby
The Isle of Mull, just across the Sound of Iona, boasts a wealth of wonderful walking. Head out for a relaxing loop around Fionnphort, with its fine, white sandy bay edged by dramatic rocks. Or, for a more challenging and adventurous walk, head for the island's only Munro, Ben More. The out-and-back route from the coast at Dhiseig to the summit of Ben More covers a distance of around 6 miles (9.5km) with an elevation of 3,100 feet (945m). If you're visiting between August and October, contact the the Benmore Estate (01680 300229) for deer stalking dates – there's no stalking on Sundays.

Opposite: Iona Abbey.

HOW TO GET HERE

Public transport Take the train to
Oban and the ferry from Oban to
Craignure, then a bus from Craignure
to Fionnphort and the passenger
ferry from Fionnphort to Iona.
Car Car ferries from Oban, then drive
on the A849 to the passenger ferry
at Fionnphort. Satnav: PA66 6BL
(Fionnphort)
OS map Explorer 373
Start/finish Iona ferry jetty, PA76 6SP,
grid ref: NM286240

DIRECTIONS

Start/finish: Iona ferry jetty

1. Follow the road inland from the jetty, passing
   the island's shop and following signs to the
   abbey. Continue on the road around the
   right-hand bend and past the school; carry on
   along the road and up a slight hill to reach the
   abbey on the right.

2. Continue to walk along the road, passing a
   row of white cottages on the left. Soon after
   the cottages take a left over a stile onto a
   footpath. Follow this path, marked by wooden
   posts, across a field and up the steep hill to the
   summit of Dùn Ì.

3. Return by the same path to the road. Turn left
   and follow the road to its end at Ardionra.

4. The next section is croftland and animals are
   often grazing freely; please keep your dog on a
   lead. Follow the path across the croftland and
   through several gates to the beach. Turn left
   and walk along the beautiful sandy beach to
   the far end.

5. Return the same way, without the ascent of
   Dùn Ì (unless you fancy it again).

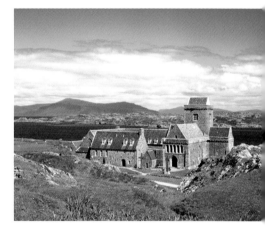

DOG-FRIENDLY AMENITIES

The Argyll Hotel is set within the main village street,
overlooking the beautiful Sound of Iona. Serving a
range of local and organic food, and with a number
of cosy rooms, this is a perfect base for exploring
the island. All rooms are dog-friendly, along with
part of the restaurant. www.argyllhoteliona.co.uk

Index

Acknowledgements

Our huge thanks to all the wonderful dogs and their owners who posed for and provided photos, generously shared recommendations, and came along on walks for the purposes of this book, including E, H & Kepi, Tracy Purnell @inspire_adventure_wales; Renee, Ewen, Bailey and Bosco; Emma, Gordon, Charlie, Aron and Holly; Zana, Joe and Pippa; Bridget, Alex and Stevie; Dr Corinne Scott and Sconepal Ole; and Geoff and Imogen.. Thanks to dog-friendly accommodation providers National Trust Holidays; Another Place, Ullswater; Steve and Kate Hare at Lana's Lodge, Mullion; to Sophie Bolesworth photography and to Ruffwear for their support. And a big thanks to all the team at HarperCollins and National Trust Books, including Evangeline Sellers, Peter Taylor and Emily Roe.

Image credits